Strategic Transformations
in Nigerian Writing

Strategic Transformations in Nigerian Writing

Orality & history in the work of Rev. Samuel Johnson
Amos Tutuola, Wole Soyinka & Ben Okri

ATO QUAYSON

Lecturer, Faculty of English
& Fellow, Pembroke College
University of Cambridge

James Currey
OXFORD

Indiana University Press
BLOOMINGTON & INDIANAPOLIS

First published in the United Kingdom by
James Currey
73 Botley Rd
Oxford OX2 0BS

and in North America by
Indiana University Press
601 North Morton Street
Bloomington, IN 47404

British Library Cataloguing-in-Publication Data
Quayson, Ato
  Strategic transformations in Nigerian writing : orality &
  history in the work of Rev. Samuel Johnson, Amos Tutuola,
  Wole Soyinka & Ben Okri. - (Studies in African literature)
  1. Nigerian literature (English) - History and criticism
  I. Title
  820.9'9669
    ISBN 0-85255-543-1 (James Currey Paper)
    ISBN 0-85255-544-X (James Currey Cloth)

Library of Congress Cataloging-in-Publication Data
Quayson, Ato.
  Strategic transformations in Nigerian writing : orality & history
  in the work of Rev. Samuel Johnson, Amos Tutuola, Wole Soyinka & Ben
  Okri / Ato Quayson.
      p.   cm.
  Includes bibliographical references and index.
  ISBN 0-253-33343-1 (alk. paper). — ISBN 0-253-21148-4 (pbk. :
  alk. paper)
  1. Nigerian literature (English)—History and criticism.
  2. Literature and folklore—Nigeria—History.   3. Literature and
  history—Nigeria—History.   4. Yoruba (African people)—
  Historiography.   5. Soyinka, Wole—Knowledge—Folklore.
  6. Tutuola, Amos—Knowledge—Folklore.   7. Okri, Ben—Knowledge—
  Folklore.   8. Johnson, Samuel, d. 1901.   9. Nigeria—
  Historiography.   10. Oral tradition—Nigeria.   I. Title.
  PR9387.Q39   1997
  820.9'9669—dc21   97-10960
              1 2 3 4 5 02 01 00 99 98 97

Typeset by
Long House Publishing Services, Cumbria, UK
in 10/11 pt Palatino
Printed by
Villiers Publications Ltd
London N3

To Alo Denkabe, for intellectual rigour
and Mawuena, for love and much else

Contents

Acknowledgements

This book is based on research carried out for a Ph. D at the Faculty of English, University of Cambridge. A Yoruba proverb has it that when farmland is cut out of the forest, it is impossible to tell which came first, the farm or its boundaries. It is with a sense of the fruitful interactions I have had in the course of my research and of writing this book that I wish to thank the following persons and organizations:

Dr Anil Seal and The Cambridge Commonwealth Trust for a scholarship to come to Cambridge; Tim Cribb of Churchill College for being a great supervisor and friend and for his unusual knack of being able to comprehend my ideas as I uttered them in sentences of various stages of incompletion; Dr Karin Barber and Dr Paulo de Moraes Farias of the Centre for West African Studies of the University of Birmingham for their unflagging interest in my efforts at making sense of Yoruba and Nigerian culture; Prof. John Peel of SOAS for enthusiastic discussions; Professor Gillian Beer of the Faculty of English, Cambridge for reading an early version of my introductory chapter and for her sharp eye for ambiguities; Professor Ruth Morse, Fitzwilliam College for reading the last version of the same chapter and for her patient comments; Dr Keith Hart, Director of the African Studies Centre, Cambridge for fruitful discussions on a wide range of issues from the status of the contemporary nation-state to football; and Colin Wilcockson, Director of Studies at Pembroke College for constant encouragement.

A trip to Nigeria opened up a whole new dimension to questions of the relevance of literary studies to the situation in Africa and I wish to thank Professor Dapo Adelugba, Dr Harry Garuba, Dr Niyi Osundare and Dr Olusegun Oladipo of the University of Ibadan for showing me how to combine literary scholarship with an unremitting concern with the condition of ordinary people. I also wish to thank Professor Abiola Irele for his generosity in sharing his work and ideas on the subject-matter of this book.

Thanks are also due to the President and Fellows of Wolfson College, Oxford for granting me a Junior Research Fellowship on which I spent a pleasant year at Oxford. Also to the Master and Fellows of Pembroke College, Cambridge for providing a cheerful and excellent work environment.

I wish to register a very special thanks to my former teachers at the University of Ghana, Legon. To Professor Anyidoho, Mary Keleve, Dannabang Kuwabong, Larbi-Korang, Rev. Kudadjie and all those who shared their minds with me, this book is a tribute to their unsung and heroic efforts at pursuing rigorously high standards in spite of the general conditions of disillusionment. To Alo Denkabe, this book is partly dedicated for his great intellectual inspiration. What I owe to him intellectually I cannot fully formulate in words; if I say this here, it is for the world to know how crucial dedicated teachers are to what we all ultimately become.

This book is also especially dedicated to my wife, Mawuena, as a tribute to her unflagging faith in this project even when I was in doubt. She, Jijo and Abena were usually my first audience and sat patiently through it all while my life took on the hue of my ideas and I metamorphosed without notice from caring parent and husband to intolerant and untidy scholar. To them, a proverb: When there is space in the heart, there is space in heaven …

To all who have contributed in numberless and nameless ways to the success of this book, *Ayékoo, Esé púpò'o*.

Note on Orthography

All Yoruba names in this book, for the sake of simplicity, have been spelled without tone accents and subscript marks, as is common in most English texts. However, all Yoruba titles and names of special cultural practices without equivalent in English are given with full tone marks and subscripts and are further italicized.

1

Introduction

African Literature & the Question of Orality

> The problem is to constitute series: to define elements proper to each series, to fix its boundaries, to reveal its own specific relations, to formulate its laws, and, beyond this, to describe the relations between series...
>
> Michel Foucault
> *The Archaeology of Knowledge*

> The main problem of a literary criticism that aims to be in all respects a *historical* discipline is to do justice to both aspects of its object: to work out a system of concepts both historiographic and rhetorical.
>
> Franco Moretti
> *Signs Taken for Wonders*

The epigraph from Franco Moretti articulates a central problem of literary criticism: how to be historical while paying attention to the specific details of literary discourse. But every time the delineation of a literary history is attempted, it immediately gets entangled with a concomitant desire to constitute series. The quest for literary history itself is a curious one as it presupposes a potential order in the universe of literary discourse which it is the critic's duty to bring to the surface. It is also important because the order is frequently an after-effect of the critical enterprise, whereby it is criticism that suggests the order which is then made increasingly coherent by the deployment of particular grids of analysis. And so it has been in the criticism of African literature.

One of the most abiding interests of African literary criticism has been to demonstrate the continuity that African literature written in Europhone languages has with indigenous sources. It is the guiding principle behind a work such as Emmanuel Obiechina's *Culture,*

Tradition and Society in the West African Novel, in which he argues elegantly for the perception of traditional sources in the process of the 'domestication' of the novel form in West Africa. Obiechina sees the novel as reflective or mimetic of traditional beliefs and practices in an almost unmediated way, being interested, as he is, in showing how the cultural and social background 'gave rise to the novel there, and in far-reaching and crucial ways conditioned the West African novel's content, themes and texture (Obiechina 1975: 3). In Obiechina's study, 'culture', 'tradition' and 'society' become paradigmatic of the real West African world reflected in the novels he analyses. In this way, the novels become amenable to a positivist anthropological harvest in which details are read directly from cultural background to fictional world and back again. Even in a more recent and sophisticated inflection of literary anthropology applied by Christopher Miller (1990), a broadly eclectic theoretical position is produced only to place the texts to be studied finally within what has been described by Uzo Ensowanne (1990) as a grid of Africa's 'immobilized antiquity' from which a largely unproblematized African culture can be shown to be reflected in the texts.

The general tendency has been to show how the peculiar configuration of orality and literacy in African contexts lends a special quality to African literature. This is joined to the impulse towards defining an ambit of 'authenticity' for African literature (see Eileen Julien 1992: 3–25). At certain key moments, this has led not only to confused categories but also to a pedantic urge to differentiate what can be considered African literature from what cannot. The prescriptivist standpoint of the notorious troika of Chinweizu, Onwuchekwa Jemie and Ihechukwu Madubuike in *Toward the Decolonization of African Literature* (1980) on what is admissible as African literature represents a bizarre and often criticized articulation of the quest for authenticity (e.g., Soyinka 1975b; Appiah 1988).

These tendencies have had significant implications for the terms that govern the criticism of African literature. Not only has an assumption of organicist relationships between traditional resources and African literature been sustained, but a notion of literature being either a receptacle or mirror of culture has also been dominant. This is displayed not so much in the statements that are made about literature as in the methodology that is employed to clarify the relationship between literature and indigenous resources. The enterprise of criticism is undertaken in a largely positivist framework. It is shown, for instance, how folk materials such as songs and stories are incorporated into the plays of Efua Sutherland; how the imitation of the forms of indigenous oral poetry is undertaken in the work of writers like Okot p' Bitek; and how proverbs and other rhetorical devices are manifested in the work of Chinua Achebe.[1] In each of these instances, the work of criticism is seen to be fulfilled when the elements of orality are identified and explained. This explanatory impulse is tied directly to the processes by which the African nation-state was inserted into the global economy at independence, with the need to show the rationalism of indigenous systems as a necessary concomitant of the emergence of fully fledged new states.

The noting of indigenous influences on African literature was part of the project of defining the national status of the emerging litera-tures, especially after decolonization. As Anthony Appiah points out, it reflects the recapitulation of 'the classic gestures of nation-formation in the domain of culture' (1992: 98). By a complex – and yet common – series of moves, this kind of apparent literary criticism manipulates a nationalistic and Africanist idea: first, there is a nostal-gic yet unifiying gesture toward a unified structure of feeling (to take advantage of Raymond Williams's term); second, that structure is identified with the idea of a homogenous orality; third, the idea of a homogenous orality provides the ground for a distinctively 'African' society and culture. Writing from the perspective of academic philosophy, Paulin Hountondji describes this tendency as 'the myth of primitive unanimity', and attacks its proponents for adopting an essentialist approach to the question of African Philosophy (Hountondji 1983: 56–62). His anger is to be appreciated, but it is necessary to note that these tendencies have some value especially as they attempt to downplay putative ethnic differences in the constitution of the African nation-state.[2] In my view, it is the effects of their unexamined assumptions for the evaluation of cultural forms that is problematic. And these assumptions are problematic not just for the definition of an African philosophy. The unanimist postula-tions have as their corollary the postulation of an a-historical relation-ship between orality and socio-cultural formations such as literature. Since the structure of orality is taken to be largely homogenized and literature is taken to reflect such an entity, the differing relationships established between literary texts and contexts of orality are easily elided. Furthermore, because literature is analysed largely within a reflectionist paradigm, with all the implications of its privileged activity in showing up an unmediated truth believed to inhere in reality, the literary activity is never juxtaposed to other discourses that draw on indigenous resources. Literature is dissociated from historiography and social theory and the varied play-offs that may be said to transpire between different socio-cultural standpoints in their use of indigenous resources is never raised as an issue. Even though writers and critics have in their various ways pursued questions of literary history in African writing, the question of possible paradigm-atic shifts in various literary uses of orality and in the face of changing socio-cultural and political realities has only been sporadically formulated (e.g., Soyinka 1963b; Priebe 1988; Irele 1990a; Harrow 1994).

Irele's and Harrow's efforts are particularly interesting as explications of the main parameters defining the field. In an essay entitled 'Tradition and the Yoruba Writer: D. O. Fagunwa, Amos Tutuola and Wole Soyinka', Irele writes with the benefit of a focus on the indigenous resources available in a single culture and echoes T. S. Eliot's celebrated 1919 essay to argue that the three writers he examines exemplify a 'Yoruba literary tradition'.[3] He examines the ways in which the three writers deploy Yoruba oral traditions in their work, and intimates that their writings establish a bridge between the traditional cultural heritage and Western metropolitan culture. Like many other critics of African literature, Irele's concern is to typify the continuities between oral traditions and writing in English. His effort is significant because he also attempts to show how the relationships with a body of indigenous resources is expressed diachronically across various literary texts and how differing attitudes to the same body of resources is registered. Irele's movement towards a properly historical analysis of the uses of orality in literature is, however, partially undermined by his dependence on Eliot's notion of literary tradition.

It is important to recall Eliot's conception of literary history.[4] For him, the really good writer relates to the totality of the mind of Europe reflected in the European literary heritage. He argues that the original creative imagination is indebted to the whole literary heritage and that, with the contribution of a new work, the arrangement in the old order of the heritage undergoes modification within and among its various elements. The literary heritage is at once inert, as is suggested in its figuring as 'monuments [that] form an ideal order among themselves', but also amenable to modification and change with the introduction of 'the new, (the really new) work among them'. Eliot's formulation harbours an important contradiction in that on the one hand literary tradition is perceived as monolithic while on the other it is seen as open to change and mutation. Terry Eagleton sees this as reflecting the dual impulses towards grasping the tradition as a self-transformative organism 'constantly re-organized by the present', while simultaneously endowing 'this radical historical relativism' with the status of 'absolute authority' (1981: 54). Eliot's conception of a literary tradition has an implicit idealist bias to it which seeks to comprehend change while foregrounding the growth of an undifferentiated literary consciousness. Robert Weimann criticizes this tendency for its implicit dissociation of the literary sensibility from historical consciousness and argues that it is a function of a crisis of alienation for literature as well as literary criticism (Weimann 1977: 85–6).

In my view, however, additional problems with Eliot's notion of tradition lie elsewhere. One key implication of his formulations is the prioritization of dead writers. His notion of great poetry is premised on the belief in literary value acquired through age or pastness. This is evident from his insistence on speaking about the relationship between living poets and the dead ones. The implied classicism in this posture is what Eagleton identifies and criticizes, but what is of added importance is that the relationships that such a methodology would discern as significant would be only those between living poets and a literary archaeological archive. The potential relationships between living poets is bracketed out of consideration, so that it is impossible to delineate the gradual formation of a literary heritage in the discernible relationships that inhere within the present as well as between the present and the past.

Eliot also operates with a notion of the heritage as library or written archive. This notion of heritage-as-library informs his assertion of 'the importance of the relation of the *poem* to other *poems* by other authors'. But the notion is also implied in his remark that 'Shakespeare acquired more essential history from Plutarch than most men from the whole of the British Museum' in support of the fact that 'much learning deadens or perverts poetic sensibility'. The notion of the library with all its conceptual boundaries encapsulated in writing as a locus of consciousness is what is affirmed in such remarks. Yet, at the same time, Eliot opens up a space for considering the place of present perceptions lying outside the realm of writing in his discussion of the processes that go on in the mind of the writer. The implicit psychologism of the process that he elaborates may be said to derive from his own experience. The important thing is that he also suggests that the mind of the writer works with present emotions. Following this trajectory of his formulations, it is possible to consider the effect of other things like lived experience, oral traditions and contemporary conceptual resources for the work of poetry.

Abiola Irele filiates his own analysis of a Yoruba literary tradition to Eliot's notions while shifting the precise focus of his formulation. The Yoruba literary tradition is invoked not so much as a means of tracing the movement of literary value and taste but as a means of delineating a cultural praxis. This shift from literary value and taste to that of praxis is one which we shall return to later in defining the ambit of this book. Irele transposes Eliot's notion of a grand chirographic literary heritage into the sense of a common stock of beliefs and symbols. The transposition is important because it signals a shift of the grounds of Eliot's formulations to open up a space for a discussion of oral traditions. He justifies recourse to Eliot's formulations in this way:

[W]hat strikes one as significant about this essay is the original understanding which it offers of the meaning of 'tradition' – as not so much an
abiding, permanent, immutable stock of beliefs and symbols, but as the
constant refinement and extension of these in a way which relates them to
an experience that is felt as being at once continuous and significantly
new. (Irele 1990a: 174)

It is evident from Irele's understanding of Eliot's formulations that
he differentiates literary texts from the symbols expressed in them
and then brackets out the texts altogether to centralize the sense of a
stock of beliefs, ideas and oral traditions as constitutive of the literary
heritage. Since symbols and beliefs are not the exclusive property of
texts, but inhere vigorously within the space of experienced culture,
Irele's transposition makes Eliot more amenable to application in the
context of an indigenous conceptual space. Thus, Irele is able to assert
the central premise of his own perspective, which is that there is a
continuity between the putative indigenous resource-base and the
context of literary writings, what he perceives as an 'elaboration in
literature of a continuous stream of the collective consciousness, from
the traditional to the modern' (*ibid.*). He moves on later to speak of the
African writer's concern to work out a 'spiritual coherence' and a
distinctive mode of thought and feeling. At the same time, he is
concerned to show the relationships between one writer and another.
Whereas Eliot's concern was mainly with a single set of relationships,
that between texts within a heritage, Irele had the added problem of
defining not only that set of relationships but also the one between
indigenous oral resources and the work of the writers. He never
makes this dual perspective fully explicit, and leaves us to decode
them from his mode of literary analysis. Whereas the relationship
between the writers is elaborated in great detail, those between them
and their indigenous resource-base is almost taken for granted. Irele's
scheme inscribes an idealist notion of consciousness which he sees as
flowing uninterruptedly in the two directions of his concerns. Even as
he attempts to differentiate his enterprise from Eliot's, he inadvertently reproduces the informing philosophical premise of Eliot's
own formulations. Significantly, however, even while Irele implies an
idealist mode of continuity, he affirms that the writers are not
unconscious slaves of what they take from the resource-base but that
they transform what they appropriate. Thus he points out, and rightly,
that Fagunwa gets 'beyond the limitations of the [oral] tradition in the
context of an extended literary medium', and that Soyinka approaches
the resource-base with a highly self-conscious artistic agenda (178;
189). In this way, a notion of strategic choices exercised in filiation
with the indigenous conceptual resources is intimated even if not
fully elaborated because of the largely idealist evolutionary paradigm within which the whole critical enterprise is caught.

Involved in Irele's analysis of the relationships between the writers is the notion of literary influence. This is particularly evident in his analysis of that between Fagunwa and Tutuola. He insists that Tutuola is a lesser artist than Fagunwa and that 'the praise and acclaim lavished upon Tutuola belong more properly to Fagunwa, who provided not only the original inspiration but indeed a good measure of the material for Tutuola's novels' (184). Irele's notion of influence is grounded on the implicit prioritization of the earlier writer against the later. But, as Michael Baxandall argues in relation to art criticism, this implies a reversal of what really pertains in the relationship between earlier and later practitioners within the same field. He rightly points out that it is rather the case that later writers and artists 'draw on, resort to, avail [themselves] of, appropriate from, have recourse to, adapt, misunderstand, refer to, pick up, engage with, react to, quote...' For him, the relationships between earlier and later artists requires a vocabulary that demonstrates the agency of the succeeding ones.[5] Indeed, it is arguable that literary influence is more like an act of perception that triggers further literary action. Between Fagunwa and Tutuola, then, it is fair to say that the latter writer discursively activates the folkloric intuitions earlier deployed in literary discourse by the former. Furthermore, though the observation that Tutuola was familiar with Fagunwa is a viable one given the fact that Fagunwa has been the dominant influence in literary curricula in the Western states of Nigeria for a long time, it seems inaccurate to suggest that Tutuola owes his originality to the earlier writer when the resources that Fagunwa drew upon were common stock to all Yoruba.[6] Irele steps out of this notion of influence when discussing the work of Soyinka. In analysing Soyinka he emphasizes his artistic agency in relation both to the work of others as well as to the elements of the conceptual resource-base. This shift brings him close to Eliot's notion of the activity of the writer in the present in re-ordering the sense of the past. It is the more germane to our own analysis and is one which we will adopt in elaborating the work of the writers in this book.

If Abiola Irele's filiation to Eliot's central notions imported an idealist conception of literary continuity into the field of Yoruba literary history, Kenneth Harrow's recent *Thresholds of Change in African Literature* (1994) is significant in that he centralizes the notion of tradition as a literary system whose changes are signalled from within itself. Starting from the premise that change is a key pre-occupation of African writers and shows itself both in the dilemmas confronting characters as well as in the intertextual relationships between texts, Harrow notes that 'emergence is always potentially present as each work appears, as each text is read/written' (4). He is careful to point out that his notion of change does not involve any simple notion of evolutionism in which succeeding stages are of a necessity improvements over former ones.

To aid in theorizing the question of change in African literature, Harrow turns to Russian Formalism and Kuhn's notion of paradigm shift in the history of science and deconstruction. For him, these three furnish useful means by which to grasp the shifts from one type of literary style to another while at the same time helping to highlight the significance of anomalies, defamiliarization and the dispersal of meanings as mechanisms of literary change. He creates a barrage of neologisms to account for the changes in African literature, linking them to a periodization that matches the political movement from decolonization (Laye, Achebe) through post-independence disillusionment (Soyinka, Ngugi) to the contemporary stage of a post-revolt consciousness. However, while making evident the need for a self-conscious use of theory in analysing African literary history, Harrow manages to focus on the literary field as if it were an autonomous field divorced from others. He gains great subtlety in focusing on the literary field as a system that extends diachronically and whose inner workings lead to transformation, while eliding the question of the external contexts that partly account for these inner workings. In a review of Harrow's book, Lyn Innes (1994) notes that 'there is little discussion of the differences between various ethnic traditions or between anglophone and francophone traditions in Africa'. The sense of a culturally decontextualized machinery of literary practices is difficult to shake off completely on encountering his study.

Part of the problem with Harrow's model derives from two things, namely, the urge to see the whole of African literature as the expression of a single *tradition*; and, the perception of this tradition as somehow divorced from local political or cultural influences. The key consequence of these two problems, it seems to me, is that he centralizes the literary field as semi-autonomous and affirms a critical responsibility to the aesthetic field as a separable one from the cultural or the political. In this respect, his analyses are vastly different from Abiola Irele's.

If Irele seemed to produce an idealist notion of the organic links between indigenous resources and African literature in his early reliance on Eliot, his later visits to the question of tradition in African literature have framed the issue in a more historical and problematic way. Tracing the varying ways in which Africans and peoples of African descent have sought to rejoin an African ethos from the mid-nineteenth century to the present day, Irele points out in 'African Letters: the Making of a Tradition' that 'tradition' is often a *theme* in African letters. He writes: 'What matters is the *affective* stance that tradition determines and the imaginative projections and intellectual constructions that it conditions in the specific historical context of its thematization within African discourse' (Irele 1995: 73). Through the different phases of this thematization, from cultural nationalists such as Blyden in the last century, through the Negritude movement of the sixties to Ngugi's radical formulations in more recent times, there has been a consistent attempt to shore up a viable sense of identity and selfhood in the face of the perceived ruptures that colonialism has wrought on the African psyche. Thus, a certain agonistic tone is inscribed in the thematization of tradition in African letters.

Irele's historical formulation of the theme of tradition in African letters sets a broader framework within which to pursue the questions he raised in the earlier essay 'Tradition and the Yoruba Writer'. But if I turn here away from a continental-type of study as exemplified in Harrow's work and towards a more localized basis co-terminous with Irele's focus, it is not to use the term 'Yoruba' to pinpoint a set of ethnic particularities. It is not even to write an 'archaeology' of Yoruba writing, since I do not propose to look at the work of people such as Zulu Sofola, Simi Bedford, Akin Isola, Femi Osofisan, Femi Oyebode, Oladele Taiwo, Niyi Osundare and numerous others. Rather, it is to help define a regulative perimeter for a discussion of putative indigenous conceptual resources from which the writers draw for their writings. By its very nature, this book does not pretend to be exhaustive and extensive; rather it is partial and illustrative. And so I look not at the complete corpus of Nigerian writing or even of the writing of the various figures in the study, but at a selection of their writing to make a specific set of points to do with orality, cultural nationalism, mythopoeia and liminality. I discuss the resource-base of Yoruba orality as a means of outlining the production of a broad conceptual system whose elements can be said to be transposable into an indigenous sense of things for both Yoruba in particular and Nigerians in general. My concern in this book will be to show how the set of concepts made available by the Yoruba writers are no longer limitable to the Yoruba but have become available for conceptualizing a larger sense of identity. This will particularly be illustrated in the filiation of Ben Okri to the writing of Soyinka and Tutuola. For, now, the thematization of tradition is perceivable as a strategic quest in which Africans have located themselves simultaneously in relation to an African ethos as well as to the rest of the world more generally. Following Eileen Julien (1992), the questions to be formulated are the relations that each writer has to indigenous resources and the implications that derive from this for questions of literary history. The key issue at hand, as she puts it, is not 'the orality of Africa but rather the intellectual categories of orality and writing that we use … how the category of 'African orality' permeates literary criticism, how it is subject to ideological pressures, and how it has come to define and confine the scope of our interest in and perception of African writing' (7).

Additionally, I will try to show how the relationship between literature and indigenous conceptual resources is part of a larger set of relationships which cuts across texts from other cultural standpoints. To ground this point the historiography of the Rev. Samuel Johnson will be explored to show how he deploys resources of Yoruba orality to create a specific mode of historiography within the new literary paradigm he exercises. This added perspective will help to define the ambit of the relationships between orality and written discourses as one of the strategic deployment of orality for different purposes. By adopting a perspective that embraces Johnson's historiography of the late nineteenth century as well as literary writing cutting across a large part of this one, I shall attempt to outline a literary tradition not solely in terms of literary value but also in terms of the strategic location of each of the writers in relation to indigenous resources as well as to larger historical realities. In this way, I hope to move on to a general analysis of the differences between them as well as of how a process of transition may be read out of the trajectory of the totality of their literary practice. A focus on imaginative literature alone would impoverish such an analysis by forcing us to see it as a separate activity divorced from a broad regime of cultural discourses.

Yoruba culture itself precludes cursory characterization. The first thing that must be noted in discussing the Yoruba is the fact that the name 'Yoruba' as a generic term conceals a wide variety of peoples often holding allegiance primarily to specific tribal groupings. The Yoruba consider themselves primarily as Oyo, Ekiti, Ijebu, Egba, Ilesha, or Ondo among others. The various 'traditional cultures' of these peoples are characterized by their diversity and constant creative revision and recycling.

Set against this diversity is a current towards perceiving a common heritage, albeit problematically constituted. All Yoruba peoples derive descent from the city of Ife and the mythical Oduduwa, though, as Robin Law (1973) points out, the variants of the Oduduwa myth are ultimately contestations for power amongst the various tribal groupings. A general Yoruba pantheon of orìṣàs (gods) also plays a part in the process of perception of a common culture, though, once again, the number of gods and their significance differs from one locale to the other.

Among the numerous orìṣàs, however, a number have acquired prominence because of the cults associated with them that have drawn adherents across the various tribal groupings. The most important of these are Eshu, trickster-god and overseer of the proper conduct towards sacrifice; Ogun, the god of iron and war; Obatala, creator-god and god of the disabled; Shopona, god of small-pox; Shango, god of lightning and Orunmila, god of Ifa divination.[7] *Orìṣà* worship includes special songs, rituals, and perhaps costumes, a series of priests and the use of a sacred grove or temple at which sacrifices are made. Also important is the fact that a Yoruba may belong to more than one cult group. For this study the most significant aspect of these *orìṣàs* and their cults is the fact that they have generated a configuration of myths, rituals and other symbolic practices which offer a viable conceptual resource-base for various purposes.

A common cosmic perception has been abstracted by scholars from the various cultic configurations inherent in oral traditions and also from things like art and child-naming procedures. The Yoruba universe is a three-tiered one with *Ọrun* (Sky) being the abode of Olorun (another name for Olodumare); *Ilé* (Earth) being home of Onile the earth goddess; and *Aiyé* (World) being the general abode of men. Within this system the real world finds its place. *Orìṣàs* are in the realm of Olorun, and they are conceived of as intermediaries between Olorun and men. Also in that realm are the spirit children or *abikus* trapped in the cycle of rebirth and the spirits of the ancestors, who have a special relationship to the world of men and manifest their presence in various *egungun* festivals. The world of the living is in a constant interactive relationship with the world of the *orìṣàs* and that of the ancestors through the various cultic and ritual practices that circulate within the culture (see Okedeji, 1966).

Also significant in the relative stabilization of what is considered Yoruba culture was the general movement towards setting the language down in writing, a process which was spearheaded by the clergy. This process was a long one with debates on orthography raging into the middle of the twentieth century. As the language came to acquire a significant status in the formal education system of Western Nigeria, there was a growth of a class of people who could read and write in the local language thus giving them a sense of community beyond their individual tribes.[8] To this was added a long process of collecting and commenting upon oral forms such as proverbs, *oríkì* (praise-names and epithets), myths, folktales and Ifa divination verses by scholars and commentators such as Lijadu, Bascom, Beier, Idowu and others, introducing a trajectory of the stabilization of cultural resources. That this process was contributed to both by Yoruba themselves as well as Westerners is itself a signal of the importance of world-historical processes in the formation of what is now taken as Yoruba culture.

The fashioning of present-day notions of what constitutes Yoruba culture can also be traced in the hundred years of vigorous and successful Yoruba cultural nationalism dating from the middle of the last century and originally pioneered by a cultural elite who were initially mainly clergymen. This nationalism was rapidly adopted by a huge intermediate class and disseminated through popular theatre, fiction and music.[9] Within these various processes, a systematization of Yoruba culture took place whose significance, above all, is that it tended towards a stabilization of the myriad variants of the myths and oral traditions thereby establishing a viable resource-base mediated by historical processes which was relied upon for different uses.

An aspect of this process that needs to be highlighted is the part played by a general notion of hybridity and inter-cultural exchange in Yoruba culture. Olabiyi Yai points out that 'the Yoruba have always conceived of their history as diaspora' (1993: 30). Ifa divination inscribes this notion within its practice by dividing the world into five regions and by requiring that *babaláwo* (diviners) greet all five regions of the world. That this practice might date from the culture's gradual opening up to the rest of the world cannot be denied, but the point is that even in what is taken to be the most distilled expression of the culture's *morés*, which is what Ifa is held to signal, there has been an inscription of the efficacy and necessity of cross-cultural interaction. As Yai further asserts:

> The intellectual climate of the region was and still is largely characterized by a dialogic ethos, a constant prurit [*sic*] to exchange ideas and experience and material culture. Each city was a locus of intellectual interaction between intellectuals (*babaláwo*, herbalists, poets, artists) and Ile Ife was regarded as a sanctuary and the university par excellence in the etymological sense of the word. (31)

In many ways it is this notion of the necessity for interchange that has informed the activity of some of the culture's most vigorous thinkers and cultural nationalists such as Rev. Samuel Crowther, Herbert Macauley, Wole Soyinka and Hubert Ogunde. The activity of all these people has been to act as cultural brokers to the rest of the world. And it seems that this has been facilitated not just by the processes of history, which defined a constant dissolution as well as merging of identities especially after the collapse of Old Oyo, but also by the fact that the practice of Ifa divination itself centralizes this predilection within traditional culture. In a comparative analysis of Yoruba with Ashanti culture, John Peel points out that it is the peculiar place that Ifa occupies among the Yoruba that has allowed the culture to open up more smoothly to world religions without violence to itself, while Ashanti culture was constrained to resist for a long time any such adoption. This is because whereas Ashanti culture was grounded on the hegemonically affirmative ritual of *Adaduanan* (the commemoration of a forty-two day cycle), which foregrounded the position of Ashanti chieftaincy, Ifa managed to domesticate all external influences and to suggest that they were only extensions of Ifa itself (Peel 1987: 106–12). Given the evident dialogism that Yai sees as central to Yoruba self-conception and the absorptive flexibility that Peel notes as definitive of Ifa divination, it is easy then to understand how with the processes generated by the formation of Nigeria, Yoruba cultural concepts could enter a process of cross-cultural exchange without any sense of violence done to a notion of ethnicity. The predilections of Yoruba culture support a process which is inexorable in the space of the nation-state because of the interaction of different peoples in the space of a common nationality. Ethnicity becomes fluid in such a context, only coagulating into concrete positions in time of crisis. What Ben Okri expresses in his filiation with a discernible Yoruba cultural resource-base is a preparedness to take the conceptual resources made available by Yoruba writers as a means of expressing a sense of identity embracing all available indigenous resources. In that sense, he is himself mediating the dialogic and hybrid sense of indigenous resources from a national and not an ethnic position for contemporary uses.

As in most contexts of orality, Yoruba traditional oral forms exhibit a high level of polysemy in terms of the materials employed in each genre. The notion of 'genre' as employed by Western critical theory can only serve as a heuristic device due to the high levels of inter-change and transference of materials between the various discernible traditional modes. Indeed, as is pointed out by Karin Barber in an examination of the discursive relationships between ese Ifa (Ifa divination verses), alo (folktales) and oríkì (praise poems or epithets), Yoruba oral genres 'tend to be highly incorporative and porous' (Barber 1991b: 13). She also notes in a study of the constitution of orìsàs that their attributed features are frequently marked by inconsistency, fragmentation and merging. These, she writes, 'need to be treated not as accidental and regrettable untidiness, but as central features of Yoruba religious thought and practice' (Barber 1990: 317). The discernible incorporativeness and porosity inherent in traditional culture have important implications for the exact methods of relating them to literary writings.

It is clear that to speak of the oral background to literary writings is to implicitly invoke a notion of the intervention of writing in a conceptual arena of flux. Though it is important to demonstrate the specific strategic configurations of the oral traditions that each writer draws upon, it is useful to conceptualize this as a process by which writing attempts a stabilization of flux in oral traditions. This process is by no means a one-way street. It may be shown that the configurations in literary writings also feed back into the oral context even if not to the same degree. Although the question of the flow of symbols and concepts from the literary into the context of orality falls outside the ambit of this book, it must be remembered that in focusing on the impact of a context of orality on the literary arena there is a foreclosure of a potential area of interest which can also aid in defining the transition of cultural values.

Certain questions offer themselves immediately we attempt to transcend the limitations of the dominant critical attitudes with regard to orality and African literary history: How do we define orality in all its potential multivalence? How do we move from there to describe the relationships between literary production and putative resources of orality? How do we define the relationships between different writers in their different locations with respect to indigenous resources? And how do we account for the shifts and changes in the specific deployment of resources in the indigenous conceptual resource-base as partial responses to the stress of socio-political changes in the state itself?

The issue of orality, and the implications it has for the human psyche is a contentious one.[10] One highly significant advance over the generally binaristic frameworks within which questions of orality and literacy are pursued is provided in an article by Matei Calinescu suggestively titled 'Orality in Literacy: Some Historical Paradoxes of Reading' (1993). His central thesis is that literacy (both reading and writing) have always relied on resources of orality. In the history of the evolution of literacy, these have sometimes been quite explicit, as in the early Latin and Greek scripts which did not have spaces between words and so perforce had to be read aloud to make sense of their meanings. In more modern times, he argues, it is important to note the degree to which literacy always depends on the possibility for oralization. This is because processes of verbal recall, either in the form of paraphrasing, summarizing, rephrasing or oral commentary are a valued part of any literate culture. It is not idle to note, in addition, that dictionaries often have phonetic transcriptions of words as if in a permanent mnemonic effort to remind people not to forget how to pronounce them. As he puts it, quite bluntly: 'Oral-cultural memory is deeply involved in both writing and reading' (178). To take his point about the mutual imbrication of orality and literacy for analysing the relations between indigenous orality and African literature, however, the crucial point has to be made that orality has to be taken as a cultural rather than as merely a techno-logical concept. For, the means by which people remember are ultimately tied to important cultural forms of coding. Furthermore, the 'sedimentation' of oral discourse on the written one does not reside solely in the mimesis of verbal speech and in the forms of oralization as is arguably the case in poetry. It also lies at the level of the reproduction of cultural codes and signifiers which may be shifted not just between an oral frame and a written one within the same language but may be seen as transferable between different languages. It is not for nothing, therefore, that the traditional culture portrayed in a work such as Achebe's *Things Fall Apart* is never mistaken for a Japanese one. It is not just that the novel mimetically invokes Igbo forms of oral discourse, it also imitates a general cultural discursivity.

And yet the relationship between orality and African literature cannot be fully explored without recourse to notions of intertextuality, since, arguably, even oral forms of discourse are ultimately texts in their own right (see Irele 'Orality, Literacy and African Literature' 1990). In most literary uses of the term, the focus is on relationships between written texts, with elements from culture and society constrained to make their appearance only as they are literary elements in an implied intertext. From its very first introduction by Julia Kristeva in the late 1960s, the term was postulated as defining a relationship between texts. The term was introduced by her in discussing the ideas of Mikhail Bakhtin and a radical notion of the non-referentiality of literature was secreted into the inaugural act of intertextuality's introduction (see Kristeva, 1981: 66, 87; see also Clayton and Rothstein 1991). The term gains great conceptual rigour in the hands of nuanced readers such as Michael Riffaterre (1984), but with the added insistence that 'reality' is only admissible into account as it is textualized within an intertext made available for displacing or affirming the 'mimetic' activity of the literary text.

John Frow undertakes a radical critique of some of the implications of the term intertexuality. The most interesting point he makes is that the text 'has not only an intertextual relationship to previous texts ... but also an intertextual relationship to itself as canonized text' (Frow 1986: 230–1). Intertextuality needs to be seen in the whole complex of expectations that a reader brings to bear on the text and the interpretive grid has an important bearing on the 'subject position' and the 'textual relations' that are constituted (155). Even though he criticizes the use of the term especially as applied by Kristeva and others, he does not abandon it altogether, but attempts to open up a space with it by which to discuss the status of the real from a Marxist perspective. He suggests that the real is represented in literature as a set of codes of literary and/or cultural authority. As he puts it:

> The representation of the 'real', in other words, is an intertextual reference to cultural modes of authority; what we take for granted as reality are the codes of cultural and literary convention. (154)

Earlier on in his discussion, he maintains that 'literary texts thematize their relation to social power by thematizing their relation to the structure of discursive authority which organizes the linguistic form or the play of languages in their own textual structure' (129). Frow may be faulted for the implication of the unmediated impact of socio-political structure on the configuration of the text. His formulation gives too much priority to the external effect of the real in 'organizing' the form of the play of linguistic registers within literary discourse. However, a number of positive implications are derivable from his formulations. The first is that the authority of the real is submitted to a series of literary norms which makes it recognizable as well as distorting it for the sake of conforming to those norms. Thus his notion of thematization can ultimately be read as the activity of literary norms in relation to dominant fields of reality. Secondly, it is important to draw attention to his notion of the relationship of the literary to reality as that between *codes*. The notion of an inter-relationship between different semiotic or significatory systems needs to be highlighted. In this way, an implicit element of the term intertextuality deriving from its relationship to semiotics can be brought into account. As Leon Roudiez (1981: 15) points out in trying to clear Kristeva's use of the term from misconceptions, her focus in introducing it was on 'the transposition of one or more systems of signs into one another'.

Yet the notion of an interrelationship between orality and literature renders the term intertextual fragile as descriptive of such a relationship because of the privileging of the physical text that the term implies. This is because the semiotics of a culture does not always require prior textualization. This is a particularly relevant premise in the general context of an indigenous resource-base which may be said to be constituted not just by representative oral and written texts, but also by motifs, symbols, ritual gestures and even unarticulated assumptions. It is useful, then, to transfer the notion of an inter-semiotic relationship between systems, left implicit in the usage of the term intertexuality, to a new terrain that would not privilege physical texts as such. The codes of the interrelating cultural, sociological and literary systems undergo transposition into one another to produce in literature something not always recognizable as belonging to any system. The idea of literature we may derive from a notion of an inter-semiotic space is not of the literary text as reflective surface but as an arena of what Alain Viala (1988), in outlining a sociology of literature, describes as 'prismatic effects'.

I wish to propose the term 'interdiscursivity' to account for the relationships between African literature and contexts of orality. The term 'interdiscursivity' may be used to describe the discernible relationships that inhere between literary texts and the field of conceptual resources. The text would no longer be seen as a mirror of discrete cultural elements but rather the prismatic field of interaction between cultural discourses and literary ones with all the potential of transvaluation of the real that this makes possible. In this light we may describe literature as not a mere precipitate of culture but as a process of meditation upon it. The term interdiscursive can also be used to denote the relationship between texts, since, in many ways that relationship is between different discourses constituted at the meeting point between the literary and the non-literary. When we speak of the relationship that Okri establishes with the work of Tutuola, for instance, we are speaking not only of a relationship between identifiable motifs available through a common recourse to the form of the folktale, but of a relationship between one configuration of the relationship between literature and orality and another, differing configuration. It is the articulation of the different configurations that requires theorization and not just the *intertextual* relationships between the texts. In pursuing the interdiscursive relationships between African literary texts and the contexts of orality it is also important to pay particular attention to the historically contigent nature of interdiscursive configurations. It is important to locate interdiscursivity within specific historical contexts so as to account for discernible changes. In this way, it should be possible to move from the mere detailing of indigenous items in African literary texts to a more rigorous understanding of the relationships between literature, society and culture.

The question of literary history in the context of African writing is best pursued within a notion of the strategic recourse to indigenous resources, with particular attention to the interdiscursive space within which this is undertaken. By analogy with Said's notion of the strategic formation of Orientalism, the literary writings of Johnson, Tutuola, Soyinka and Okri will be treated in this book collectively as a strategic literary formation in their deployment of indigenous resources. But whereas in Said's usage, the term firmly links Western knowledge with a will-to-power that subserves the project of subjugating others, I would like for my purposes to shift the axis of the term to place it within a notion of a 'will-to-identity' in African literature. The notion of a will-to-identity yields a simultaneous concern with the African nation-state as the implicit horizon, the political unconscious of the literary enterprise as it were, as well as a concern with projecting a viable identity outwards into the global arena. And so it is possible to discern in the writers to be discussed a constant concern with the processes of nation-state formation in both direct and indirect ways, revealing an imaginative sensibility that has the political horizon as an important defining signified. This notion of African writing as a will-to-identity may be traced to the sentiments expressed by writers such as Achebe in his 'The Novelist as Teacher' (1975) and Wole Soyinka in the introduction to *Myth, Literature and the African World* (1976) and in numerous other pronouncements about the function of African writing in seeking to recuperate a sense of self-worth for the African psyche.

In relation to the projection of indigenous resources, a variety of positions may be discerned. In the writings to be discussed here, the basic tendency that is elaborated is one towards mythopoeisis rather than straightforward realism. The resource-base of mythopoeia itself generates an interesting configuration of ideas to do with heroism and the establishment and transgression of boundaries. These ideas furnish a sort of subtext to the work of the writers we will look at, in that there is frequently an elaboration of liminal boundaries from various perspectives in their work. To highlight this particularly subtle seam in addition to the central concern of tracing a specific literary history in Nigeria would then be fruitfully to heed the suggestions delivered by the two epigraphs with which this chapter was opened: to pay close attention to the constitution of series and the elements proper to them in a literary criticism that is at once not just literary and historiographic but also interdisciplinary.

Notes

1 These specific examples are taken from Eldred Jones's editorial article 'Myth and Modernity: African Writers and Their Roots', *African Literature Today* 18 (1992): 1–8. It offers a concise example of the general practice of detailing the elements of orality in literature which are then further elaborated by the articles that follow in this special issue entitled 'Orature in African Literature Today'.

2 The essentialism involved in scholarly ideas about African life and culture have come under serious criticism in recent times particularly from Anthony Kwame Appiah in his influential *In My Father's House* (London: Methuen, 1992). But nowhere have the essentialisms been more forcefully and convincingly deconstructed than in an essay by Denis Ekpo entitled 'Towards a Post-Africanism: Contemporary African Thought and Post-modernism', *Textual Practice* 9.1 (1995): 121–35. Ekpo makes the exciting observation that the notions of Africanness that have dominated African thought so far have actually had a debilitating effect on the development of sustained analysis precisely because they derived congenitally from a Western Logos and stabilized the West within a moral framework. For him, this has disastrous consequences and he advocates a new mode of analysis that would move into an understanding of colonialism not in moral terms but in terms of the perfection and operation of a *system*. It is to systems and their attendant games, therefore, that he would have us turn our attention as a way of mastering the ways by which to gain *cognitive* rather than moral control over the West.

3 This essay was first delivered at the Weekend Seminar on Yoruba Language and Literature, University of Ife, 1969 and published in Adebisi Afolayan (ed.) *Yoruba Language and Literature* (Ife: University of Ife Press, 1982). It was subsequently republished in Irele's collection of essays, *The African Experience in Literature and Ideology* (Bloomington: Indiana University Press, 1983) rpt 1990. All my references are to the version in *The African Experience* (1990).

4 All quotations will be taken from Eliot's 'Tradition and the Individual Talent', in *Selected Prose of T. S. Eliot*, edited with an introduction by Frank Kermode (1919; London: Faber and Faber, 1975): 37–44.

5 Michael Baxandall's list of words and phrases denoting the agency of later writers and artists in relation to earlier ones runs up to forty-six. See his *Patterns of Intention:*

On the Historical Explanation of Pictures (New Haven and London: Yale University Press, 1985): 58–9.

6 Apart from his novels being required reading in schools in Yorubaland from the early 1940s, Fagunwa also designed Yoruba readers which proved to be very useful for use in the teaching of the language. For a careful analysis of the educational debates in which Fagunwa became involved, see T. A. Awoniyi, 'The Role and Status of the Yoruba Language in the Educational System of Western Nigeria: 1846–1971', diss., University of Ibadan (1973): 253–9.

7 Idowu settles on these figures on the basis of their position in the oral traditions. From a study of the sources these *orìṣàs* are noted to have been closest to Olodumare from earliest times. See *Olodumare: God in Yoruba Belief* (London: Longman, 1962): 70–106.

8 J. F. Ade Ajayi gives an account of the specific processes in 'How Yoruba was Reduced to Writing', *Odu* 8 (1960): 49–58. Also Awoniyi (1973) already cited. It is pertinent to note also that the transition to a literate tradition in Yoruba led to the constitution of what may be called a Yoruba *koiné*, specifically of a written standard based on the Oyo dialect into which Samuel Ajayi Crowther began to translate the Bible. This development was crucial in promoting a modern pan-Yoruba consciousness, given expression in the term 'Omo Oduduwa' ('Children of Oduduwa'). It is significant that the term is reprised in the name of the Yoruba cultural association (Egbe Omo Oduduwa) that formed the genesis of the Action Group, the political party founded in the fifties by Obafemi Awolowo. These points were persuasively brought to my attention by Abiola Irele in personal communication.

9 For a wide-ranging discussion of this process in the West African sub-region in general, see *Self-Assertion and Brokerage: Early Cultural Nationalism in West Africa*, edited by P. F. de Moraes Farias and Karin Barber (Birmingham: Centre for West African Studies, 1990).

10 The first initial impulses in historical, anthropological and cultural studies of orality and literacy came from people like Eric Havelock in his *Preface to Plato* (1963). At the same time the work of Parry from the 1920s (collected in 1971) and Lord (1960) set new standards and issues in the field. Goody and Watt were the earliest to attempt to typify the different implications of orality and literacy on the human mind in their seminal article 'The Consequences of Literacy' (1968). Walter Ong produced his interesting survey of the issues in *Orality and Literacy* (1982), and his, along with the work of Goody and others who apply a technologically deterministic notion of literacy with all its implicit privileging of Western culture, have been criticized by Ruth Finnegan in 'Literacy versus Non-Literacy: the Great Divide' (1973) and in her *Literacy and Orality: Studies in the Technology of Communication* (1988). Brian V. Street has also criticized the earlier model from a more ideological perspective in his *Literacy in Theory and Practice* (1984).

2

Nutritive Junctures

Rev. Samuel Johnson
& Yoruba Historiography

In many respects Rev. Samuel Johnson's *The History of the Yorubas*[1] offers a challenge to any paradigm of literary history we might like to construct for Yorubaland and for Nigeria more generally. Positioned as it is in the late nineteenth century, the work combines an overview of the processes of the formation and later fragmentation of the 'nation' of the Yoruba through a careful interweaving of oral and literary sources. *The History* provides a multi-layered dimension to traditional historiography, a rich interface between orality and writing that has not yet been fully explored by scholars of Nigerian history.[2] Completed in 1897 but not published until 1921, *The History* attempts to project a pan-Yoruba identity by focusing on the rise of Oyo (or 'Yoruba proper', as Johnson calls its people), its growth in status among Yoruba states and its gradual eclipse due to the rise of other military and metropolitan centres such as Ilorin and Ibadan. It also relates the circumstances that led to the establishment of the British Protectorate in 1893. So broad is the scope of the work and so beautiful its composition that it has been praised by scholars as the principal glory of Yoruba historiography (see Law 1976; J. D. Y. Peel 1989). To turn to *The History of Yorubas* in opening a study of Nigerian literary history is not merely to gesture a commitment to inter-disciplinarity; it is also deeply to acknowledge the indispensibility of this work for understanding a period of cultural transition in its fullest complexity, just as the traditional boundaries of a 'Yoruba' culture were being formed in the face of wider historical processes that were to integrate it into a larger nation that was to become Nigeria. An exploration of *The History* will help to demonstrate the variety of strategic uses to which oral traditions are put in the context of transitional cultural and historical processes.

The History's pre-eminent status as a source of information on

eighteenth- and nineteenth-century Yorubaland has led later historians to rely heavily on it as an authoritative source of oral traditions
dealing with that period. The mode of its appropriation by academic
historians, however, reveals an unconscious impulse to define the
work in a limited and monologic relationship to academic historiography. The usual approach adopted by academic historians is to
cross-check the accounts in Johnson's work against parallel accounts
from neighbouring tribes or against written accounts by travellers
and missionaries where they are available. If, as is often the case,
there are no available parallel accounts, academic historians attempt
rationalizations of the accounts and quickly move on to their own
conclusions. At other times, the rationalization of the accounts is
done more subtly by means of citing or quoting Johnson in such a
way as to limit the margins of improbability involved in the magical
and supernatural aspects to some of his accounts.

An example of this is to be seen in the way in which Gaha, one of
the most powerful Prime Ministers of Oyo, is variously handled by
Johnson, S. A. Akintoye and R. S. Smith. Gaha's power is generally
acknowledged as symptomatic of the decline of Oyo in the eighteenth century. Johnson says this of him:

> Gaha was famous for his 'charms'; he was credited with the power of
> being able to convert himself into a leopard or an elephant and on this
> account was much feared. He lived to a good old age and wielded power
> mercilessly. He was noted for having raised five kings to the throne, of
> which he murdered four and was himself murdered by the fifth. (178)

In Johnson's hands, Gaha is lent legendary awe. This would con-
ceivably derive from the way in which he was traditionally perceived
in the oral accounts. Akintoye writes of him in terms that completely
distance any sense of awe from this seemingly all-important figure:

> By the end of the eighteenth century, however, the empire [i.e. Oyo] was in
> decline. A clear sign of this decline is seen in the career of the _Basorun_
> (Prime Minister of the Empire) who held all authority in the empire in the
> hands of himself and his children and reduced successive Alafins to mere
> puppets. (Akintoye 1971: 33)

Gaha is not even mentioned by name. Indeed, his name is tucked
away in a footnote to the main text. In the case of Smith, he discusses
Gaha's prowess and even reproduces the same passage we have
quoted from Johnson, with the important difference that he omits the
first sentence of the passage referring to Gaha's charms and his ability
for uncanny metamorphoses (see Smith 1988: 38–40). In _The History_,
unlike in the other accounts referred to, historical figures are often
attended by the same discursive strategies that attend legendary and
mythical ones, thus blurring the distinction between history and
legend. The discourses of academic historians, on the other hand,

entail the suppression of the legendary tendency in line with affixing historical 'facts' and figures in a rationalistic discourse that can be submitted to verificatory procedures. The urge of academic historians to establish a scale of factuality and to differentiate the probable from the less probable leads to a suppression of the cultural signification of *The History*, because apart from bracketing out the legendary elements they also ignore the discursive properties of the work that derive from a context of orality.[3]

The urge to establish a scale of factuality by academic historians relates to attitudes in a broader field of scholarship to do with orality in Africa. It has to do with the attitudes towards oral traditions in general and the means by which to derive 'History' (as a Western and academic category) out of them.[4] Nowhere is the problem of conceptual categories better articulated than in Jan Vansina's landmark contributions to the historical study of oral traditions. His *Oral Tradition* (1965) inspired great efforts in this direction by proposing a methodology by which to isolate the distorting impact that things such as generic conventions and cultural imagery have on the properly historical aspects of oral traditions. In this methodology, oral traditions are placed in an interpretative framework that brings them as close as possible to written documents. Essentially, however, the fine differentiations necessary to arrive at the historical matter in oral traditions are also differentiations to bring them in line with the conceptual form of archival documents.[5] Thus, what is at play in this methodology is a chirographic impulse to treat oral traditions as written documents would be treated, excluding the problematic parts that would relate to the dynamics of orality that might disturb the chirographic paradigm. Even when, as Vansina does in an important advance over his earlier work, oral traditions are recognized as possessing significance for various disciplines, the stress for the historian is to recognize their multivalence the better to abstract a historical core (Vansina 1985: 28–9). In this way, the procedures serve to suspend the cultural signification inherent in the oral materials in order that an unproblematic historical core be retrieved. It is this attitude that has been operating implicitly in the ways in which Johnson's *History* is appropriated by academic historians as a source of oral traditions about the Yorubas. In my view, a proper appreciation of *The History* requires that it is treated first and foremost as a cultural product, with an awareness of all the multivalent potential that it derives from its background of orality.

Johnson relied on two main sources for information on Yoruba history up to the later part of the nineteenth century. With respect to the ancient and mythological period, he relied on the 'bards' or official court historians, while in relation to the period from the time of *Aláàfin* Abiodun, the last powerful king of Oyo in the late eighteenth century, he turned to eye-witness accounts of events.[6] The 'bards' Johnson refers to were the *Arǫkin*, a composite organization consisting of two principal groups: the *Onisèkèrè* (*sèkèrè* drummers) with the *Ológbò* at their head, and the *aro* drummers with the *Alaro* as their leader. They were responsible for reciting the history and *oríkì* of former kings on important occasions. They also had a role as social critics and often modulated the nature of potentially disruptive information to be given to the king, especially that to do with bereavement. Their role in the king's court seems to have been all-important, and though they now no longer enjoy the same prestigious status, they still exist as a semi-professional group on call to perform on important occasions in the modern-day *Aláàfin's* court.[7] Given the admitted importance of the *Arǫkin* in contributing to *The History*, it is useful to attempt an abstraction of their historiographic principles to aid us in grasping the peculiar quality of the work.

We must attempt to abstract the historiographic principles of *Arǫkin* practice with the awareness that the *Arǫkin* are not the only sources of history in Yorubaland. Oral traditions are freely available in the culture, and there are often contestations as to the provenance and significance of some of the traditions. Because of this, historians advise that official accounts be always tested against accounts derived from unofficial sources (Law 1973; Folayan 1975). Official sources do not have a monopoly of what constitutes history in Yoruba culture. To typify Yoruba historical consciousness from official sources, then, is to point out the historiographic practices pervasive in the culture and not just limited to official sources of history.[8] To do this, however, is not to pretend to be able to exhaust the full discursive potential of oral traditions in Yorubaland, something that would require a more comprehensive analysis beyond the ambit of this book.

In Yorubaland, historical narratives are known as *ìtàn*. Deidre La Pin typifies it in her study of Yoruba storytelling as including the 'acts of the *òrìsà* and great men; the origins of peoples, lineages and towns; battles lost and won; and the establishment of religious or political institutions' (La Pin 1977: 31, 44–53). The *ìtàn*, as an oral mode of relaying the traditions, give scope for the inclusion of a wide variety of other oral genres such as songs, *oríkì* (praise-poems and epithets), proverbs and etymologies in the historical framework of their narratives. Significantly, however, the other oral genres included in the *ìtàn* are themselves potential historical modes. This is particularly true of *oríkì* , which offer historical materials by means of a tightly woven concatenation of the praises and attributes of persons, lineages, clans and gods. The key to unravelling *oríkì*, as Karin Barber points out, is the context of performance where the opportunity is offered for observing what chanters of *oríkì* are doing (in the Speech Act theory sense of the word), because the form depends a great deal on the action of the performer in linking up with the performances of previous performers and also in constituting the identity of the subject of the *oríkì* (Barber 1989; 1991a: 67–86). More importantly, they establish a symbiotic relationship with the *itàn* in the context of ritual ceremonies such as those relating to the worship of the *òrìsàs*. Though *itàn* are the modes in which knowledge about the *òrìsà* is circulated in everyday contexts, *oríkì* are the main modes for the propitiation of the *òrìsà* in ritual ones. And quite often, the attributes that the *oríkì* isolate and concentrate upon become detached from their initial contexts and are transferred from one *òrìsà* to another, in a fluid reconstitution of identity. Because of this reconstitutive feature of *òrìsà* identities, Karin Barber argues that a useful mode of entry into the identity of *òrìsà* is through their *oríkì*, which would help to make sense of the discernible inconsistencies in the *itàn òrìsà* (Barber 1990). Thus both *oríkì* and *itàn* are inextricably linked not only in the construction of the identities of *òrìsà*, but also of clans and personages as historically knowable entities with specific modes of emergence, development and change within Yoruba culture. This observation is particularly important because the oral narrative forms are always articulated within certain practical contexts that require a special relationship to be established between the audience, the oral genre and the cultural values being articulated. As a means of entry into the historiographic practice of Yoruba culture, the symbiotic relationships between various oral genres point to the fact that history, as derived from the oral traditions in the culture, is a tissue of various interrelated signifying practices. When oral narrators narrate history it is with a repertoire of all the various oral genres available in the culture which they continually scan to make meaning. As Farias notes in relation to the *Aróķin*: 'What is recorded of the *Aróķin* practice seems to be best described in terms of an inherited repertoire of appellations, tableaux, glosses, and narratives which can be accessed at any point and need not be scrolled down in ordered chronological stages' (Farias 1992: 290).

The active interrelationships of various oral genres in the body of the *itàn* permit the oral narrators to establish specific relationships with their audience. The *Aróķin* recited their *itàn* to the accompaniment of music from drums and other instruments. This is clear from the fact that the two groups into which they were traditionally divided derived their identities from the different drumming instruments central to their vocation. It is conceivable that such musical instruments were a necessary accompaniment to the reciting of oral traditions at court or other public gatherings to arrest and hold the people's attention. The music aided in creating a dramatic social space within which the audience were drawn into participating in the historical consciousness activated by the *Arǫkin*. What is more interesting, however, is that even when the context does not seem to demand musical instruments, oral narrators still evoke putative theatrical conditions by interspersing the narration of oral traditions with songs. This is evident from Farias's interviews with the *Arǫkin*. The *Alusèkèrè* Beelo twice breaks into songs during a lengthy answer to the question about the founding of the *sèkèrè* drums (Farias 1992: 277, 288). And several times during Adeyemi's accounts and in La Pin's historical narratives, songs feature as a common part of the narratives. The contexts in which some of La Pin's *ìtàn* are told is particularly interesting because they were recited in response to the researcher's prodding. The audience was often composed of not more than three people including La Pin herself, but this did not prevent the narrators from introducing songs into their narrations.[9]

Yet, in my view, the most important conceptual grid on which the historical consciousness converges and which offers opportunities for narrator/audience participation is not the songs but the anecdotal organization of narratives. It is noticeable that the narrative structure of the *ìtàn* is essentially episodic, and proceeds by relating the anecdotes of great persons. This anecdotal thrust, however, is not so much a special feature of the historical narratives as it is a general paradigm for organizing social interaction in oral cultures in general. Anecdotes are a common part of everyday life in oral cultures, and La Pin notes that in Yorubaland they form a large part of interpersonal interaction. For her, anecdotes are a means of persuasion and illustration that speakers often employ to convince their listeners. Thus, a Yoruba speaker launches into anecdotes to clarify a point and to help bring his/her audience to a value judgement on the reported experiences related by the speaker (La Pin: 17–20). It would seem, however, that anecdotes in oral narratives signal additional aspects. Since face-to-face communication is of great importance in passing on information in oral cultures, it would seem fair to hypothesize that the face itself becomes one of the organizing units for the construction of a conceptual grid. By a metonymic analogy, the face stands for what we might term 'character-in-action'. It would seem that anecdotes mark in the narrative space the essential face-to-face contact that is the main mode of communication in the wider social space. In this sense, anecdotes abound in the historical narratives so that the audience can relate quickly to the meaning of the narratives by grasping the modalities of action accorded individuals in the anecdotes. The anecdotal framework of oral narratives foregrounds character-in-action as against abstract processes and is designed to fulfil different needs from history in literate cultures.[10]

To scholars treating oral traditions as history, the *oríkì*, proverbs and songs we have noted as featuring in the *ìtàn* are known as 'clichés' or stereotypes. In conjunction with episodes and personal reminiscences, it is one of the principal elements from which oral historians compose history. Clichés are deceptively simple statements of meaning that refer to a more complex reality, sometimes in the past. They occur in 'several linguistic forms, but they are commonly proverbs, sometimes songs or chants, and typically in oral traditions elementary narrative themes like the arrival of a foreign hunter who settles as a king among local people' (see Joseph Miller, 1980: 7; also Vansina 1985: 137–46). To these scholars, the clichés are often geared towards affirming the present institutional status quo or of validating the cultural value-system. It seems to me, however, that despite the obvious presentist impact of the clichés in oral traditions and of oral traditions generally, they have uses other than affirming the status quo. Furthermore these elements can be detached from their initial contexts for application in other contexts. And it is not always that this is done in affirmation of the present arrangement of things.

An example of more critical applications of oral traditions is provided in a study by Bruce Lincoln. Among other things, he shows how in Iran during the time of the Shah, the Shah and his enemies drew on different moments from the past as they struggled to construct different kinds of societies in the present. Whereas the Shah relied on the history of the Achaemenians (Cyrus the great, Darius I, Xerxes I) by which to construct an imperial and non-Islamic Iran, the mullahs turned to traditions of the martyrdom of Husayn from whom the Shi'ites draw inspiration and refigured the story so as to portray the Shah as Yazid, Husayn's murderer (Lincoln 1989: 32–7). And with reference to Yoruba culture, Andrew Apter (1992) shows, among other things, how the multivalent potential inherent in installation practices of Yoruba kingship were deployed in the political context of the 1989 Elections for the affirmation of opposition against the political status quo in the Ogun State of Nigeria. It becomes necessary, then, for us to shift our attention away from functionalist analyses of oral traditions and the elements in them towards grasping the strategic reasons for their transfer and application in different contexts. Furthermore, it is important to remember that the transferral of materials from oral traditions is not limited only to the clichés but may also involve wider conceptual and discursive frameworks moving between one context and another. We shall come to see later in the discussion how the reliance on oral narrative materials for the writing of *The History* produces a specific cultural understanding in relation to nineteenth-century cultural nationalism.

It is useful, in turning to the work itself, to outline its general divisions. I set out the work's general outline in the form of a table to make for easier reference:

Subject	pages	no. of pages
a) *Ethnographic Background*		
Language and Grammar	xxiii–lv	33
Mythology	1–25	25
Religion	26–39	14
Government	40–78	39
Names	79–89	11
Geography	90–94	5
Land Law	95–97	3
Manners and Customs	98–140	43
b) *Narrative History*		
Mythological Founders	143–154	12
Historical dynasties and the processes of state formation (inter-state wars, diplomacy etc.)	155–461	306
c) *'Documentary' History*		
Contemporary sections including texts of letters and other documents; the British Protectorate.	462–650	188
Appendices (containing texts of treaties and other agreements and lists of kings, military leaders and notable events)	651–671	20

Section 'a' of the work provides the bulk of the ethnographic materials relating to the Yorubas, while section 'c' outlines the events that led up to the establishment of the British Protectorate and also provides the texts of documents and treaties illustrating specific aspects of the process. I label this section 'contemporary' only in as far as the events reported occurred within the mature lifetime of Johnson himself. It is also 'contemporary' because of the growing activity of the missionaries and the British admininstration which paved the way for the establishment of the Protectorate over Yorubaland. Johnson was often an active participant in affairs at this stage. My focus will be mainly on section 'b', which contains the bulk of materials deriving from oral traditions. I shall, however, examine the discursive texture of the other sections and discuss the relationship they have with the middle section. The section divisions relate mainly to the general emphasis of their content and are not meant to be hard and fast. There are obvious areas of overlap between them.

The first indication that the work is not interested merely in narrating a 'history' is the extent of ethnographic materials provided in the Introduction. Most histories of the Yorubas open with brief introductions to the geography and culture of the people. *The History* does the same thing but to an extent that completely confounds the boundaries of an ordinary 'introduction'. It has 173 pages devoted to explaining every imaginable aspect of Yoruba culture. The chapter on 'Manners and Customs' (98–140) includes sections on diet, dress, funeral practices, and even has diagrams and sketches illustrating different Yoruba facial marks. These ethnographic materials are posited as generally belonging to all Yoruba peoples. Apart from the chapter on 'Government' (40–78), which relies heavily on the political organization of Oyo, all the other ethnographic details are posited as deriving from a pan-Yoruba ethos. In describing the naming ceremony of children, for instance, he asserts that it is evidently an ancient ancestral practice. Since he has earlier on affirmed that 'all the various tribes of the Yoruba nation trace their origin from Oduduwa and the city of Ile Ife' (15), the placement of such a cultural practice within the formulation of ancestral origins generalizes its application to embrace all the different Yoruba peoples. The vast stock of ethnographic materials in the introduction establishes a putative pan-Yoruba cultural archaeology.

Significantly, however, the ethnographic details are not confined to the first part of the work. There are often further elaborations of some of the ethnographic details given in the introductory sections. Though court officials such as the *Osi'wefa* and the *Ilaris* are introduced early in the introductory sections, we learn more about them and the ways in which their positions evolved much later in the work. It is interesting to learn, for instance, that *Ilaris* played a vital role in inter-tribal diplomacy and that their names were often decoded as a means by which to gain insight into the position of the *Aláàfin* in relation to important political issues.[11]

It is the middle sections of the work that betray the imprint of the discursive mode of oral traditions. The questions that need to be asked in relation to this section are: What is the effect of the transferral of materials deriving from oral traditions to a written framework? What conceptual and structural character does it lend *The History*? In the only full-length study of *The History* to date, Michel Doortmont characterizes *The History* as a collection of not very well connected praise-songs, engineered into a seemingly coherent epic tale. The foundation for this epic is formed by a king-list, which has in turn been copied in one form or another by many historians, as constituting the chronological framework in which Oyo history can be set. (Doortmont 1994: 79)

The items that arrest Doortmont's attention are the multiplicity of songs framed into a seeming epic, and the king-list which has been highly influential in later histories of Oyo. His perception of the pervasiveness of songs is quite interesting and requires comment, but we will set that aside for the time being and focus on the function of the king-list in the work. The various accounts in *The History* focus on the doings of kings, war-lords and their closest associates and the narrative as a whole unfolds as a chronicle of episodes in the reigns of various kings. This framework has been useful for later historians as a means of chronologically mapping various events in Yorubaland, and though this has been afflicted by some uncertainties because of the differences in the composition of various king-lists from the same period, it is still very useful.[12] It seems to me, however, that the importance of the dynastic framework lies not just in the possibilities it offers for chronological mapping, but rather in the opportunities for circulating accounts and anecdotes within the framework of the dynastic grid. In other words, the king-list is a centripetal organizing principle around which accounts can circulate. This grid has many uses for Johnson. The accounts have a thematic disposition and also yield stereotypical patterns. Farias notes how the traditions relating to the reigns of Shango and that of Ajaka his brother can be read as forming a thematic patterning. He suggests that the descriptions of these reigns in Johnson's *History* read like perceptions of kingship attributing two opposite but complementary natures to it; in his words 'the capacity for disorderly but creative violence and the capacity to establish peaceful order' (Farias 1992: 119–20). The thematic disposition of the accounts also allows Johnson to derive Christian notions of retributive justice from some of the patterns. This is seen in his comments about the deserved fate of Dado, an Ibadan war-chief and about the death of Ogunmola's son Ilori which he regarded as being a punishment for the father's over-ambition and deception.[13]

The accounts and anecdotes are often introduced with some editorial flourish such as 'as an example of such and such, the following story is told…' or 'several anecdotes were told of so and so, such as what follows…'[14] Setting himself aside from the anecdotes in this manner shows a consciousness of setting the oral accounts down in writing. It is a sign of the confluence of oral and literate attitudes to the project at hand. Furthermore, it reveals a desire to tell them as they were told and to gain some objectivity.

And yet, from the point of view of his relationship to the historical discourse he constructs, perhaps the greatest significance of the anecdotes lies in the freedom they allow him for inserting himself into the historical narrative as a self-conscious narrator of oral traditions. Johnson depicts a range of attitudes to the accounts he relates that reveals their significance as a framework that allows him to insert himself as a narrator. In a sense, the editorial flourishes mark the precise points at which he himself takes on the garb of an oral narrator. This becomes evident when we note that there is a full range of literary and narrative devices in the accounts which are amenable to elaboration. Among these are characterization, dialogue and scenic description. Johnson's relationship to this freedom for elaboration is partly depicted in the extent of dialogue and speeches he attributes to some of his characters. An interesting example is the speech of Lakanle, the _Otun Kakanfo_ (Commander of the Right Flank) of Ibadan forces during the early period of their expansionist campaigns. Lakanle remains at home at the start of an important Ibadan campaign on the side of the Ijebus against the Egbas, but comes hurriedly to the field of battle in response to his routed army's desperate calls for help. We are told that on arrival at the camp he 'assumed no lofty airs' nor did he 'allow one word of reproach to fall from his lips'. Instead, he addresses his men with words of encouragement:

> Fellow countrymen and companions in arms, I am not more surprised at your valour and prowess than at your chivalry in inviting me to share with you the honours of the field. For what can I do singly without your aid… Be of good cheer, my brave men, and this time tomorrow let victory crown our efforts. (254)

To this the soldiers 'gave long and loud shouts and were heard at a very great distance'. The whole speech characterizes Lakanle as a war-chief with deep humanity, concerned for the welfare of his soldiers as well as that of the families they left behind.[15] From the _ìtàn_ in La Pin's study and also in Adeyemi's work, there is no evidence of long speeches such as this one. What there is is frequent but brief dialogue. The fact that Johnson puts together such a long speech shows that he has imaginatively entered the conceptual space of the history he is narrating to animate the figures whose role he is exploring.[16]

The scope of his imaginative entry into the materials is also discernible from the extent of identification he establishes with certain characters. Most of the accounts are narrated with some measure of warmth, but it is difficult to escape the impression sometimes that Johnson operates with a scale of preference in relation to the figures he describes. Something of this is seen in his handling of chief Ayo of Abemo. Ayo is first introduced as being the leader of a band of chiefs who left Ijaye for Abemo (238). The narrative later focuses on him and the civil conflicts he had to resolve in his town. What is most striking about the second introduction of Ayo is that he is described in the context of some physical surroundings:

> But Ayo, instead of entering his house remained squatting on a mat in the square in front of his compound, close by the spot where his women folk were dyeing cloths, his horse standing by his side, and his spear stuck in the ground close to him. (269)

We notice how calmly Ayo blends with his environment and how the hint of domestic activity of the women nearby suggests a peaceful everyday atmosphere. The mention of his horse also contributes a sense of intimacy while his spear stuck in the ground introduces a sense of stillness into the picture. This picture is even more striking because Ayo is reported as having just broken camp on hearing about the reported treachery of one of his war-lords. A sense of tranquillity attaches to him once again when the circumstances of his death are being related. He has to depart Abemo because of a plot against his life, but after a short ride, decides to wait for his pursuers. This is what we see:

> He dismounted at a certain spot and sat under a tree, his horse standing by him. He sent away his little band of followers in order to die alone like a soldier. Here he calmly awaited his pursuers. (272)

Once again we notice the presence of his horse beside him. We also observe his consideration for his followers and the calmness with which he awaits his enemies. All this builds Ayo up in an endearing light. And when we are told later in a flashback that he was fond of drink and that he sometimes joked with his friends about their drunken escapades, the picture of a humane character is complete (272–3). What seems to influence Johnson in his portrayal of Ayo is his difference from other war-chiefs, for Ayo was 'by nature generous and merciful, in which respect he was most unlike his bloodthirsty peers of that age' (273). Thus, the light in which Ayo is portrayed relates to the perception of the moral value of his character. The description of Ayo differs in certain respects from that of other characters described in *The History*. Apart from there being few scenic descriptions, very few of the figures are ever depicted as possessing a personal foible of positive value.[17] Though the precise extent of his elaborations is difficult to establish, it is fair to suggest that Johnson had endless opportunities for identifying with the figures he describes and allowing himself to expand their characters in various directions. In doing this he engages with the conceptual format of characterization which we earlier termed character-in-action. For Johnson, as for oral narrators and their audiences, characters are an important part of the narratives because they act as conceptual grids on which significant ideas are put. Thus when Johnson elaborates his characters in this way, he is encoding a value system in the general discursive ways in which they would be encoded in the oral culture. In an important sense we could say that Johnson not only relates the oral traditions, but also *elaborates* them by taking on the freedom available to oral narrators. Because the main mode of narrative progression in *The History* is by way of anecdotes, he has the freedom to take on the narrative consciousness of oral narrators even as he attempts to place an objective distance between himself and the accounts he relates. Thus, one effect of relying on the historiographic discourse of his oral narrators is to render history as a told story with all the imaginative freedom that an orally told narrative affords.

This brings us to another point raised by Doortmont in his characterization of *The History*. The observation that the work is a 'collection of not well connected praise-songs, engineered [by Johnson] into a seemingly coherent epic tale' is an important one. It indicates that the songs in *The History* are a dominant feature of the accounts. The striking multiplicity of the texts of songs and ditties in *The History* becomes even more pronounced in accounts of wars. In a particularly telling section relating the circumstances leading to the Ijaye war and its aftermath (331–6), Johnson provides the texts of five songs in the space of just six pages. Of the five songs, three are attributed to the common people, one is attributed to Kurumi the Ijaye war-chief, and the last is given to the bard or praise-singer of one of the Ibadan war-chiefs. The songs capture the spirit of the times. They are composed of gnomic and proverbial sayings and deserve attention both as literary forms and as commentaries on the unfolding events. The song that the people of Ijaye sing in mockery of Adelu, the *Aláàfin* of Oyo is a case in point:

> L'aiye Onalu li ro'kan le okan
> L'aiye Kurumi li ro'gba ro'gba
> L'aiye Adelu ni ipele di itẹle idi

> In Onalu's time we used changes of dress
> In Kurumi's time we used cloths of fine weave
> In Adelu's time our best became our everyday. (334)

The Ijaye chief is called by two different names in the first two lines, as if to suggest a multiplication of his power and of the benefits deriving therefrom. As Johnson himself observes, the description of the conditions under Adelu is highly ironic because the line echoes a proverb that suggests that in time of poverty, people are forced to wear their best clothes even on everyday occasions. This ironic twist gains force by coming after two parallel constructions which are praises of the conditions under Kurumi. The last line gains even greater ironic sharpness if we propose a translation which is even more literal than Johnson's. It would go something like this:

> In Adelu's time the fine cloths for our shoulders became that by which we covered our bottoms.

The last line gains in irony if the phrase '*itẹlẹ idi*' is translated as 'the cloth with which the lower parts of the body is covered'. This interpretation revolves around the word *idi* because, depending on its tonal inflection, it could either mean 'bunch of firewood' or 'buttocks'. From the context, it seems to be the latter word, but either way it is difficult to miss the irony tipping over into sarcasm of the last line of the song.[18] The songs, then, draw on various poetic resources of the Yoruba language. Not only do they reflect the resources of Yoruba orality, their frequent appearance in Johnson's text suggests an oral as well as written conception to the work. The frequent songs are as if to dramatize the historical accounts and to invite the audience/reader to participate in the history he is outlining. Even in cold print, the songs capture some of the tension of the lived experience of the events he describes.

As we have already observed, the *ìtàn* in Yoruba culture make room for the expression of different oral genres within their narrative framework. The songs in Johnson's *History* are thus best understood in conjunction with the many *oríkì*, proverbs, and etymological explanations that frequently feature in the text. Taken together, these items lend *The History* a peculiar conceptual and structural imprint by being transferred from oral narrative contexts to be discursively reproduced in the body of a written and extended historical narrative. Because of the focus on anecdotes, much of the events described occupy a foreground by being linked to the actions of important characters. In this foreground, however, the various etymological explanations, *oríkì*, and songs act as intermediary teloi of cultural significations. They feature in the English-language text as obvious 'quotations' from another culture and thus attract attention to their status as culturally significant teloi. And because Johnson refuses to paraphrase them but rather renders them as closely as they would appear in Yoruba culture itself, these items have the effect of bringing the written history as close as is possible to the mode of oral history itself. In a discussion of the dismissive attitudes of Enlightenment historiographers in relation to the perceived irrationality of eighteenth-century historical discourse, Hayden White suggests that the problem of the Enlightenment historians lay not in their inability to understand the irrational in history, but rather in 'their incapacity to conceive of historical knowledge in general as a *problem*. This is because they drew the line too rigidly between 'history' on the one hand and 'fable' on the other, without recognizing the general difficulties in setting down truths about the past in the form of historical knowledge' (White 1978: 140). In my view, the problem of history-as-knowledge would also relate to the difficulties in separating historical knowledge from the cultural discourse in which it is couched. And this becomes even more problematic when re-reading a history that derives from a context of orality from the vantage point of literacy. In a sense, Johnson's *History* illustrates this problem. It is written so as to constitute a problem for the historical understanding whose contours can only be fully grasped if the traditional culture upon which it relied for its historiographic principles is understood. Furthermore, its reliance on oral historiographic principles is a strategic one that can only be understood if it is placed in the larger context of events in nineteenth-century Yorubaland and Nigeria. In that sense *The History* is written so as to require some preliminary conceptual adjustments by any reader unfamiliar with the oral modes of Yoruba discourse and with the context of the period in which it was written. Thus, the discourse of *The History* interweaves points of cultural intensity in the form of *oríkì*, proverbs, and etymologies to foreground itself as primarily a cultural product within a wider socio-cultural reality.

The third section of *The History*, which I term 'Documentary', reveals different features from the 'Narrative' middle sections of the work. In this part of the work, Johnson inserts the complete texts of letters and treaties giving as few comments as possible. Chapter XXVII of the book, which discusses the peace negotiations between Yoruba chiefs and the British administration, spans 15 pages, five of which are filled with the texts of various documents. Subsequent chapters are much the same. This section reads like a comprehensive diary of events with frequent references being made to people and dates. It is as if the work moves into a new conceptual mode.

The perceivable shift into a new conceptual mode is not accidental. It is signalled in this section of the work by frequent references to writing as a means by which the characters set down their positions in relation to political issues to be discussed. There is an early casual reference in Chapter XXVI to one Mr A. F. Foster, 'by whom the letter to Mr Olubi was written for the king' (462) but the reference to writing and its importance in negotiations becomes pronounced at a meeting with the Governor. We are told that the Governor had several interviews with the *Aláàfin's* messenger in order to learn from him particulars about the state of affairs inland. He also held meetings with the representatives of the Oyos and Ijeshas in Lagos, but these fell to undermining each other's positions to gain favour for their respective tribes. The reported reaction of the Governor is fascinating as it reveals the foregrounding of writing as a necessary first step towards future action :

> Under the circumstances the governor asked the messenger to put down in writing his opinion of the situation, the exact state of things, and his reasons for believing that the people wanted peace and that the Lagos Government's interference would be acceptable. And this he did in a letter addressed to His Excellency on the 28th of November, 1881. (466)

The question of the significance of writing is given centrality again, but with an ironic emphasis when we are told that to a request by a member of the Oke Igbo delegation to Lagos that the *Aláàfin*'s messenger divulge the purpose of the king's message, the retort of the members of the Oyo delegation is that since a messenger is not allowed to know the contents of a sealed letter, they are incapable of divulging its purpose (469). Though orality is clearly a dominant mode of interaction, writing seems to become the new focus for the construction and negotiation of various discursive positions in relation to politics.

The consciousness of writing and of dealing with written documents is what alters the quality of the report of events in this part of *The History*. Johnson seems to wish to allow the various documents to speak for themselves. But, because these documents have been set down in writing, they establish boundaries between their content and that of the rest of the narrated events. Unlike the accounts that populated the middle sections of the work, these documents contain no accounts amenable to imaginative entry and embellishment. Since, as we have noticed, Johnson attempts to establish some measure of objective distancing by allowing his sources to 'speak for themselves', he is forced by the boundaries inherent in these documents to surrender the freedom he exercised when acting as a narrator of oral traditions. In a sense, he is forced by the nature of the events he is describing at this stage to go as close to a Western mode of historical reconstruction as possible and this mode is modulated for him by the nature of the written sources he is working with. This relates not only to the fact that documents were available for this period, but also to the fact that he has now entered a historical zone in which Western culture is itself a dominant player.

Some questions need to be posed in evaluating the contribution of *The History* to the formation of a Yoruba consciousness: what was the purpose (or purposes) of writing *The History*, since it is evidently not just interested in history as such? What does it signal about the general uses of orality in the period when it was written and in subsequent periods? Johnson himself provides part of the answer in the very first paragraph of his work:

> What led to this production was not a burning desire of the author to be in print – as all who are well acquainted with him will readily admit – but

purely a patriotic motive, that the history of our fatherland might not be lost in oblivion, especially as our old sires are fast dying. (vii)

In this he reflects the concerns of the time. Newspapers of the period give evidence of the concern of the people that 'our Folklore, Legends, Histories, Parables, Aphorisms, Allegories & Co., are within the ready grasp of Oblivion'.[19] Indeed, the era saw a flowering of writings related to different aspects of Yoruba culture. *Iwe Owe*, a collection of proverbs, was published by S. A. Allen in 1885, D. B. Vincent's *Iwe Alo*, a collection of riddles, came out in the same year, and E. M. Lijadu's works on Ifa came out in 1897 and 1908. *The History*, then, becomes a sort of compendium of all these, since in its single texture it discursively weaves proverbs, songs, *oríkì* and other cultural materials. The statement of intent that Johnson provides can however only be part of the answer. The desire to conserve oral tradition is only a subsidiary one; the main reason, which is ultimately of over-riding importance, is the desire to project a unified Yoruba 'nation'.

It is all too easy to take for granted the rationality underpinning the urge to document and store aspects of Yoruba culture and history, but what this concealed was the spectacular production of a notion of nationness and of a homogenous people who had not begun to perceive themselves as such until very late in the century. Their perception of being part of one people could be said to have developed and gained coherence contemporaneously with the process of the deployment of notions of nationness and unity. What were the informing sources of the idea of the 'nation' by which Johnson and others organized Yoruba culture and history? How did this idea retain its contours in the process of outlining a history for peoples who saw themselves as first and foremost members of smaller ethnic communities?

The idea of the nation that Johnson made use of may be traced to his knowledge of classical European civilizations. He laments in his preface that educated Yoruba 'are well acquainted with the history of England and with that of Rome and Greece, but of the history of their own country they know nothing whatsoever'. On further examination, this turns out not to be an idle rhetorical jibe. Doormont details in his study of Johnson the type of education that prospective church workers in the period were exposed to. More significantly, he argues persuasively that aspects of the plotting of *The History* seem to bear comparison with Xenophon's *Anabasis*, *A history of the times* and *Hellenica*, texts that were on the curriculum of the CMS Training Institution which Johnson attended. Doortmont notes that particularly in Johnson's references to supernatural interventions in the unfolding of certain events, there seems to be a conflation of a Christian notion of divine intervention with one that uncannily parallels that shown in Xenophon's accounts of Greek history (Doortmont 1994: 64–76).

One thing that may be extrapolated from the conflation of classical and biblical influences in Johnson's work is that both Xenophon's works as well as the Bible dealt intensely with the formation of societies and their attendant heroic traditions, thus providing attractive models of action that could easily be conjoined to traditional notions of Yoruba heroism. In both the classical and the biblical sources, the chosen people are often defined in relation to others, either barbarians in the case of the classical texts or Philistines and other 'unchosen' people, in the case of the biblical accounts. In both cases there is also a strong mythographic consciousness at play in which the supernatural, in terms of gods or God, are seen to freely participate in the theatre of history. In an important sense, the older sources defined the historical peoples in terms of an epic trope. This epic trope was a historiographic organizing principle that allowed the narrativization of the fate of a people sharing a common consciousness of their role in history. Furthermore, such epic tropes lent themselves to teleological narrativization that touched on and became meaningful for reflections on present arrangements of things.

None the less, it is not completely accurate to see the idea of the nation as deriving solely from the classical and biblical texts that Johnson steeped himself in. The formation of the idea had a lot to do with developments in the idea of nation-statism in Europe at the same time. As Basil Davidson (1992: 118–19) puts it: 'The nineteenth century in Europe, above all its middle years, were the nation-state's great gestation period; and the births that would follow were many.'[20] Though it is difficult to demonstrate with specific references, it is not outrageous to hypothesize that the Western Christian missionaries would frequently have discussed notions of progress with an implicit assumption of the European state as a paradigm for the articulation of such progress. Even with an active cultural nationalist of the status of Edward Blyden writing in the period, the notions of the special qualities of the African race were built on the implicit assumption of a European paradigm of the nation (see Law 1990: 84, 88; also Ajayi 1962).[21] More significantly, Blyden's ideas were known to have been actively discussed in the educated circles of Lagos from as early as 1883 (Lynch 1967: 222) with he himself visiting Lagos three times, in 1890–1, 1894 and in 1896–7. As Law notes, these ideas must have reached Samuel Johnson through the educated circles in which he and his brother Obadiah moved.

It is at the interstices of all these factors that Johnson's notion of the Yoruba 'nation' was located. However, it is only to an acute sense of his people's emergence into an arena of wider historical processes that we should ultimately attribute the triggering impulse for *The*

History. Their mode of emergence, of course, cut in two directions. On the one hand the collapse of the Oyo Empire by the turn of the nineteenth century led to an upsurge of intertribal conflict and new processes of societal and state formation. And, on the other, their history was inextricably intermeshed with the appearance of British imperial power and all that it represented in cultural and political terms. The idea of the nationness of the Yoruba could not have been sustained without reference to this dual projection of significance both inside and outside of Yorubaland. This duality, of the constitution of an inside identity inextricably entangled with a looking outwards, may itself be taken as the dominant structuring impulse behind Johnson's consciousness, especially as this related to the processes of the formation of his sense of selfhood as a Saro and former freed slave. For, as John Peel (1989: 203) notes in assessing the contribution of the Saros to the constitution of Yoruba identity, 'the Saros' personal experiences of loss and dislocation were quintessential of the upheavals of the country at large.' We may add that their experience was also one of a cultural liminality that allowed them to be active in the production of a horizon of significance beyond their local tribal groupings.[22]

Scholars have variously commented on Johnson's avowed choice of the histories of Oyo and Ibadan to represent that of Yoruba-speaking peoples in general. He has been accused of practising some sort of 'substitutionism', writing the history of Oyo and Ibadan as if it was the history of all Yoruba-speaking peoples (Law, 1990). Indeed, the Oyo–Ibadan nexus of his history was resented by members of other tribes and led to harsh criticisms of the patent Oyo bias in his work. This 'substitutionism', however, is a crucial manoeuvre that reveals the motivation behind the process towards erasing differences in the construction of a pan-Yoruba identity. The 'substitutionism' can be perceived in the discourse of 'metonymy'. If metonymy is seen to be the general discursive strategy that substitutes the part for the whole, there is an important sense in which that part can be foregrounded not just as a part of a whole, but as an indestructible whole in itself, thus countering the perception of fragmentation. Johnson takes Oyo and Ibadan to stand for all the Yorubas, but these two, as metonyms for the Yoruba-speaking peoples, are located within the state of perplexing fluidity and constant flux that *The History* so painfully details. The dominant impression that emerges about the people is a sense of incessant assimilation and dissociation of identities and peripheral groupings: the Hausa mercenaries invited to Ilorin quickly became a force for the Islamization of its people, finally leading to its becoming an Emirate; Ibadan and Abeokuta are population centres that grow out of the refugee problems generated by the incessant wars in the north between the Oyos and the Ilorins

(*The History*: 193–4, 197–205). What Johnson does is to affirm the history of Oyo and of Ibadan as metonymic of the fate of all the people, for in the cultural continuity that Oyo represented, and in the multiplicity of identities that Ibadan embraced, the general fate of the Yorubas was mapped out in the processes of real history. In the cases of both Oyo and Ibadan, they had managed to establish large empires that brought the various Yoruba peoples under a single umbrella. His attempt to project a unified Yoruba identity through the focus on Oyo and Ibadan as metonyms is then a significant negotiation of the harsh reality of fragmentation with which he was accosted. It is a discursive strategy that maps an integrated homogeneity across splintering identities. Johnson does not allow the violent contradictions among the Yoruba people to act as an interruptive factor to the strategic discourse of projecting a homogeneous pan-Yoruba identity.

Yet he demonstrates a contradictory posture in carrying out this enterprise. On the one hand, he affirms the vitality of Yoruba culture by providing a wide range of ethnographic materials relating to the culture and also by depending on a non-Western episteme for the articulation of his historical discourse. There are several points at which he is openly critical of certain Western practices which he perceives as threatening to the integrity of his culture. He argues forcefully that the introduction of Christianity and the spread of British influence had introduced irregularities in local naming practices with ridiculous results. He also laments the increasing tendency among his people towards presenting 'words and phrases which are idiomatic English in Yoruba words'. This he perceives as a corruption of Yoruba language due to contact with the West (*The History*: 87–9). In spite of these patriotic sentiments, however, Johnson at various times attempts to place some of his people's social practices within Christian or foreign frameworks so as to lend them a new kind of legitimacy. This is evident in his attempts to trace an Eastern origin from which his people's ancestors could be said to have migrated. Even more striking are his suggestions that some important events are a fulfilment of a divine plan. At several other times too, he casts sceptical and aspersive remarks on some of the accounts he reports, suggesting they are the workings of immature and uncivilized minds.[23]

These contradictions become clearer when placed in the wider context of intellectual developments in Nigeria from the late-nineteenth to early-twentieth centuries. They were contradictions that marked the intellectual milieu of the period. The arrival of freed slaves and a gradual Christianization of large sections of the people in some metropolitan centres like Lagos, Oyo, Abeokuta and Ibadan led to the growth of a highly talented and energetic class of intellectuals who had affiliations with the Christian church. By the latter half of the nineteenth century, these local church officials began to feel restive in their subordinate positions under Western missionaries. The dissatisfaction led to an upsurge of intellectual activities designed to assert the viability of local culture.[24] Newspapers were one means for the expression of this dissatisfaction. Christian missionaries helped found Abeokuta's *Iwe Irohin* in 1859, but it was Lagos that was the base of a vital indigenous newspaper movement. The establishment and success of *The Lagos Times* in 1880 paved the way for the expression of nationalist sentiments by the Lagos elite. *The Lagos Times* was edited by Mojola Agbebi, a committed cultural nationalist, and was successful as a bold and uncompromising denouncer of wrong. Other papers followed suit and soon there was a vigorous atmosphere of criticism against the colonial government.[25]

It is evident that Johnson's text was a representative example of cultural expressions in that period. As has already been noted, some of the expressions of the vitality of traditional culture were articulated with certain Western analogues of nationhood in mind, with the consciousness of race as a central tenet in the equation. At the same time too, the efforts towards a viable identity were undertaken with a sense of the desirability of some of the things in Western culture. This led to a conflation of values which was even projected onto the general social demeanour of the intellectuals. As Ayandele (1966) tells us:

> They [the intelligentsia] retained parts of indigenous culture that were deemed valuable and borrowed judiciously from the European civilisation they so much execrated. Realising that complete cultural independence was impossible, they evolved a new synthesis which was neither reactionary traditionalist nor European-imitative but sufficiently African in appearance to satisfy their race-pride and sentiment. (259)

Thus the pursuit of identity was done with an implicit consciousness of its being articulated at the conjuncture of two cultures. For Samuel Johnson, this sense of a conjuncture is expressed not just in the contradictory posture that may be detected in his handling of his materials, but also in his bold attempt at expressing his people's historical consciousness in a literate mode. As I have already pointed out, one of the ways of achieving this was to reproduce the discourse of Yoruba historiographic practice as closely as possible to create a cultural statement within the new literate means of expression. With this, he achieves a relationship to the debates on cultural nationalism of the period which both embrace and go beyond them to look to the future. His project links up with other attempts at projecting identity at a cross-cultural conjuncture which have been marked in other fields. In an interesting conceptual parallel to the project of *The History* in the twentieth century, the African Church of Orunmila articulates biblical themes by means of the discursive strategies of Ifá divination texts (see Barber 1990). In this, the Church of Orunmila demonstrates the same impulse that motivated *The History*, but from a profoundly theological and philosophical position. We can see, then, that the impulse towards drawing from the oral traditions is one that marks various discourses in both the Yoruba and the English language. It is useful to bear this in mind when we turn to examine the literary writers and the strategic relationships they establish with the traditional resource-base in all its varying manifestations.

Notes

1 Rev. Samuel Johnson, *The History of the Yorubas*, edited by O. Johnson (1921). Page references in the text refer to this edition.

2 Michel R. Doortmont seems to be the only person so far to have devoted himself consistently to the work of Samuel Johnson. See his 'Samuel Johnson and *The History of the Yorubas*: A Study in Historiography', unpublished MA diss., University of Birmingham 1985, and 'Recapturing the past: Samuel Johnson and the construction of the history of the Yoruba', unpublished Ph. D diss., Erasmus University, Rotterdam, 1994.

3 The question of the role of the supernatural in oral traditions has been analysed by several scholars and will not concern us here. For examples dealing with its significance in the oral traditions of different cultures, see E. R. Dodds, *Greeks and the Irrational*, (Berkeley: University of California Press, 1951); also Robin Horton, 'African Traditional Thought and Western Science', *Africa* 37.1 (1967): 50–71.

4 The problem of the constitution of a universal category of History deriving inspiration from a Western paradigm has been examined by Robert Young in *White Mythologies: Writing History and the West* (London: Routledge, 1990). Among other things his investigation of 'the history of History' shows how attempts to decolonize the category are continually being undertaken by various post-colonial writers. It seems to me, however, that the category can be even further problematized by viewing it from a radical context of orality and the form in which historical knowledge is constituted in predominantly oral cultures.

5 For a critical assessment of this tendency in the study of oral traditions, see Renato Rosaldo, 'Doing Oral History', *Social Analysis*, 4 (1988): 89–99; Joseph C. Miller, 'Introduction: Listening for the Past in Africa', in *The African Past Speaks*, ed. Joseph C. Miller (Kent: Dawson, 1980): 1–60; also Joseph Ki-Zerbo's general introduction to Unesco's *General History of Africa Vol. I*, especially pp. 7–11.

6 Robin Law has suggested that Johnson may well have been overly sanguine in believing he had eye-witness accounts referring so far back. See Law, 'How Truly Traditional is Our Traditional History', *History in Africa* 11 (1984): 195–221.

7 My account of the *Arǫkin's* past and present status relies on the analysis of their position offered by Agiri, 'Early Oyo History Reconsidered', *History in Africa* 2 (1975): 1–16 and P. F. de Moraes Farias, 'History and Consolation: Royal Yoruba Bards Comment on their Craft', *History in Africa* 19 (1992): 263–97.

8 I shall be drawing my examples for Yoruba historiographic practice from three main sources, namely de Moraes Farias, 'Royal Yoruba Bards', already cited, and his 'Yoruba origins revisited by Muslims' in Farias and Barber, *Self-Assertion and Brokerage*: 109–47; Deirdre La Pin's 'Story, Medium and Masque' (1977); and '*Iwe Itan Oyo*: A Yoruba traditional history and its author', a history of Oyo dating from 1914 by Michael Adeyemi and edited by Toyin Falola and Michel Doortmont in

Journal of African History, 30 (1989): 301–29. Together, these offer collections of oral traditions and also important commentary on oral narrative practices in Yorubaland.

9 See especially nos. 345, 346 and 347 in the appendix to her study, recorded the same day, one after the other. These are in Volume II of her dissertation.

10 However, it might well be that there are grounds for seeing this feature of oral narratives as fulfilling a Formist historical mode in Hayden White's sense of the term. Formism is that historiographic mode in which the 'depiction of the variety, colour, and vividness of the historical field is taken to be the central aim of the historian's work'. The difference, though, is that as a discourse the formism of Western history is not aimed at eliciting people's participation in the historical consciousness directly, whereas oral historians attempt to elicit such participation by focusing intently on character-in-action. Obviously, it is necessary to place the historical discourse in its proper cultural context. See Hayden White, *Metahistory: The Historical Imagination in Nineteenth-Century Europe* (Baltimore: Johns Hopkins University Press, 1973): 13–21.

11 The *Osi'wefa* are first introduced on p. 59, but there is an elaboration of the way they attained their high position on pp. 162–3. The *Ilaris*, on the other hand, are first introduced on pp. 60–3, but their role is continually elaborated throughout the text. The role of Oba'kosetan ('the King is not ready') for instance, is particularly interesting and he is mentioned variously on pp. 468–70, 514, 526 and 531. For the role of other *Ilaris*, see pp. 171–2, 211 and 466. See also Richard Olaniyan, 'Elements of Traditional Diplomacy: An Assessment', in *Yoruba Oral Tradition*: 293–332 for an exposition of traditional Yoruba diplomacy drawing on Johnson and other sources.

12 For discussions of the discrepancies between Johnson's king-list and those of other Oyo historians see Law, 'How Truly Traditional is Our Traditional History' and also B. A. Agiri, 'Oyo History Reconsidered' already cited.

13 Johnson, 237–8, 349, 435. But for a discussion of stereotypical patterning and their significance in both the accounts given by the *Arókin* they interviewed and in Johnson's *History* see Farias, 'Royal Yoruba Bards': 285–6.

14 Examples of such editorial flourishes abound, see, for a few examples, pp. 146, 169, 206, 242, 372 and 397.

15 There is something to be said for seeing this as Johnson's manipulation of rhetorical speech genres from classical accounts. Doortmont shows that his education included a fair amount of study in the classics.

16 Other examples are Elepo's parable, 290–1 and *Aláàfin* Majotu's speech to his chiefs, 214–15.

17 Consider, for instance, the positive character portraits he gives of figures like Abiodun, 192, Elepo, 302–3 and Oluyole, 305–7. These contrast with the vengefulness of Odarawu, 169 and the perverse sexual habits of Prince Adewusi, 214–15, and the numerous negative traits he gives of other figures. In all these the judgement he passes is implicit in the manner in which the figures are presented.

18 I am indebted to Professor Dapo Adelugba of the University of Ibadan for taking me through the nuances of these lines in the Yoruba language and for pointing out the subtle irony of the last line.

19 *Lagos Observer,* 27 October and 3 November, 1888. Cited by Law in 'Yoruba Historiography'.

20 The literature on the formation of nation-states is rich and varied. One thing to be noted in passing is that the dual processes of internal class and gender formations in Europe, going hand-in-hand with imperialist expansion that had begun earlier but burgeoned in the period, ensured that European nationalism was a multifarious phenomenon. See especially E. J. Hobsbawm, *The Age of Capital* ([1962]; 1995) and Laura Ann Stoler, *Race and the Education of Desire* (1995) for respective treatments of the rise of nationalism and of bourgeois gender values as they related to imperial expansion.

21 Edward Blyden's key writings in this respect were *Christianity, Islam and the Negro Race* (1887), *West Africa Before Europe* (1905), and *African Life and Customs* (1908).

22 The Saros were freed slaves from Sierra Leone. Often devout Christians, they formed the earliest church workers. Among important Saros in Yoruba cultural nationalism were people like Samuel Johnson himself, Bishop Ajayi Crowther (who first translated the Bible into the Yoruba language), Rev. James Johnson and many others. For a general account of the activities of the Saros and of other cultural nationalists in this period in West Africa, see Robert July's *The Origins of Modern African Thought*, London: Faber, 1968.

23 For some instances of Christian interpretations, see pp. 9, 29, 33, 188, 211, 296; and for sceptical remarks, pp. 29–30, 33, 174.

24 For a concise analysis of the role of the Church in early Nigerian cultural nationalism, see J. F. Ade Ajayi, 'Nineteenth-Century Origins of Nigerian Nationalism', *Journal of the Historical Society of Nigeria* 2.2 (1961): 196–210.

25 For a lively analysis of the activity of the newspapers in this period, see Omu, 'The Newspaper Press in Southern Nigeria, 1800–1900' in *Studies in Southern Nigerian History* (London: Frank Cass, 1982) edited by Boniface I. Obichere.

3

Treasures of an Opulent Fancy

Amos Tutuola
& the Folktale Narrative

Amos Tutuola's writings provide a curious angle to the notion of a strategic formation in Nigerian literature. The publication of his first books in the 1950s generated mixed responses, with non-African critics seeing in them a fresh and bewitching type of storytelling while African commentators deprecated his ungrammatical English and were at pains to show his debt to Yoruba folklore.[1] Eustace Palmer was later to say, in summing up the early controversy, that early readers had assessed Tutuola by the wrong standards. It was better to view him as a 'brilliant teller of tales' instead of a novelist (1979: 12). Other critics accepted this standpoint but went on to assert that his work revealed a profound grasp of mythic patterns (Gerald Moore 1980). Yet others saw him as a 'riddler' creating works whose central aim was to confound efforts at easy interpretations, while a few others saw him as the teacher of a new humanistic code (Priebe 1980; Achebe 1980).

Two general tendencies have characterized the criticism of Tutuola's work. On the one hand, there have been strenuous efforts to show his debts to Yoruba storytelling traditions. This has often been done by tracking his sources and showing how much he depends on motifs, themes and tales from Yoruba folklore. The other tendency has been to trace universal patterns in his work. This has been particularly true of the comments of critics like Gerald Moore (op. cit.) and Harold Collins (1969, 1980). It seems to me, however, that the general effect of these two tendencies is to undervalue Tutuola's own role as a creative imagination, making him a slave of totalizations deriving either from his culture or from universal mythic paradigms.

In this chapter, I would like to examine Tutuola's work in the light of three contexts. Firstly, I shall examine his work in relation to traditional cultural resources. His resources, for me, include both Yoruba folkloric materials and the literary production of earlier writers such as Fagunwa. As has already been noted, Fagunwa was a dominant figure on much of Yoruba literature from the mid-1940s when his books were introduced into the curricula in the then Western Nigeria (see Awoniyi 1973; also Isola 1988). My focus will be not so much on tracing his reliance on specific themes, motifs and stories, but on the discursive use he makes of them in order to create a universe which is both Yoruba and also peculiarly his own. Secondly, I shall examine the interface that he generates by transferring the folktale narrative into a literary mode of discourse. Thirdly, I would like to explore Tutuola's work in relation to his contribution to a cultural identity for both Yorubas and Nigerians at a time when questions of cultural nationalism had acquired a fresh urgency. I shall try to show how the veritable tensions his work generated among his early Nigerian critics relate to the contradictions in identity-formation in the period leading up to self-rule. For this exercise, I shall draw mainly on *The Palm-Wine Drinkard* and on *My Life in the Bush of Ghosts*.[2] Of all his six published books, these first two generated the greatest controversy among his local critics and therefore offer a useful means of relating his work to the general context of identity-formation.

Tutuola's debts to Yoruba folklore have been well documented (see, especially, Lindfors 1980). It is generally accepted that he was heavily dependent on the themes, motifs and tales of Yoruba story-telling traditions for his narratives. What is not realized is that though he articulates a Yoruba folkloric intuition, his art form has no direct parallel in Yoruba storytelling traditions. The hallucinatory realms he elaborates and in which he places a superhuman hero in one quest or another are not mentioned by any of the critics of Yoruba storytelling traditions. In an early analysis of Yoruba folktales, Adeboye Babalola tells us there are three broad categories of the folktale available to the traditional raconteur: those that are essentially mythological but slightly didactic purporting to explain the origins of some human characters and natural phenomena; humorous tales 'just for fun'; and expressly didactic folktales conveying specific morals.[3] Ayo Bamgbose, in a later effort, classifies them into 'Moral Stories, Tortoise Stories, and "Why" Stories.' In the most comprehensive analysis of Yoruba storytelling traditions to date, La Pin adopts a subtler classification drawing both on the classifications of the storytellers themselves as well as on the modal inflections of particular story materials. For, as she tells us, every set of materials is meant to evoke a particular response or mood and thereby establish a specific relationship with the audience (La Pin 122–33, 142–58). Apart from 'Charters', which are mythological stories taken to be largely factual, other narrative types she identifies are 'Romance', 'Parable', 'Formulaic Tales', 'Fables', and 'Song-Stories' (op. cit. 43–132 *passim*).

The first thing to be noted about these three taxonomic sets is the general disagreement about the specific generic types of folktales available in Yoruba culture. Furthermore, none of the sets cater for the type of supernatural stories that feature in Tutuola's books. This is in spite of the fact that all three critics mention the presence of the supernatural element and attempt to explain the cultural function of this element in the tales. La Pin's 'Romance' type comes closest to the mood of Tutuola's tales in which a hero undertakes difficult tasks and finally conquers all the anxiety-generating forces that confront him. One of the stories she collects is particularly interesting because it centres on the adventures of a hunter in the realm of spirits of dead people.[4] However, the spirits in this tale are signally different from those in Tutuola's stories. They behave much like human beings and have none of the ferocious and grotesque physical characteristics that mark the spirits in Tutuola's narratives. The differences between his type of ghostly stories and those that are collected by La Pin and others become even more problematic when we consider the fact that in *Bush of Ghosts*, the spirits in the book are far more grisly than those that feature in the earlier work set among the 'Deads' in *The Palm-Wine Drinkard*. The spirits in *Bush of Ghosts* have not lived on earth at all and are a species of supernatural denizens of the other world. Is the silence about the ghostly type of stories Tutuola sets down a curious oversight or do they represent taxonomically recalcitrant types?

It appears that the tales Tutuola sets down are an uncommon type of cautionary tales told to children which seem never to have crystallized into a definable genre. These normally involve the most frightening aspects of life outside the village community. Cautionary tales often draw on traditional travel narratives and on the experiences of hunters in the forests. The bush is the antithesis of settled communities and is conceived of as the problematic 'Other' harbouring all sorts of supernatural forces. This notion is further reinforced by the stories that circulate about hunters' encounters with strange creatures on their hunting expeditions in the bush. Thus, what Tutuola elaborates are the more harrowing aspects of cautionary tales, though he also draws upon other motifs and themes common to the more established genres told to children for entertainment.[5] The interesting thing about Tutuola's handling of these materials is that he brings together a whole range of oral genres such as riddles, proverbs and etymological tales so that his narratives become concatenations of several elements from Yoruba storytelling traditions and thus cannot be easily limited to one mode or genre. Furthermore, he interweaves the cautionary vein with humour, giving the cautionary mode an inflection that does not seem to be present in the oral contexts in which cautionary tales are used to frighten and inform children about the spirit world.

If this is the case, then we need to re-interpret Tutuola's celebrated acquisition of the tale that forms the basis of *The Palm-Wine Drinkard*. We are told that one Sunday morning he went to see a very old man on his father's farm. The old man roasted a big piece of yam for him and then regaled him with fresh palm-wine. This is what happened:

> He started to serve the wine with bamboo tumbler. This bamboo tumbler was as deep as a glass tumbler, but it could contain the palm-wine which could reach half a bottle. Having taken about four, my body was not at rest at all, it was intoxicating me as if I was dreaming. But when he noticed how I was doing, he told me to let us go and sit down on the bank of a big river which is near the farm for fresh breeze which was blowing here and there with strong power. Immediately we reached there and sat under the shade of some palm trees which collected or spread as a tent I fall asleep. After an hour, he woke me up, and I came to normal condition at that time.
>
> When he believed that I could enjoy what he wanted to tell me, he told me the story of the Palm-Wine Drinkard.[6]

Tutuola was 32 years old then. We must note that in relation to the 'very old man' he must have seemed merely a boy. The tale is told well after the drinking has taken place and not during it, as if to suggest it was an appendix the old man was adding to their experiences that afternoon. It is difficult to know how much of *The Palm-Wine Drinkard* was due to the old man, but we would not be wrong in surmising that the old man told this particular tale to put their own palm-wine drinking into a wider and more problematic context. In a way, it was to suggest to the young writer some of the dangers of prodigious drinking and the need to seek broader modes of social action. In this sense, the word 'enjoy' in the last sentence of the passage is ironic. Tutuola was not meant just to enjoy the tale, but was also meant to be cautioned even as the plot of the narrative acted as a cautionary structure for the Drinkard in the tale.

This interpretation would definitely not be sufficient for explaining the level of grotesque elements in *The Palm-Wine Drinkard*. For this, we have to look to Tutuola himself. This is particularly important because though his later works have the element of the grotesque, he is not quoted anywhere as attributing them to any other old man or person.[7] Tutuola's own input is discernible partly in the embellishments to the tales he incorporates in his work and partly in the nature of ghost-figures he creates. Many variants of the tale of the headstrong girl who refuses eligible bachelors and finally ends up with a ghost or other horrifying creature exist in the folklore of several West African communities (see Lindfors, 1980: 235–7). In *The Palm-Wine Drinkard*, it features as the long tale of the 'complete gentleman' (17–31). Palmer points out that in a Yoruba version published in Ogumefu's collection of legends, the 'complete gentleman' is originally a head and not a skull and belongs to a country entirely populated by heads. He comes to the human world because he has a longing to see it and borrows his parts from humans. On arrival at a town, it is initially he himself who is attracted to a group of dancing girls, one of whom he persuades to marry him and return with him to his own country. When the bride realizes that her husband is nothing but a head, she runs away horrified to her home, and since the head has now neither body nor limbs, is unable to pursue her. In another version the girl is saved by a wind which her mother causes to blow her home, and in a Sierra Leonean version the gentleman sheds only his clothes, not the parts of his body (Palmer 1979: 15–16). Though, as Lindfors rightly points out, it is difficult to know what exact variant Tutuola uses of any tale, it is still possible to trace the changes he makes in the central elements of the story so as to refocus it in the light of his own purposes. The central narrative elements of the tale of the 'complete gentleman' may be schematically set out as: (a) a young girl is deceived into following a spirit normally appearing in the guise of a handsome young man; (b) a spirit in the guise of a handsome young man comes to woo a young girl and (c) her painful discovery and later escape. These three elements can be elaborated in different directions so as to give differing emphases to the tale.

The girl's plight, which in the context of several variants ends in her learning a well-deserved lesson about the gap between appearances and reality, is altered in the context of *The Palm-Wine Drinkard*. Here, the focus is shifted onto the stature of the hero in rescuing her. She is rescued by a hero whose bravery and prowess have been demonstrated in the context of earlier trials he has successfully passed prior to undertaking her rescue. Furthermore, the villain is made much more formidable. He possesses terrible medicines which need to be taken account of in undertaking the rescue. In this way, the rescue of the hapless girl forms an aspect of building the credentials of the hero. This would explain the fact that even after he has the lady safely delivered to her home, the Drinkard returns to the skull family house to 'investigate' and enters into a serious contest with the villainous skull whom he defeats by superior magic (30–1). In addition to establishing the credentials of the hero, the tale is also designed to lend a touch of romance to the proceedings. The fact that the girl is rescued by a hero and not by some force in nature immediately makes room for the elaboration of romance between her and her rescuer. The Drinkard wins the young girl's hand as a reward for his endeavours, so that a continuity is established with other events in the narrative. Later, the girl will give birth to a strange child who emerges full-bodied from her thumb. She will also become a partner in all the Drinkard's adventures. In this way, Tutuola appropriates the tale of the 'complete gentleman' but shifts its axis so that it does not remain only a cautionary tale to young girls but additionally becomes both a means of reinforcing the heroic qualities of the hero and also a test connected with matchmaking. If we turn to Vladimir Propp's classification of the function of folktale segments, we can say that Tutuola's changes to the tale lead to a change in its function in relation to the consequences that derive from it for the rest of the narrative.[8] Though the young girl does learn a lesson, the significant consequence for the rest of the narrative is that the hero acquires a bride and not merely that the young girl learns a harsh lesson. Interestingly, the functions of the 'complete gentleman' tale are multiplied by being placed within the context of a larger story which exerts different thematic pulls by virtue of being a weave of different folktale segments.

Tutuola's particular imprint can also be discerned in the extent of elaboration he gives to the grotesque elements of the tales he uses. In the tale already referred to, the complete gentleman joins a 'skull family' of like members who seem to be well organized in their own world. The young lady is given a frog as a stool on which to sit and is guarded by one of the skull people. A supernatural cowrie is strung to her neck and it gives off an alarm in the form of a scream so loud that 'even if a person was four miles away he would not have to listen before hearing' (*The Palm-Wine Drinkard*, 27). He is adept at creating a memorable range of grisly spirits. From the *Bush of Ghosts*, we have spirits such as the piece of land that screams when it is stepped on, the huge ghostess with thousands of heads stuck all over her body, and the television-handed ghostess whose body is dotted with sores 'with uncountable maggots which were dashing here and there on her body'.[9]

The variety of spirits testifies to an opulent imagination. But taken in the generality of their manifestations, the spirits create different moods in the two books. This is partly because of the nature of the heroes and the particular relationships they establish with the realm of spirits in the narratives. In *The Palm-Wine Drinkard*, because the hero has an unambiguous titanic stature from the very outset of his journey into the spirit-world, the variety of spirits serves to register the multiplicity of impediments to the fulfilment of his quest. We might describe the mood that the spirits in this narrative engender for the hero as one of frustration. In *Bush of Ghosts*, the mood is decidedly different. Since the hero is only a seven-year-old without any magic or supernatural power, he is frequently a passive object of the machinations and desires of the denizens of the spirit-world. He is frequently transformed into different animals and objects, and in one disconcerting instance is turned into a pitcher with only his neck and head sticking out. Not only is it impossible for him to eat when he feels hungry because his mouth keeps changing into a small beak on the touch of food, he also attracts the attention of several animals in the forest. A boa constrictor attempts to devour him, and succeeds in swallowing him up to the neck, after which it is obstructed by the body of the pitcher and so has to let go (66–71). The atmosphere that this and other ghostly incidents create is one of extreme anxiety. In a sense, the spirit-realm of *Bush of Ghosts* is the crucible of a nightmare through which the boy has to journey to acquire strength only at the end of the journey. As Geoffrey Parrinder observes in the introduction to the book: 'It has a nightmarish quality of its own, and one feels the bewilderment and fear, repugnance and despair, and also intoxication and exaltation, which one would expect to experience in the company of ghosts.' Parrinder's assertion of the emotions we vicariously feel because of empathy with the hero's predicament is noteworthy. It is important to add, however, that from our observations about the quality of the mood in the two books, we cannot claim that an encounter with ghosts would be attended by a homogenous range of emotions. The variety of spirit-figures in the two books and the different emotions they evoke relate to different though related attitudes to the spirit-world. On the one hand, it is perceived as harbouring immense potential which may be harnessed by a hero with the requisite magic and courage. And, on the other, it is the object of awe and immense terror. But, once again, it is possible to be initiated into its processes and to harness its potential through patience and resilience. In both cases the differing epistemological emphases of the spirit-world render it an object for exploration for the imagination. Tutuola explores its varying significations by way of dominant Yoruba cultural symbols and the free rein of a fertile imagination.

The changes that Tutuola makes to the materials he uses can also be seen at the level of his choice of heroes. This is better understood if the mode of heroism displayed in his writing is compared with that portrayed in Fagunwa's work. All the heroes of Fagunwa's books are hunters who set out into the forest for one reason or another, encounter a host of challenges, overcome all these and return home more experienced. The heroes of Tutuola's narratives also end up overcoming the impediments in their way. Some important differences emerge between the two types of heroes, however. In Fagunwa's writing, the heroic vocation is a natural corollary of the occupation of his heroes. In Yoruba culture, hunters are highly regarded as heroic role models. We have the assertion of Abiola Irele:

> The very choice of the hunter as the central figure in Fagunwa's principal novels and in the human scheme of his narratives is of great importance, for the hunter represents the ideal of manhood in traditional Yoruba society. There is a real sense in which the hunter can be said to be a 'given' hero in the Yoruba imagination, as exemplified not only in numerous folktales, but especially in the *ìjálá* poetry, the themes of which are specifically organized in relation to the hunter's perception of the world

of nature, and which express the particular ideal that he pursues: the unique combination of physical and spiritual energy that is the privilege of man in the universal order, and which the traditional image of the hunter represents in the highest degree. (Irele 1990a: 180)

The cultural status of hunters is partly derived from the historically important role they played as scouts during wars. Because they had such intimate knowledge of the forest and were traditionally organized into professional groups, they often formed the core from which the army was recruited. Since Yorubaland was sited mainly in the forest belt, it is easy to appreciate why knowledge of the forest would constitute a privileged type of knowledge. Added to this was the fact that the forest was thought to be the abode of spirits which only the hunters, under their tutelary deity Ogun, could face and conquer.[10] Thus, by drawing his heroes from the class of hunters, Fagunwa postulates heroism as a 'natural' extension of certain figures. In contrast, Tutuola's heroes have none of these natural advantages. In fact, in *The Palm-Wine Drinkard*, the hero is decidedly anti-heroic at the beginning in terms of his attitude to work. The opening of the book quickly emphasizes this:

> I was a palm-wine drinkard since I was a boy of ten years of age. I had no other work more than to drink palm-wine in my life. In those days we did not know other money, except COWRIES, so everything was very cheap, and my father was the richest man in our town.
>
> My father got eight children and I was the eldest among them, all of the rest were hard workers, but I myself was an expert palm-wine drinkard. I was drinking palm-wine from morning till night and from night till morning. By that time I would not drink ordinary water at all except palm-wine. (*The Palm-Wine Drinkard*, 7)

The hero here is clearly an inordinately lazy person. In a culture in which hard work is particularly respected, such a figure would stand as an anti-hero. The hero of *Bush of Ghosts* is also of decidedly small stature. As has already been noted, not only is he just seven years old when the book opens, he is often shown to be a victim of circumstances. Having no juju or supernatural powers, he is often at the mercy of the spirits he encounters. It is only much later, as the narrative progresses, that he acquires facility in the ghost-language and his own reserve of magical powers which help him defeat a powerful sorcerer spirit in a contest, heal the television-handed ghostess of the sores that have covered her body for two hundred years and also carry out other magical feats.

The significance of these differences in the type of heroes that Tutuola chooses in contrast to Fagunwa is that whereas in Fagunwa's narratives, the cultural status of the hunter makes their brand of heroism a culturally given part of their character, in Tutuola's narratives the choice of heroes problematizes the culturally derived structure of heroism. Interestingly, Tutuola settled for this type of hero only after experimenting with the hunter type of heroic vocation. In the manuscript of a less known earlier work entitled *The Wild Hunter in the Bush of Ghosts* which was completed in 1948, the hero is a hunter and has all the characteristics of a typical Fagunwan culture-hero.[11] Though this earlier work provided some of the materials for *The Palm-Wine Drinkard* and *My Life in the Bush of Ghosts*, he departed from the influence of Fagunwa which is discernible here, not only in terms of the choice of hero, but also in some of the incidents and Christian sentiments. By changing the type of hero that appears in his later work, Tutuola ensures that heroism derives from the processes of adventure and the confrontation of challenges to which the hero is exposed. In the case of the boy in the *Bush of Ghosts*, we can even say that he acquires heroic stature in a process of maturation akin to the structure of an initiation rite.

It is important to note, however, that though Tutuola partially problematizes the cultural conceptions of the heroic vocation, this is articulated within the same notional structure that informs the Yoruba mythopoeic tradition itself. For it is evident that his heroes subsist on the heroic potential inherent in the mythopoeic structure of folktales in which heroes are larger than life and are almost akin to gods. It is no accident, for instance, that at a point in *The Palm-Wine Drinkard*, the hero asserts that he is 'Father of all the gods' (10). With the implications of such an *oríkì* attaching to his character, he finds it impossible to escape the trials that are set him. As he tells us when he is asked to go and rescue the headstrong girl from the 'complete gentleman', his initial hesitation has to be set aside when he remembers his *oríkì*:

> I was about to refuse to go and find out his daughter who was taken away from the market by the curious creature, but when I remembered my name, I was ashamed to refuse. I agreed to find out his daughter. (*The Palm-Wine Drinkard*, 17)

Tutuola's choice of heroes, then, involves a simultaneous differentiation from and affirmation of the culturally accepted modes of heroic vocation. That the full implications of his partial differentiation are not fully worked out might be attributed to his lack of awareness of the full potential of what he was doing in his writing. In Chapter 6, we shall see how Ben Okri reaps the problematic potential of the mythopoeic heroic vocation in *The Famished Road*.

The effects of Tutuola's handling of the folkloric form ramify at other levels as well. He generates significations in the narratives that go to problematize the hero-quests that dominate his materials. These often reside at the level of sub-texts that the narrative structure of his books conceal from view. Something of this uneasy concealment is discernible in *The Palm-Wine Drinkard*. As has already been noted, the opening of the narrative shows us a socially irresponsible figure who drinks prodigiously and lives off his father's indulgence. The indulgent father even goes as far as engaging a palm-wine tapster to keep his son's drinking requirements constantly satisfied. Not long after this initial situation, both father and tapster die 'suddenly' and the Drinkard loses all his friends. At this point, the hero is faced with a small-scale existentialist problem, for, being addicted to palm-wine and singularly lazy, he is incapable of fulfilment in the new order of things. He becomes restless. His quest for the tapster, then, may be read also as a quest for a form of social being. But, at this point, social being for the Drinkard is somewhat interfused with an impulse towards hedonism and the satisfaction of personal desire for greatness. From this perspective, the numerous ghostly encounters he has on the way to finding the palm-wine tapster constitute potentially tragic barriers to the achievement of the goal of social being.

The events of the narrative later subvert the assumptions on which this quest is undertaken, but should also be considered as a subversion of our own reading procedures if they have focused solely on the finding of the tapster as the sole goal of the narrative. We, like the Drinkard, discover that the tapster cannot return with him and that the narrative has other important lessons to offer. The Drinkard is rewarded with a magical egg that can supply all his needs and, by implication, also ensure him an acceptable form of social being. Indeed, he does seem to achieve temporary greatness and is surrounded by adoring people. He returns home when there is a great famine, so that the egg proves particularly useful:

> As I had become the greatest man in my town and did no other work than to command the egg to produce food and drinks, so one day, when I commanded the egg to supply the best food and drinks in the world to these people, at the same time it did so... (*The Palm-Wine Drinkard*, 122)

Unfortunately, the egg gets broken due to the greed and restlessness of the people, and it no longer produces sumptuous repast even when taken and 'gummed together'. When the people realize the egg can no longer supply their needs, they all return to their homes 'one by one, but they were abusing me as they were leaving' (122). By this point, the narrative has completely marginalized the tapster quest and replaced it with other significations. Once again, the Drinkard's hopes of acquiring a mode of social being that involves the satisfaction of his personal pleasures and the possession of good standing with the people undergoes a momentary reversal.

The final emphasis of the narrative is not on external aids to social being, but on the intrinsic value of wisdom subserving communal interests. The Drinkard resolves the conflict between Earth and Sky and thereby solves the problem of the drought that afflicted his people. The narrative possesses an essentially optimistic view of the human capacity for victory over tragic odds and so it re-integrates him into his society, affirms a communalistic ethic and helps him achieve an acceptable form of social being. His final integration with his community is signalled by the appearance of the first-person plural pronoun in place of the first-person singular which has dominated the text up to this stage:

> [T]he great famine was still going on seriously in every part of the town, although when I saw that many old people began to die every day, then I called the rest of the old people who remained and told them how *we* could stop the famine. *We* stopped the famine thus: *We* made a sacrifice of two fowls, 6 kolas, one bottle of palm oil, and 6 bitter kolas … the sacrifice was to be carried to Heaven in heaven.
>
> First *we* chose one of the king's attendants … then *we* chose one of the poorest men in the town … at last *we* chose one of the king's slaves who took the sacrifice to heaven for Heaven who was the senior to Land and Heaven received the sacrifice with gladness. (*The Palm-Wine Drinkard*, 24–125, italics added)

It is significant that the Drinkard is moved to join forces with his people on seeing how the famine was ravaging the helpless aged. No longer does the Drinkard stand as a hero facing odds on the strength of his own personal stature. He now subsumes his talents to communal democratic processes and, by this, achieves at-onement with his people. He also adopts an attitude of respect to the desires of the elderly, something which in a traditional culture would be crucial for defining a socially acceptable role.

As has been noted by many commentators on the folktale, folktales are often the conduit for the socialization of their audience into the cultural *morés* of the society (e.g., Eliade 1963; Godelier 1977; and Zipes 1983). The type of socialization that the folktale achieves derives from its ability to combine a totalizing metaphysical imperative with the dictates of entertainment. When the evil are defeated and the brave made triumphant, it is as if to assert such values within a culture and to affirm a cultural order that respects these values. It would seem, however, that in the context of Tutuola's narratives, the totalizing imperative that is part and parcel of the folktale form is at various times shown to be inadequate. In the *Palm-Wine Drinkard*, the structure of the narrative demonstrates a keen sense of the limitation of any human heroism based on a limited personal basis. At the end of the book, we see that heroism is subsumed under compassion and community, showing that heroism centred on the individual ego is not adequate to the dictates of social existence. That this sense of heroism partly derives from Yoruba culture itself it would be difficult to deny. But, by stringing together a collection of folktale fragments and imposing his own design on the whole, Tutuola generates a conceptually multivalent type of heroism that prevents us from focusing solely on a monologic type of heroic vocation. In this way, he generates significations that the folktale in oral culture might leave muted or unarticulated because of its totalizing imperative.

The form of *My Life in the Bush of Ghosts* lends further credence to this point, though from a different perspective. The ghostly adventures that the young boy undergoes are framed within references to events in the real world in the first and last sections. The opening section paints a picture of domestic strife arising from polygamous arrangements, the jealousy of rival wives, and the effect this has on the emotions of the children. This section finally ends depicting the ravages of war. The young boy is separated from his elder brother with whom he was hiding on some part of the road, and with the sounds of guns receding in the direction that his brother took, he takes stock of his plight:

> Now it remained me alone in the bush, because no brother, mother, father or other defender could save or direct me if and when any danger is imminent. (*Bush of Ghosts*, 21)

The palpable bewilderment of the young boy is a direct consequence of the domestic and social dislocations which have been painted for us.

After detailing the boy's adventures in the bush, the narrative, in its last sections, returns to resume the life of members of the boy's family after the separation. Like him, they have suffered intensely due to the ravages of the war, except that their suffering is wholly in the real world. His mother was sold into slavery and his brother spent many years 'in various towns' as if to parallel the younger brother's adventures in various ghost-towns. The theme of their lives has been suffering and change, though they have all managed to survive against the odds. In a crucial sense, their existence has been analogous to that of the boy in the bush of ghosts. This time, the metaphysical imperative has been used to adumbrate social concerns, because the theme of both life in the bush and in the real world has been that of suffering and anxiety that ends in the triumph of the human spirit. And this emerges because the adventures in the spirit-realm, which form the core of the narrative, are framed within social referents that have no direct relationship to the spirit-realm. Unlike the references to aspects of the real world such as churches, schools and televisions associated with ghostesses which we find in the spirit sections, the references to the real world in the framing sections have a different effect on the narrative. Whereas the references within the spirit-realm sections show the capacity of the folktale intuition for reflecting the terrain of the real world, the references in the framing sections interact with the spirit-sections so as to produce counter-posing or parallel conceptual effects. In this particular instance, they suggest that though the real world is substantially different from the world of spirits, it is logically equivalent to it in terms of the dis-locations inherent in both.

Yet it must be noted that though the metaphysical imperative of the folktale is partially challenged, this is done in terms which make the folkloric intuition finally dominate the narratives. This is best understood when we consider the fact that Tutuola's narratives establish boundaries between the real world and the esoteric one and suggest that it is entry into the esoteric world that generates the ghostly adventures. In both *The Palm-Wine Drinkard* and *Bush of Ghosts*, the sense of a threshold crossed by the hero is made evident. In *The Palm-Wine Drinkard*, it is marked by the river which lies between the ghost-world and the Drinkard's town and which the mountain-spirits cannot cross. Chased by mountain-spirits, he transforms him-self into a self-propelled pebble that bounces just ahead of the spirits till it bounds across the river. He is instantly free from pursuit because the mountain spirits cannot cross the threshold marked by the river.[12] In *Bush of Ghosts*, the boundary is more clearly demarcated, even though when crossing it at the beginning the young boy is oblivious of its significance:

> But as the noises of the enemies' guns drove me very far until I entered into the 'Bush of Ghosts' unnoticed, because I was too young to know that it was a dreadful bush or it was banned to be entered by any earthly person. (*Bush of Ghosts*, 22)

These boundaries demarcate the real world from the spirit one and suggest that it is the world of spirits that embodies the chaotic and anxiety-generating forces of nature. Whatever inkling there is of these forces also inhering in the real world is subverted by this dichotomizing gesture and the fact that much of the narrative focuses on the adventures in the ghost-world. Thus, we can say that Tutuola gestures towards the cleavages in the metaphysical imperative of the folktale intuition within which a social problematic is articulated but that his narrative form is so dominated by that imperative that the social concerns can only be glimpsed as undeveloped potentialities.

The significance of Tutuola's dichotomizing gesture is explicable on an even wider level if it is seen as a trope and placed in relation to the work of Soyinka and Okri. The Tutuolan tales are analogous to rites of passage especially as described by Arnold Van Gennep ([1908], 1960). Van Gennep divides the rituals of rite of passage into three phases of separation, transition, and re-absorption. These phases are conceptually defined as the pre-liminal, the liminal, and the post-liminal respectively. Victor Turner expands on Van Gennep's central concepts and adds that the area of the liminal is an area of anti-structure and ambiguity. It is an area which involves the conceptual denuding of initiands to establish a sense of community and equality before a re-absorption into the society can take place (Turner 1969: 94–111). In extrapolating from Van Gennep, Turner later comes to perceive the notion of liminality as a theme or trope by which to explain several aspects of both traditional as well as contemporary culture (Turner 1977; 1990). This opens up a space for us to consider the notion of liminality as a trope which may be seen to be operative in the work of Tutuola and the other writers.

In the folktale form as elaborated by Tutuola, there is a recourse to a specific signification of the liminal phase. The spirit threshold in his tales is a zone of liminality which reveals a strong sense of anxiety attached to the crossing of the boundary between the real world and that of spirits. In Yorubaland, as in most parts of Africa, the spirit-world of the ancestors and gods is accessed through special rituals. There is a danger inherent in crossing into the spirit-world without proper preparation. As Mary Douglas ([1966], 1992) points out in her studies of purity and pollution, the danger that attaches to the crossing of boundaries is a function of the anomalous status of the marginal and the in-between. The liminal and/or marginal is not fully integrated into social structure and its affective status is one of danger because it is perceived as anomalous. In Tutuola's narratives, the person who crosses the liminal boundary becomes an immediate centre of potential meanings. The violent adventures that his characters undergo can all be read as a process of affirming the problematic status of the protagonist because of the entry into the realm of spirits. We shall see how in the work of Soyinka and Okri there is a recourse to the trope of liminal boundaries and of liminal characters for varying definitions of the relationship between the real world and that of spirits and of forms of heroic vocation. This trope gets reproduced partly because all three writers draw on conceptual resources of an essentially mythopoeic bent. The trope is an important part of the conceptual resource-base. In a sense, then, Tutuola's dichotomizing gesture is part of a larger cultural meditation on the conceptual status of boundaries even if this is only a subliminal dimension of the indigenous resource-base.

What would we say are the general effects of the transferral of the oral narrative modes of the folktale into a literary medium? Obviously, the transferral from the context of oral narration into one of literary narration has implications for the relationships that are established between the folktale forms and their audience. Many of the tales and fragments that Tutuola weaves into his narrative still bear the marks of their original purposes within oral culture. Several narrative units in his books end with etiological closing formulas which show they were meant to explain some aspects of natural or cultural arrangements. We notice endings such as 'Since that day that I had brought Death out from his house, he has no permanent place to dwell or stay, and we are hearing his name about in the world,' or quasi-etiological ones such as 'It was on that day that I believed that if there is no noise of a creature in a bush or if a bush is too quiet there would be fear without seeing a fearful creature.'[13] Stories are also often rounded off with formulaic expressions tying up the themes that have just been explored such as 'This was how I got a wife,' or, 'That was how we were saved from the Unknown creatures of the Unreturnable Heaven's town,' or 'This is how I escaped from the 'homeless-ghost' who was carrying me about...'[14] Formulaic endings are a mark of storytelling in Yorubaland and are also widespread in West Africa.[15]

A notable implication of Tutuola's deployment of such techniques in his narratives is that by stringing such stories together as he does, he prevents the affirmation of closure that these formulaic endings would signify in the context of oral storytelling. He generates a sense of the provisional nature of such closures. For, in stringing together all these stories, he suggests that there are numerous stories to be told and that they can be added *ad infinitum* depending on the opulence of the narrator's imagination. This becomes particularly relevant when we remember that the narratives are largely episodic and that within each episode Tutuola often interrupts the flow of the narrative to introduce other episodic digressions before returning to the main frame of his narrative. This is particularly evident in *The Palm-Wine Drinkard*. Good examples are the interruptions in the tale of the 'complete gentleman' when, instead of going right ahead and telling us how he rescues the young lady, the hero digresses to tell us the circumstances surrounding her kidnapping. The principle is also operative in the 'Red People's Town', when there is a pause to allow the king to tell us how his people acquired their strange skin colour. At another point the Drinkard interrupts the narrative to give us details of two riddles, to which he invites us, as readers, to respond.[16] Tutuola structures his materials in a loosely episodic format, but the various episodes are often strung together in the form of embeddings. The whole narrative is composed of framing episodes within which, very often, another tale is embedded.[17] In this way, the sense of the presence of an abundance of stories that presumably informs the oral culture is transferred into the written medium. The sense of opulence that is thus registered derives precisely from the fact that the narratives are episodic and the formulaic endings are not erased in the process of transferring them into the literary mode. The formulaic details, together with the highly episodic structure are reminders of the oral basis of the tales. To have erased them would have been to make the folkloric intuition subserve a novelistic discourse, something which Tutuola was not interested in doing.[18]

Some questions need to be addressed in evaluating Tutuola's contribution to a strategic formation in Nigerian literature. Though his narratives express the ultimate triumph of the human spirit, his choice of these particular materials for writing when more humorous forms were available in the culture (stories of Ijapa the trickster Tortoise come to mind) raises a number of questions. Why did both he and Fagunwa turn to these grisly forms and why did they choose to elaborate narrative forms whose original audience was mainly children?

At some risk of incongruity, I would like to suggest that their choice had to do with Christianity and the ways in which it gave the realm of the supernatural a repulsive charm. Even though Yoruba culture has proven itself open to other religious forms of thinking, it is still the case that the monotheistic thrust of Christianity forced traditional forms of worship into a less than positive light.[19] This contradiction is partly glimpsed in the fact that Christians turn to traditional forms of healing only when more modern methods seem inadequate. But even then, this is sometimes undertaken with much self-doubt and questioning of motives. In Wole Soyinka's *Isara* (1990) a novel in which he tries to re-create the atmosphere in which his father grew up, a picture is painted of a society in flux. This period was the inter-war years, a period whose influences would have affected both Fagunwa and the much younger Tutuola born in 1903 and 1920 respectively. In a poignant passage, Soyinka depicts the conflict in the heart of Christians through a debate between Soditan and his wife (fictional *alter egos* of Soyinka's own parents). The debate is over the question of allowing Soditan's wife to undergo certain rituals that her father-in-law wants to perform to help alleviate her chronic stomach pains. Both man and wife are devout Christians, but Soditan thinks it is time to give traditional rituals a chance, even if from a distance. He even suggests that the ritual to be performed is no different from the Christian practice of giving thanks or of almsgiving, but this leads to a heated argument between man and wife. The wife speaks first:

'Let me say this, dear. The way I see it, *saara* is a kind of thanksgiving… What Father is saying in this letter is something else; *etutu* is like a secret ritual.'

'Why secret?' He pushed the letter towards her. 'Where does it say so in the letter?'

'Oh, you know what I mean,' she protested.

'No, I do not know what you mean. There is nothing secret about it. Or we can go to Isara if you like – that would take the secrecy out of it. He invited us – or rather, you. So, go and find out what it's all about. If he embarks on anything that contradicts your Christian teaching, you withdraw.'[20]

Traditional ritual can be indulged in if it does not contradict Christian teaching. At the same time, the tension between Christianity and traditional religion seems to make the rituals even more desirable in a problematic way. If we transpose our insights to an examination of the cultural environment surrounding Tutuola and Fagunwa's work, we find certain parallel impulses. Christianity had already raised a challenge against the main traditional belief system as it was expressed in òrìṣà cult groups and their ritual practices and offered a counterposing religion that sought to answer questions about the relationship between man and the Unknown. The cults carried on with undiminished vitality, but in the minds of more sensitive Christians, the traditional cosmogony required rationalization. The efforts Christians made at such rationalizations varied, but one coherent expression was provided in E. B. Idowu's *Olodumare: God in Yoruba Belief* published in 1962, in which there was an attempt to describe Yoruba religious beliefs with the aid of implicit Christian conceptual analogues. Other significant attempts from a more popular perspective could be seen in the expressions of Africanist churches such as the Aladura Church of the Lord which sought a syncretic mixture of Christianity with forms of traditional religious worship.[21] In both these efforts, the attempts were aimed at engaging with institutionally dominant aspects of the Yoruba traditional belief system in the light of the meeting between Christianity and traditional religion.

The experiments with the folktale that Fagunwa undertook must be seen in the light of these developments, though here the contradictions between the traditional belief system and Christianity did not appear problematic. In the eyes of Fagunwa, the cautionary structure of ghost narratives produced a perfect terrain for the testing of the Christian spirit that would be acceptable to Christianity while drawing heavily on traditional modes of discourse. Thus, he took the form of the folktale and interwove Christian messages into it. The influence of John Bunyan's *Pilgrim's Progress* is not hard to discern in this scheme of things, though the allegorical mode of Bunyan's book was replaced with the colourful variety of local Yoruba spirits. As we have already noted, Tutuola's early work seemed to have been heavily influenced by Fagunwa to the extent of displaying Christian sentiments. In *The Wild Hunter in the Bush of Ghosts*, the hero twice appeals to his readers to write letters to him for enquiries about their relations in Heaven and Hell. As Bernth Lindfors notes, it is clear that 'Tutuola started off from a position much closer to Fagunwa spiritually than has hitherto been recognized.' He adds:

They both began as didactic writers combining Christian theology with traditional Yoruba moral wisdom, but, Tutuola after initially following

Fagunwa's example in Africanizing Bunyan, returned to more indigenous sources of artistic inspiration and wrote less homiletic secular sagas.[22]

In his later works the moralizing and homiletic edge which characterizes Fagunwa's handling of the folktale is completely abandoned. This is because, though a Christian, he had none of Fagunwa's missionary zeal. It seems to me, however, that the effect of his Christianity manifested itself elsewhere. For Tutuola, all the vague stories about spirit-figures encountered by hunters in the bush acquired a strange intensity precisely because they were at threat of being lost to the conceptual force of Christianity. To what extent he saw this as a danger for the whole culture it is futile to speculate, but he has been quoted as saying that 'it seemed necessary to write down the tales of my country since they will soon all be forgotten' (quoted by Claude Wauthier 1966: 74). What he preserved was not just the folktales but also the sense of awe and wonder that must have attended his frequent hearing of these types of cautionary tales. It is possible to argue, then, that both Fagunwa and Tutuola settled on these types of tales instead of the more popular tales of Ijapa the Tortoise, precisely because it was these residues from childhood which challenged their new found Christianity. In a sense, settling on them was a way of coming to terms with the awe and terror that their new religion asserted was inherent in the relationship between man and the spirit-realm.

The response of Tutuola's early critics is a pointer to the strength of repression that attended such childhood awe. This repression was even more complicated because the period leading up to Independence was itself perceived as one which required an engagement with realism and rationality. In any case, Fagunwa had already got all the praise for experimenting with the folktale form in a fluent and competent Yoruba which showed Tutuola's work to be an anaemic imitation. Traditional Yoruba directed this type of storytelling mainly at children. It was therefore not difficult for his audience to appreciate his experiments. With Tutuola, however, the dynamics of publication altered the impact his stories would have had. Not only was he first read by adults, he was read by Western adults who saw in his writing important messages for the adult world. This was obnoxious and intolerable for an African intelligentsia poised for self-rule and eager to express their capacity for rationalistic engagement with the problems of the real world. In the era leading up to Independence and after, the dominant mode of cultural discourse emphasized realism, since this seemed to be the only rational way of engaging with the social world. Even in the burgeoning Market Literature of the private Onitsha presses, the dominant concerns were with real social issues.[23] Tutuola's narratives were clearly an embarrassing diversion from the dominant mode of cultural discourse among those most concerned with cultural identity. Thus, the intensity of the criticism he faced in his early days was a function of his perceived divergence from the dominant realist mode that governed cultural discourse of the time.

If we want to speak of Tutuola's contribution to a strategic formation in Nigerian literature, we must see in him the simple desire to express marginal forms of the folkloric intuition in an idiom that would bring it to the centre of cultural debates. Not only that, his was the expression of a repressed cultural potential which would have been the reserve of anthropological research for discovering aspects of Yoruba belief systems. By transferring this material into a literary mode of discourse he unconsciously cleared a space for the articulation of the repressed in a culturally meaningful way. Though his early critics failed to appreciate his work, it is significant to note that attitudes to him have undergone a complete change, so that now he can be seen for what he really is: a traditional raconteur seizing the opportunities made available by modern culture to express himself in a new medium, thereby challenging fresh perceptions of both the medium and the message.[24]

Notes

1   The early debates are well set out in *Critical Perspectives on Amos Tutuola*, edited by Bernth Lindfors, (London: Heinemann, 1980). See especially the reviews by Dylan Thomas and Babalola Johnson for opposing views on his originality.

2   *The Palm-Wine Drinkard* (1952; London: Faber, 1990); and *My Life in the Bush of Ghosts* (1954; London: Faber, 1990), abbreviated to *Bush of Ghosts*. Page numbers given in parentheses in the main text are to the later editions. I shall also dispense with the use of '[sic]' as a mark of a typographical or other error in the texts of Tutuola's works since his grammatical 'errors' and his special vocabulary add to his peculiar appeal.

3   Adeboye Babalola, 'Yoruba Folktales', in *West African Review* (July, 1962), 41–9. He gives a fuller treatment in 'Yoruba Literature' in *Literatures in African Languages*, edited by B.W. Andrezejewski et al., (Cambridge: Cambridge University Press, 1985): 157–76; Ayo Bamgbose, 'Yoruba Folktales', *Ibadan* 27 (1969): 6–12. See also, Oyekan Owomoyela, 'Tortoise Tales and the Yoruba Ethos', *Research in African Literatures* 20.2 (1989): 165–80 in which he argues that the title of 'trickster' in Yoruba folktales is properly speaking to be given both to Ijapa the tortoise as well as to Eshu, the trickster god.

4   No. 41 of her collection. See also numbers 170 and 174.

5   Olusegun Oladipo, personal communication, University of Ibadan, 15 June 1993. Dr Oladipo is an academic philosopher with a particular interest in the traditional Yoruba world-view and how this can be related to contemporary social and political concerns.

6   As reported by Arthur Calder-Marshall in a review of the *Palm-Wine Drinkard* in *The Listener*, 13 November, 1952. Reprinted in Lindfors, ed., 4–5.

7   It is important to note, though, that the spirit-realms in his later books shed some of their vitality and colour. By the time of *Pauper, Brawler and Slanderer* (London: Faber, 1987) the story is set mainly in the real world despite a reference to being set in a period two thousand years ago. The few extraordinary figures that are encountered

in the story have none of the grotesque elements and just serve as magical helpers and *dei ex machina*.

8 Propp discusses such changes in function in relation to the assimilation of segments with more than one structural function for the tale. See his *Morphology of the Folktale* (Austin: University of Texas Press, 1971), 66–70.

9 *Bush of Ghosts*, 96–111, 84–5 and 161–6 respectively.

10 Samuel Johnson gives an interesting account of the hunters' role in investigating supernatural happenings on pp. 165–6 of *The History of the Yorubas*. See p. 450 for an account of the role of hunters in the Ibadan home defence system and also pp. 375–6 for an account of challenges to the hunters' privileged position posed by professional warriors.

11 *The Wild Hunter in the Bush of Ghosts,* edited with an introduction and postscript by Bernth Lindfors (Washington: Three Continents Press, 1982). In fact, it is important to note in this light that in *The Brave African Huntress* (1958), Tutuola uses a hunter figure as the main focus of his book. The title of this book is in fact almost a literal translation of Fagunwa's *Ogboju Ode ninu Igbo Irunmale*, and the gender inversion may be considered significant in the way Tutuola self-consciously re-works the material he took from the older writer who wrote in Yoruba. I am grateful to Professor Abiola Irele for bringing this point to my notice in personal communication.

12 Obiechina makes the interesting observation that all the creatures in the spirit-world of Tutuola's narratives are constantly aware of the boundaries within their world which they scrupulously respect. Why this should be the case, it is hard to imagine. But it might well be that the spirit-figures are obeying the dictates of the episodic format that controls the narrative in general. In that case what they are obeying are the limitations imposed by the writer's handling of his material and not any necessary boundaries within the spirit realm. See Obiechina's 'Amos Tutuola and the Oral Tradition', in Lindfors, ed., 84–105.

13 *The Palm-Wine Drinkard*, 16 and *Bush of Ghosts*, 82 respectively.

14 *The Palm-Wine Drinkard*, 31, 63 and *Bush of Ghosts,* 53 respectively.

15 See La Pin , 39–42; also, more generally, Ong 1982: 23–7, 34–6, 60–7.

16 *The Palm-Wine Drinkard*, 18–23, 75–7, 110–15.

17 Tutuola's structural patterns fall into those that Propp shows are characteristic of the folktale. See his *Morphology*, 92–5 for a diagrammatic representation of such patterns.

18 It is interesting to note how the structure of the works of more sophisticated novelists such as Chinua Achebe, Ben Okri, Raja Rao and Salman Rushdie are highly episodic. This seems to pertain partly because all these writers depend to varying degrees on oral resources and modes of storytelling. Whether the invocation of orality necessarily generates an episodic novelistic structure as its formal corollary is a difficult point to assert, but it does seem to be a fair assumption.

19 For general discussions of the social consequences of Christianity and Western education on traditional society under colonialism see A. E. Afigbo, 'The Social Repercussions of Colonial Rule: The New Social Structures', and K. Asare Opoku, 'Religion in Africa during the Colonial Era', both in *UNESCO General History of Africa Vol. VII* edited by A. Adu Boahen (London: Heinemann, 1985): 487–507 and 508–38 respectively.

20 Wole Soyinka, *Isara: A Voyage Around Essay* (1989; London: Methuen 1990), 127.

21 J. D. Y. Peel gives an interesting sociological and historical account of the reasons for the growth of Islam and Christianity in the tolerant Yoruba system of òrìṣà cults. See his *Aladura: A Religious Movement Among the Yoruba* (London: Oxford University Press, 1968): 45–54.

22 Introduction to *The Wild Hunter in the Bush of Ghosts*, xvi.

23 The content of Onitsha Market Literature ranged from fictional romances through history, current affairs and practical concerns such as how to pass examinations and

launder clothes. E.N. Obiechina gives an interesting introduction to some of this literature in his *Onitsha Market Literature* (London: Heinemann, 1972).

24 Incidentally, Yoruba culture has produced several other people who have seen and seized the opportunities provided by modern means of communication for the expression of traditional sentiments. A case in point is Hubert Ogunde, who was one of the first popular playwrights to go into film and also Baba Sala, whose experiments with the video camera have projected his brand of comedy to a wider audience both in Nigeria and elsewhere.

4

The Space of Transformations

Theory, Myth & Ritual
in the Work of Wole Soyinka

Wole Soyinka's work represents an important phase in the strategic formation we are tracing because of his attempt at a new mythography that draws from the indigenous resource-base. His work has generated a large mass of commentary and analysis. This accords not only with the variety of his output, but also with the cultural energy with which his writing is imbued. Biodun Jeyifo notes that Soyinka's plays have an elaborate substructure of myth, ritual and symbolism which transforms them into 'haunting, apocalyptic creations of the imagination' (in Maduakor 1986: xii). He suggests that the mythic substructure and the symbolic and ritualistic framework are rarely given full thematic clarification, but are 'cumulatively elaborated in hieractic action, emblematic mime, epiphanic image [and] passages of incantatory speech and prose description' (*ibid.*). Joel Adedeji (1987: 105) shares this opinion from the point of view that Soyinka's theatre has little to do with imparting a 'meaning' or 'moral'. Its purpose is to 'set a riddle, not to tell a story'. Both of these evaluations of Soyinka's work are interesting for couching their assessment in terms of a subtext or substructure of meaning which is seen as elusive and requiring special attention to be grasped. This substratum is a function both of the literary artefact as well as of the cultural references woven into Soyinka's texts.

Several critics have sought to uncover the cultural meanings of Soyinka's plays. His work has often been explored in terms of the mythological motifs and cultural rituals evident in the plays. This emphasis has been necessary because of the need to engage with the culture-specific elements of his writings, but it has also had the effect of limiting the scope of critical questions asked of his work. Added to this aspect is the tendency to set the reading of his plays against his own critical pronouncements on the nature of tragedy. This second tendency has been generated partly by Soyinka himself due to the range of his own critical interventions in which he comments not only on his own plays but also on those of others from across the world. In this scheme of things, 'The Fourth Stage' essay stands in a special relationship to critics of his work.[1]

Focusing on Soyinka's valorization of a sacrificial ideal in 'The Fourth Stage', his tragic characters are generally seen by critics as manifestations of Ogun. Not only does this become a monotonous critical manoeuvre, it also prevents the identification of the varying attitudes that the plays have towards the indigenous resource-base. The unmediated Ogun symmetry that is seen to inhere in all the tragic characters undermines any attempt to trace the various altera-tions to the Ogun ideal which, taken together, depict a continual process of growth, contradiction and elaboration in Soyinka's work. Another implicit limitation deriving from an unmediated reliance on Soyinka's theorizing of tragedy is that the notion of a 'Yoruba tragedy' is often derived directly from the parameters by which he defines it in his own theory without an analysis of the deliberate exclusions on which his formulations are based. This makes it impossible to pose questions to his work which are not limited by the boundaries of his theorizing itself (see, for instance, Larsen 1983; Katrak 1986: 19).

The limitations of criticism of Soyinka's work derive from implicit assumptions informing the critical enterprise in the first place. Tradi-tional Yoruba culture is seen as a stabilized entity articulable in its rituals and myths. What Soyinka is seen as doing is to have captured the essence of Yoruba culture in his theorizing and to have drama-tized it in his plays. Since he speaks on behalf of his own culture, the assumption is that his theorizing coalesces the essence of the culture with a highly sophisticated mode of articulation. As can be derived from Jeyifo and Adedeji's comments noted earlier on, there seems to be an unacknowledged quest for the meanings of the plays which are seen as elusive. This also embraces a quest for the essence of Yoruba culture perceived to lie behind the plays. Between the culture and the critic, Soyinka's theory is interposed as a statement about his culture. Because of these implicit levels in the engagement of critics with the works of Soyinka, they are prevented from posing questions as to the strategic and critical manoeuvres involved in his use of the cultural matrix both in theorizing Yoruba culture as well as in guiding his literary practice. There is a sense in which, because of the difficulties in Soyinka's own prose style, his theory generates a 'tyranny of para-phrase' not only in the sense that critics have to unravel the primary meanings of his writing, but also because they are constrained to reproduce his processes of thinking. Derek Wright notes these problems in an evaluation of recent work on Wole Soyinka and points out that Soyinka's theory 'has become a kind of Bermuda triangle in which many critical commentors have lost their way' (Wright 1992:

109). Whether it is possible to completely escape these difficulties it is hard to tell, but a possible way out of the conundrum is to undertake the critical manoeuvre of paraphrase with a clear view to linking such an exercise to wider questions that lie well beyond the boundaries of Soyinka's discourse. In this chapter, I shall explore 'The Fourth Stage' essay in terms of a cultural work in which he mediates contemporary Yoruba uses of myths and rituals for new purposes. Secondly, I shall examine *The Strong Breed* and *Death and the King's Horseman* both in relation to the theory of tragedy in 'The Fourth Stage' and also as discursive re-workings of the theory as well as of elements of the indigenous conceptual resource-base.[2] There are two main things I want to adumbrate with this focus. The first is to show Soyinka's location in the literary strategic formation we are pursuing and the second is to illustrate the degree to which certain tropes of liminality get produced and sustained as the indigenous resource-base is put to new uses.

In examining Soyinka's theory of tragedy, it is useful to bear in mind the words of Lévi-Strauss concerning the continual processes of transformation in mythic systems:

> [A] mythic system can only be grasped in a *process of becoming*; not as something inert and stable but in a process of perpetual transformation. This would mean that there are always several kinds of myths simultaneously present in the system, some of them primary (in respect of the moment at which the observation is made), and some of them derivative. And while some kinds are present in their entirety at certain points, elsewhere they can be detected only in fragmentary form. Where evolution has gone furthest, the elements set free by the decomposition of the old myths have already been incorporated into new combinations.[3] (italics added)

In the case of the Yoruba the process seems to be less old myths being re-combined continuously with new forms, and more a continual interchange of elements not only between various myths, but between myths and even folktales. As Karin Barber points out in relation to Yoruba òrìsà, there is a perceivable 'inconsistency, fragmentation and merging' of the qualities of òrìsà. It is oríkì that recover something of this state of flux by processes of naming which depend on an eclectic conglomeration of references (Barber 1990b: 317–18). The oríkì òrìsà suggest something of a strategic recall of the qualities of the deities concerned. When Soyinka adopts the Ogun myth as definitive of the essence of Yoruba drama and cultural sensibilities, he takes the first step towards arresting the flux of òrìsà realities to map out conceptual parameters within which his meditations on his culture can find expression. It is a crucial intervention and is done with a large project in mind. The Ogun myth offers a huge payout of 'sign, symbol, and agency' which guides his thinking in various directions simultaneously but still keeps it within the same conceptual ambit provided by the myth.[4]

A defining structural feature of his meditations on Yoruba mythology in *Myth, Literature and the African World* is a process of what we may call 'relational differentiation'. He isolates each item in his scheme by simultaneously relating it to and differentiating it from other items. The important first step of seizing on a particular òrìṣà reality to discuss his culture involves the continuous differentiation of Ogun's qualities not only from other deities in the Yoruba pantheon but also from a Western paradigm represented in the meditations of Nietzsche on tragedy. Soyinka draws eclectically from Nietzsche. Nietzsche's move in *The Birth of Tragedy* to extrapolate tragedy from ritual and then to move from there to outline metaphysical verities inspires Soyinka in what steps to take in his own efforts at eliciting meaning from Yoruba mythology. In addition, Nietzsche's dialectical resolution in tragedy of the duality of energies represented by the Apollonian and Dionysian principles seems to have inspired Soyinka's reflections on the relationship between Ogun's energies and Obatala's serenity and their resolution in Yoruba drama. And Nietzsche's postulation of the Greek need for the Olympian gods as a means of negotiating the terrors of existence finds a corollary in Soyinka's own notions of a Yoruba yearning to bridge the gap between them and their òrìṣà.[5] However, Soyinka perceives essential differences between the Yoruba pantheon and that of the Greeks. Though he suggests that Ogun signifies the totality of Dionysian, Apollonian and even Promethean virtues, with a special resemblance to Dionysos, the rituals of Ogun's Mysteries are seen to be quite different from those of Greek gods. This is because, unlike the rituals to do with Greek gods in which, for him, the principle of illusion seems to have been fostered, Ogun's mysteries are based on a cultural appreciation of the reality of the chthonic realm (142). Moreover, there is an important difference in the ethical and moral basis of the two pantheons for Soyinka. Like Yoruba òrìṣàs, the Greek gods are seen to be given to various excesses. However, in their case, he notes that the 'morality of reparation' seems to be alien to them. Punishments occur only when the offence is an encroachment on the earthly territory of another god. He notes that in the Yoruba case, human society often exacts penalties from its gods for both real and symbolic injuries (13–15). For him this is an important index of the differences in the ethical and moral bases of the two pantheons. Whether he is correct in this assessment of the differences between the two pantheons is less important than the fact that he labours to simultaneously establish affinities as well as differences between them in aid of carving a specific identity for the Yoruba one. In a way, the process by which Soyinka attempts to differentiate his theory of tragedy from Nietzsche's involves earthing the philosopher's abstractionism in a pragmatic context. This derives from Soyinka's ultimate desire to extract a mode of action from his theory that can be applied not only in the sphere of theoretical conceptualization but also in the realm of cultural praxis.

Another manoeuvre of relational differentiation is applied within the Yoruba pantheon itself. Ogun is differentiated from Obatala and Shango in the Yoruba pantheon.[6] Whereas Obatala is seen to represent a general placidity which is perceived to be the harmonious essence of creation, Ogun's factor is seen as more energetic. For Soyinka, Obatala represents all those elements that make for harmony: 'patience, suffering, peaceableness, all the imperatives of harmony in the universe, the essence of quietude and forbearance; in short, the aesthetics of the saint' (13). In contrast, Ogun is seen as the embodiment of 'creativity' as opposed to 'creation'. This principle involves both harmony and rupture in the service of artistic production. Additionally, he is also the embodiment of challenge and the hubristic impulse of the rebel (13, 28, 30, 157–8). In relation to Shango, the two gods are differentiated in terms of the type of justice they represent. Whereas Shango's justice is primarily retributive, Ogun's stands for a 'transcendental, humane but rigidly restorative justice' (141). Soyinka evokes the serenity of Obatala and the retributive justice of Shango but avoids grounding his theory on the tragic potential of either of the two gods. He chooses to focus on Ogun, making it clear that he does so for a pragmatic reason. Ogun is the more appropriate god for present historical circumstances.

The continual differentiations of Ogun's essence both from local gods and from Western ones is a sign of an urge to carve out a space for a definition of Yoruba aesthetics and culture in a relational process of thought. By the fine differentiations he derives, Soyinka constructs the argument around Ogun in terms of a movement or process of becoming, in which the god's character is predicated on various conceptual affinities with other gods from Yorubaland and elsewhere. Proceeding from this premise, Soyinka then attempts to disencumber the Ogun myth of blurred conceptual trappings before articulating his own cultural conceptions through it. This process is marked throughout the essay by continual reversions to establish the various differences between Ogun and other deities. In addition to this, the meditations on a Yoruba tragedy are positioned as potential reflections on world tragedy in general. The realities of Yoruba aesthetics and culture are not posited in a vacuum, but are affirmed in relation to other world systems. We shall see later how this positioning is elaborated by Soyinka to help project his meditations on Ogun into an international arena of cultural discourse.

Soyinka interweaves three distinct myths of Ogun in mapping the god's singular career. The first is the myth of Orisa-nla and the emergence of all the deities from his disintegration into a thousand fragments due to being smashed by a boulder (27; see also Idowu 59–60). Ogun represents for Soyinka 'the closest conception to the original one-ness of Orisa-nla' (31). The second, which centres directly on Ogun, takes pride of place in Soyinka's theory. It is the myth about Ogun's carving of a pathway for the gods in their descent to earth (see Idowu, 85–7). He frequently refers to various dimensions of this myth throughout *Myth*. In addition to this one, there is the myth of Ogun's reign on earth at Ire and his act of precipitate violence in killing his own people when in the stupor of palm-wine (29; Idowu, 86–7). In traditional contexts, the story of Orisa-nla's fragmentation is told to account for the emergence of the numerous deities in Yorubaland and does not relate to the special qualities of any one òrìṣà. Those directly relating to Ogun circulate among his devotees and find common articulation in the rituals to do with him. Yet it is interesting to note that Ogun is linked to two different towns in his myths. According to Idowu, when Ogun carved a pathway for the gods, it is to Ile-Ife that he brought them. In fact, the deities went as far as crowning him *Osin-Imole*, which means 'chief of the divinities'. Obviously, this myth serves to validate the primacy of Ile-Ife which is generally taken to be the epicentre of Yoruba cosmogony. On the other hand, it is at Ire that Ogun was crowned king, and it was there that he later wreaked havoc. In Soyinka's reworking of the myths the focus is less on the two towns than on the various levels of signification that the myths yield. Significantly, there is no linking of Ogun with Ife at all, and his arrival at Ire is explained in relation to the mountainous nature of the area, something that appealed to a deity who wanted to be on earth but not involved with ordinary people (29). Clearly, it is more important for Soyinka to expand the myths to embrace fresh realities than to use them for their usual role of validating one town or another or the affirming of a particular social hierarchy. For him the myths yield various meanings of the deity's character. Ogun is a culture hero and a revolutionary and his actions map out the parameters of both hubris and creativity. Also crucial in Soyinka's scheme is that Ogun sacrifices himself to affirm the community's sense of corporate identity. What Ogun does for the gods is a model for what culture heroes do for their communities.

Soyinka's theorizing around the myth is grounded on a number of conceptual pre-suppositions. The most important is that for the Yoruba, time is not an abstract linear concept but the crucible where the three worlds of the living, the dead, and the yet unborn meet. As he asserts, 'life, present life, contains within it the manifestations of the ancestors, the living and the unborn' (144). He couples this initial pre-supposition with a partial echo of Nietzsche which helps him define a dimension of Ogun for heroic vocation: there is a gap, an abyss between these three realms which needs to be continually bridged by ritual and sacrifice. It is left unclear exactly where the gap lies, but it seems to be both articulated and bridged by a variety of cult practices as well as being a more generalized existentialist void or idea. When he suggests that it is a communal psychic condition, Soyinka lapses into a definition of social psychology which is not grounded on any evidence in the culture. He is evidently exercising poetic licence on this point. The significance of this manoeuvre, however, lies in the fact that it prepares the ground for defining different dimensions of heroic vocation for the culture as well as for dramatic action.

The postulated sense of a vacuum afflicting the Yoruba mind finds a correlative in the desire of the gods to achieve contact with mankind. It is this urge that provided the impulse for their journey to earth in which Ogun emerged with singular honour. In this, Ogun represents the supreme sacrifice not only on behalf of the gods but also on behalf of the communal ethos. Furthermore, his journey defines the value of the protagonist's death for the tragic action in Soyinka's view. At another level, the abyss represents special qualities of experience that challenge the will. Not only is it the 'chthonic realm', it is also a space of dissolution and disintegration, a special space of 'the inter-transmutation of essence ideal and materiality' (26). Once again, Ogun's experience is the correlative of this dimension of the abyss. Ogun is disintegrated in the abyss to re-emerge on the other side wiser and more powerful for the experience (153). Under the stress of crisis a person or indeed the whole culture experiences a déjà vu of recall in which memory reproduces the initial efforts of the god Ogun and his exercise of will in crossing the abyss. The abyss, then, is the inchoate space of both despair and its resolution (149, 150).

There is an overlap with yet another level of meaning where the transitional abyss has a special significance for the psyche of the individual dramatic actor. A dimension of the abyss resides within the votary's (and dramatic protagonist's) psyche when he participates in the rituals of Ogun or in the dramatic action of crisis. Soyinka outlines two specific areas of the votary's experience of the abyss. The first is in preparation for the experience of catharsis, when the votary is possessed by the god and becomes his mouthpiece, uttering 'visions symbolic of the transitional gulf, interpreting the dread power within whose essence he is immersed as agent of the choric will' (143). Catharsis proper is linked to the serenity of Obatala, he being the 'serene womb of chthonic reflections' (ibid.). Another dimension of the abyss for the individual actor's psyche is when he has to establish ritual empathy with the gods 'beyond the realm of nothingness (or spiritual chaos) which is potentially destructive of human awareness, through areas of terror and blind energies' (146). Whereas in the first instance the actor seems to be a passive agent of Ogun's will, in the second he is a conscious activator of the processes by which the psyche conquers the transitional abyss which is internalized by way of the tragic action. As has already been noted, Ogun's journey through the abyss of transition is presented as a parallel for the actor and his relationship to the community. In the actor's entry into and re-emergence from the area of transition, the whole community is re-energized and enriched with new strength. There is a transmission of the protagonist's strength to the participants in the choric rites who are his immediate community and symbolize the community at large.

Given the rich and varied significations of the notion of the transitional abyss for Soyinka's theorizing, it is necessary for us to pause to examine some of its implications. His handling of the notion of transitional abyss reproduces the notion of danger inherent in the crossing of liminal boundaries. We have already noted how in Yoruba folklore as elaborated by Amos Tutuola, the crossing into the bush or forest is a trigger for the harrowing experiences of the ghostly realm. Soyinka's elaboration of the abyss of transition reproduces Tutuola's understanding of liminal thresholds by suggesting that the transitional abyss is polyvalent and anomalous. That is why it threatens disintegration and requires a special effort of the will. Also, the person crossing the boundary, be they Ogun, votary or tragic actor, enters into an anomalous phase which has potential both for energizing and destroying. However, Soyinka can be differentiated from Tutuola in that he makes prescriptions for coping with the stress of transition which could be applied almost directly in the social sphere. Like the *babaláwo*, he engages with the myths of the gods to extract contemporary significance, but, unlike them, his prescription for coping with the stress of cultural transition is not propitiatory rites but an assertion of will to the utmost.[7] In elaborating what is largely intuitively grasped in his culture, he places the notion of liminal boundaries in varying contexts that allow him to meditate on a wide range of issues ranging from the relations between ritual and drama through to the personal and cultural correlatives necessary for success in a confusing and potentially tragic world. Later on in this chapter we shall see how the notion of transitional abyss and its varying significations is featured in his plays.

The notion of the transitional abyss also operates at another level of discursive significance which points to its importance in conceptualizing the relationship between Yoruba culture and the rest of the world. The transitional abyss is a strategic invocation of a particular topos which defines the consciousness of cultures meditating on their position in the world. In the view of Harry Garuba, Soyinka's deployment of the notion of transitional abyss signals a fascination with the conceptual potential inherent in the idea of the frontier for defining cultural positions in relation to a vaguely conceptualized 'Outside'.[8] Comparing Soyinka's use of the Ogun myth with the writings of early settlers in America such as Frederick Jackson Turner, Garuba argues that the notion of a frontier which needs to be crossed or pushed back is a definitive topos of cultures defining their identities at the conjuncture of vast new realities. In Frederick Turner's 'The Frontier in American History' as in early American writing, the notion of the frontier has a correlative in a specific type of character capable of crossing or conquering it, namely, one with a rugged individualism. The notion of the frontier is significant for Soyinka as he meditates on the relationships between his culture's conceptual system and its place in the world. Unlike the American frontier, which was a physical one, the one he engages with is a conceptual one which can only be articulated as it locates itself differentially within a history of such conceptualizations in other parts of the world.

It is evident that the myths of Ogun yield the notion of boundary or frontier and that his enterprise in carving out a pathway for the gods can be used to define the required dynamic of the engagement of Yoruba culture with the rest of the world. This is something Soyinka emphasizes. However, it can also be argued that the sense of a frontier is as much his own intellectual impulse as that of the myths he elaborates. In an essay suggestively entitled 'The Writer: Child at the Frontier', he asserts that the notion of the frontier is crucial for the writer's creative expression. 'If there were no frontiers in either his interior or exterior being,' he writes, 'the writer would probably erect one'.[9] The interesting thing in relation to his theorization of Yoruba culture is that this conceptual dynamic which is internal to his own creative processes is aligned to a wider process of his culture's perceived insertion into a global aesthetic arena.

We can further clarify how Soyinka uses the Ogun myth to generate a wide variety of conceptions to do with the self, drama and cultural identity by comparing his version to other uses of the myth in Yoruba culture. In traditional Yoruba culture, Ogun is the tutelary god of drivers, metal workers and also hunters. It is in the highly organized guilds of hunters that the myth is most seen to produce practical significations which are returned to time and again in defining an ambit of self-conceptualization and action. Two chants especially identified with hunters' guilds are the ìjálá and ìrèmòjé chants. Hunters' guilds were particularly associated with Oyo and both types of chants were diffused from there. Bade Ajuwon (1989), writing in a special collection of essays called *Africa's Ogun*, even suggests that knowing ìjálá chants might have been a 'password' for gaining acceptance in strange places because of the high level of organization of the hunters' guilds and their diffusion throughout Yorubaland. The *ìjálá* chants are used for a variety of ritual occasions embracing Ogun festivals, festivals in honour of ancestors and also hunters' funerals, while *ìrèmòjé* chants are specifically tied to hunters' funerals. Both of these chants depict various stages of the appropriation of the myth of Ogun. In the *ìjálá* chants documented by Adeboye Babalola (1966, 1989), the image of Ogun that emerges is of a deity with strong human affiliations and with seemingly irreconcilable contradictions. He is hot-tempered and belligerent but at the same time is protector of poor and oppressed peoples everywhere. Additionally, he is believed to be the founder of several towns and occupations. The interpretation that Babalola puts on this factor of Ogun beliefs is important:

> It is inconsequential that Ogun is the founder-king of several places, the founder-blacksmith of others, or the founder-hunter of still others. What is consequential is the composite picture each of these tales provide: *Ogun is a legitimator of beginnings, foundings, and innovations*, and each *oríkì Ogun* is a folk etymology, relevant to the specific place in which it is performed. (Babalola 1989: 168; italics added)

In contrast to the transitional space that Ogun occupies in Soyinka's theory, it emerges from the *ìjálá* chants that he is linked to beginnings and foundings. Thus, several towns and dynasties attempt to link foundational narratives to him as a means of political validation, so that even the tale associating Ogun with Ire is a manifestation of the political inflections of Ogun myths. It seems that in *ìjálá* chants there is a dual movement of appropriation of the myth. On the one hand, Ogun is defined as 'a man of the people,' a 'Robin Hood' or 'Aeneas' in Babalola's terms, living among ordinary people and suffering their tribulations with them (1989: 155). Yet, on the other hand, he is depicted as aligned to political hierarchies and his myths are seen to validate the political structure. This set of contradictions is not altogether irreconcilable, however, particularly when we bear in mind that to Ogun devotees everyone is at liberty to draw on symbols associated with him for different reasons. Because Ogun devotees share the same symbols, they are free to conglomerate in a single ritual body or to form separate groupings which draw on different variations of the Ogun theme. As one of the lines in the *ìjálá* asserts, which is pointed out by Babalola himself in illustration of this aspect of Ogun beliefs, 'Whoever does not like this should set up his own Ogun' (1989: 160).

The *ìrèmòjé* chants give a different picture of Ogun. These chants serve to affirm the value of hunters as a professional grouping by linking them to Ogun. Part of the funeral rites of hunters involves the display of the dead member's paraphernalia. The items include yam, which is Ogun's favourite food, and red palm-oil, the colour by which he is traditionally identified (Ajuwon, 176–7). The chants themselves elaborate what Ajuwon calls an 'Ogun philosophy'. The deity is perceived as a conceptual model of agency for hunters and the qualities that are emphasized are those of self-reliance, courage, heroism, mastery of medicines and knowledge of forest lore (Ajuwon, 180, 182, 184–5). The qualities that equipped him to carve a path for the gods are what get emphasized in *ìrèmòjé* chants. The appropriations of Ogun's qualities in *ìrèmòjé* chants are designed to project hunters as the ideal of heroic vocation and, as has already been noted in the last chapter, this is something that finds consensus in Yoruba culture. The difference between the qualities of the deity in the two different chants is that *ìrèmòjé* chants define an exclusive set of qualities which are seen to be most fully articulated in the vocation of hunters themselves, while *ìjálá* chants define a more popular aspect to the deity's character.

However, this interpretation cannot be taken as exhaustive. The differences in the god's qualities as seen in the two chants are ultimately tied to their different contexts of ritual performance. Whereas the *ìrèmòjé* are specialist chants, *ìjálá* are not. The question of the performance context and the differential effects it has on the interpretation of myth opens a window for our own understanding of the relationship between Soyinka's theorizing of the Ogun myth and its value to his culture.[10] In an important sense, Soyinka's deployment of the myth is itself a 'movement of transition'. Not only does he transfer the myths from its ritual contexts of performance, but by the extensive interpretation to which he submits them, their original terms are re-written so as to embrace new aesthetic, cultural and even political realities that were not within their purview in their other cultural uses. This brings us to his relationship to Johnson in terms of their differing attitudes to their cultural resources.

As was noted in Chapter 2, Johnson's mode of historiography which drew on the resources of Yoruba orality had the effect of affirming a Yoruba consciousness within the new literary mode of production. His project had certain important limitations, however, particularly in terms of the imaginative and creative freedom he allowed himself in his reliance on the cultural matrix. In many ways, Johnson reproduced the discourse of Yoruba orality with the intention of rendering its historiographic discursive strategy as truthfully as possible. Even when he took on the garb of the oral narrator, it was to render the historical narratives as 'factually' as was possible within the freedom available to the oral narrator. Obviously, he did this with the intention of rendering a reliable 'History'. On the other hand, Tutuola (and Fagunwa's) articulation of the folkloric intuition expresses the free play of the artistic imagination on the material available in the culture. That Tutuola is tied closely to the discursive strategies of Yoruba folklore is partly due to his limited resources of language and also because of his general lack of awareness of the full implications of his creative enterprise.

With Soyinka, things take a decidedly different turn. Not only is he liberally re-writing the terms of Yoruba mythology, he is doing it in the service of a clearly expressed aesthetic and political ideology. It is, as he affirms in defining the agenda of *Myth, Literature and the African World*, 'the simultaneous act of eliciting from history, mythology and literature, for the benefit of both genuine aliens and alienated Africans, a continuing process of self-apprehension' (Preface, xi). The adoption of a posture that seeks to address both insiders and outsiders is the one which he elaborates at every opportunity. This is done with a free play of the imagination in a continual productive engagement with the cultural matrix. In a note to his adaptation of *The Bacchae of Euripides*, he acknowledges his debt to his own poem *Idanre*, 'a Passion poem of Ogun, elder brother to Dionysos'. The project of his poem *Ogun Abibiman* was to 'lend' Ogun to the then South African liberation struggle, where the Yoruba deity would have led the black host alongside Chaka the Zulu. In another interesting replay of this gesture, he suggests in his after dinner speech at the Nobel Prize Banquet that Ogun is definitely the progenitor of Alfred Nobel and asks that those in the audience unfamiliar with his *Idanre* hurry to the nearest bookshop and secure themselves copies. The occasion seems quite humorous, yet though the linking of Ogun with Alfred Nobel was no doubt meant to evoke some laughter, it nonetheless falls in line with Soyinka's efforts at projecting his tutelary deity into a wider arena of cultural discourse. Whereas Johnson asserts a traditional culture enriched with Christian sentiment in support of an emergent cultural nationalism, Soyinka adopts both a national and post-national posture in drawing on indigenous resources for affirming Yoruba, Nigerian and even African verities at a world level. That Johnson and Soyinka operated different conceptual categories is pertinent as is the fact that their temperaments emerge as radically different. But it is difficult to escape the feeling that his appropriations represent a more confident assertion of cultural identity than Johnson was capable of in his historical circumstances. Soyinka's theorizing, then, represents a confident moment in the articulation of Yoruba culture, something that finds expression at various levels of the culture's relationship to itself and to the outside world.

For John Peel this is part of a larger process of the desacralization of religious symbols in Yorubaland and Nigeria. Concluding an assessment of contemporary studies of Yoruba religion, he suggests that Yoruba religion has gradually undergone a process of 'culturalization'.

In this process, though *orìṣà* rituals are actively promoted as symbols of overall communal identity, a certain inescapable displacement of their subject and significance has also taken place. As he puts it: 'Religion itself is culturalized: having always been part of culture in the broad anthropological sense, it is transformed into 'culture' in the narrower sense in which it is the concern of Ministries of Culture and Arts Councils' (Peel 1994: 164). Though he sees this process as partly due to the culture's engagement with world religions, culturalization could also be placed within a larger grid of the meeting of traditional culture with global factors. When Soyinka transfers the myths from their usual context of Yoruba ritual and into an Africanist cultural discourse in *Myth, Literature and the African World,* he seeks to forge a metaphysical African community. It is a move which Anthony Appiah (1992: 127–9) criticizes for the implications of homogeneity involved in such a move. However, such a move might also be linked to a process in Yoruba culture whereby elements of the culture are gradually entering the global aesthetic economy in a variety of ways both for general consumption and also as a means of identity formation for diasporic Africans. The project of Gates's *The Signifying Monkey* in which there is an attempt to trace the African-American popular street practice of 'signifying' to the Yoruba myths of Eshu shows that this is no idle dimension of cultural activity. It is a clear pointer to the fact that indigenous Yoruba resources are being actively recovered for the construction of identities even in the diaspora. In other words, it is a process in which Yoruba culture is being exported by the detachment of cultural elements from their ritual contexts of circulation. Soyinka channels this into an ideological direction. His projection of Yoruba culture as somehow 'African' is a movement in the de-sacralization of cultural resources for the purposes of accommodating the values of increasingly international cultural realities.

This brings us to another point. In many ways, Soyinka's theorizing of Yoruba culture is significant for providing it with a new vehicle of articulation. This does not merely involve the fact that for the first time the culture is mediated through the form of a philosophical essay. The discourse of the theorizing itself is a significant element of this new vehicle because there is a strenuous effort to foreground a 'poetic' manner of thinking about the culture. The mode of theorizing is essentially poetic, and there is a foregrounding of the linguistic means by which things are stated so that not only does the language call attention to itself, but the very logic of the theorizing depends on the relationships established between effects of language.[11] This emerges quite clearly when we pay attention to some of the processes of thought in a passage in which he links ritual music to tragic reality:

> Only the battle of the will is thus primarily creative; from its spiritual stress springs the soul's despairing cry which proves its own solace, which alone reverberating within the cosmic vaults usurps (at least, and however temporarily) the powers of the abyss. At the charged climactic moment of the tragic rites we understand how music came to be the sole art form which can contain tragic reality. (146)

We should note how 'the will' is granted a metaphorical 'voice', which it exercises in a 'despairing cry'. The way is prepared for this metamorphosis by an invocation of a sense of combat and embattlement in the word 'battle'. This is carried over into the implications of the word 'stress' which makes the soul's anguished reaction predictable. The sense of embattlement and anguish prepares the way for the emergence of the cry so that ultimately the will becomes metaphorically a 'voiced' entity. The implications of the cry of the will are extended in 'reverberating in the cosmic vault' with all the vague suggestions of a magnification of decibels. However, in terms of the development of the argument, the implications of the introduction of a voice for the will are harvested only in the apodictic assertion that music is the sole art form of tragic reality. Then, the vague suggestiveness of metaphor is turned towards progressing the argument. What emerges from this movement is a subtle shift from metaphorical analogy to apodictic statement without a conceptual break in the flow of thought. The movement can only be understood by grasping a logic that depends on the suggestiveness and ambiguities of metaphor for its clarification. The subsequent movements in the thought are to clarify the apodictic statement through illustration and differentiation. This is a significant characteristic of the discursive strategies Soyinka deploys in theorizing his culture and it points to a strongly poetic mode of thought. This, it seems to me, is what makes his theory both difficult and suggestive. The poetic vehicle within which the culture is theorized is also articulated in relation to the plays, which is where the theory is further elaborated, tested and contradicted.

The Strong Breed[12] is interesting for being an early exploration of the notion of ritual self-sacrifice and its differential relationships to the individual self as well as to the community. Based on an annual purification ritual of the Niger Delta, the play outlines the career of Eman, a man marked out for the role of ritual carrier both by his family and also by the fact that he is a sojourner in a town which chooses foreigners to act as its sacrificial carriers in annual celebrations of renewal. The play is complicated partly by Eman's identification with Ifada, a dumb boy in the household where Eman is visiting and whom the community first focuses on for the role of sacrificial carrier. A further complication derives from the flashbacks in the plot that fill out the history of Eman and map out the various moral and ethical options he has defined himself against in his development of a sense of purpose within the traditional milieu. The Niger Delta rituals of the play serve as a useful transposition of Yoruba purificatory rituals (see Awolalu, 153–5). Soyinka defines his attitudes to the sacrificial-carrier ritual as it is expressed in several local cultures and he makes his analysis of the phenomenon based on his grasp of a Nigeria-wide articulation of such rituals. Presumably, he is relying on the research he carried out in 1960–1 into indigenous rituals in the country. The play, then, may be taken as defining indigenous resources not limited solely to the Yoruba.

Most critics rightly note that Eman's attitudes to the purificatory rituals in general are crucial for an understanding of the play, but there seems to be some difficulty as to the exact nature of those attitudes. Critical opinion is that Eman grows reluctantly into an awareness and acceptance of his destiny as sacrifice and that by the end of the play he has fully accepted that destiny. Two things account for this particular perception. The first is the notion that Eman offers himself as a sacrifice for the community, and the second is the notion of intentionality involved in his actions in becoming a sacrificial carrier. Larsen likens Eman to Ogun. He writes:

> Like Ogun, Eman sacrifices himself in order that the group – in Eman's case, the villagers – may have a chance of progressing. (*A Writer and his Gods*, 91)

The suggestion here is that, like Ogun, Eman decides to sacrifice himself in order to take the villagers through the passage of transition towards greater self-awareness. In Oyin Ogunba's reading of the play, each step in Eman's career, from his very first refusal to listen to Sunma's warnings at the beginning right through to his final submission, is taken to be 'part of the making of a man who is destined (or chosen) to suffer' (1975: 104). From these readings, Eman is either an unproblematic expression of Ogun's tragic agency, or, a proof of the inexorable force of determinism aimed at affirming a communal ethos. However, there is much evidence to the contrary pointing toward the problematic status of the notion of self-sacrifice and of Eman's attitudes to it.

Yoruba notions of destiny are thoroughly ambiguous on the notion of determinism. On the one hand, there is the belief that each man has a particular *ori-inu*, or inner-head with which he or she is born. This *ori-inu* ensures that each person has a required role to play on earth. On the other hand, however, Ifa divination suggests that it is possible to alter one's fortune through properly conducted sacrifice to the *òrìsàs*. Therefore, the notion of destiny makes room for free will and the mediation of circumstances. Olusegun Oladipo argues that the concept is 'two-sided'. It is 'something given and unalterable and also something which, in certain circumstances and under certain conditions, can be altered'.[13] The Yoruba notion of destiny is far from fatalistic. Soyinka himself says that 'the sense of destiny of the Yoruba is certainly *not* resignation at all. You might say it is one of the sum total of what happens' (cited in Katrak 1986: 115). What complicates the concept in *The Strong Breed* is that not only does the candidate for the sacrificial-carrier role express strong aversion to it, but also that the very communal values upon which such a role would be based are called into question. Derek Wright (1993: 59–60) presents a useful angle to the play when he suggests that Soyinka is concerned here mainly with 'the business of ritual mechanics and the excessively literal-minded habits of thinking that inform them'. On this account, it may be argued that the play shifts the axis of concern from the validation of ritual practice to a questioning of the ethical basis of ritual in the first place.

Evidence of pre-destination in the play is quite strong, though this is qualified by the total context of events. In one particular flashback, Eman engages in conversation with his father back in his own village on the issue of his family's vocation. It has been his family's lot to carry a symbolic boat across the river every year to take the evils of the community away with them. Eman refuses to take on this vocation and his father tells him:

> Do you know what you are saying? Ours is a strong breed my son. It is only a strong breed that can take this boat to the river year after year and wax stronger on it. (133)

As Eman persists in refusing the family vocation, his father adds:

> I tell you it is true. Your own blood will betray you son, because you cannot hold it back. If you make it do less than this, it will rush to your head and burst it open. I say what I know my son. (134)

The notion of a pre-destined vocation comes out strongly here and the events in the play seem to lead inexorably towards a fulfilment of Eman's putative destiny as sacrificial carrier. But that this is granted does not mean that he ever accepts this role without question or ever grows to an awareness of its necessity in the form in which it is posed by his father. And we must note that it is not only the role of carrier that makes him uneasy in the play. He expresses uneasiness at all traditional ritual roles which are detached from questions of ethics and free will. An examination of his biography through the flash-backs reveals the lines of his character.

In another flashback, we see Eman's confinement as a boy in his village in preparation for puberty rites. Omae, an admirer later to become his betrothed, decides to risk condemnation to come and see her beloved. This makes him uneasy, for, as he tells her, to be touched by a woman at that crucial stage would lead to contamination (136–9). But Omae persists in staying with him until his tutor arrives. The Tutor turns out to be lecherous and attempts to manipulate the situation to his advantage. He dismisses Eman and tries to get Omae into his own hut to have his way with her. There is a short scuffle after which Eman emerges to intervene and oppose his tutor. The Tutor threatens blackmail, but Eman has already decided to leave the camp. This has a decisive impact on the Tutor, who, in the traditionally required way, banishes Eman from the village for a decade. We must note the affective status of the liminal phase in which Eman is, and the suggestions of pollution and danger in this part of the action. This engagement with the notion of passage and the affective status of the liminal has important consequences for the mood of the play which we shall explore later.

Several things emerge out of this episode. In the first place, Eman is caught at a certain liminal phase of a puberty rite in which, if he misconducts himself, there is danger of contamination both for him and for the community at large. The rite of passage is very important to him, because as he once tells Omae 'don't you see, I am becoming a man' (138). But the importance of 'becoming a man' fades beside the ethical issues raised by his tutor's shameless behaviour. Ethics and justice weigh for him more than simply going through a socially required process to mark development. His sensitivity to such issues places him on a different and more profound level of liminality, and when his consciousness of injustice is aroused he rejects the merely social for the sake of a profounder morality. The reasons he adduces for refusing his father's vocation are important in this respect. Apparently, after his period of banishment, he returns to his village to see Omae, and it is in this visit that his father confronts him with the question of his predestined vocation. But Eman returns a changed person. It is only Omae that makes him stay, and when she dies of childbirth, all reasons for remaining in the village evaporate. His conversation with his father is revealing at this point:

> OLD MAN: It had to be. But you know what slowly ate away my strength. I awaited your return with love and fear. Forgive me then if I say that your grief is light. It will pass. This grief may drive you now from home. But you must return.
> EMAN: You do not understand. It is not grief alone.
> OLD MAN: What is it? Tell me, I can still learn.
> EMAN: I was away twelve years. I changed much in that time.
> OLD MAN: I am listening.
> EMAN: I am unfitted for your work father. I wish to say no more. But I am still unfitted for your call. (133–4)

We must note that part of his sense of inadequacy in the face of his father's vocation is due to the gap of experience. But another reason may be ventured. He is unsuited for his father's vocation precisely because his mind leans towards questioning the efficacy of traditional rituals and their general ethical foundations. Though this point is ventured only tentatively, more evidence emerges in his attitudes to the rituals of sacrificial carrier in the village of his sojourn.

When Ifada the dumb boy is captured for the ritual but manages to escape back to seek Eman's protection, it offers him an opportunity to confront the leaders of the village about the efficacy of their rituals. As he points out, if Ifada is so mad with terror, he can be neither a willing nor efficacious sacrificial carrier. To the leaders of the village, however, the matter of willingness is immaterial. They can make the carrier willing through certain special preparatory rituals:

> OROGE [*smiling*]: He shall be willing. Not only willing but actually joyous. I am the one who prepares them all, and I have seen worse. This one escaped before I began to prepare him for the event. But you will see him later tonight, the most joyous creature in the festival. Then perhaps you will understand. (129)

Ironically, it is not an 'understanding' that comes to Eman easily because, once again, his ethical sense emerges, and he questions the ethical foundations of the traditional rituals. At all times his choice is on the side of justice, even if it carries the risk of social ostracism and damnation.

An important question needs to be addressed. If it is correct that he questions the ethical basis of the sacrifice, why then does he offer himself to act as sacrificial carrier for this same heartless society? The problem with the question as it is posed is that it takes for granted that his sacrifice was indeed for the society and not for something else. In fact, the formulation of the question in this way might even be partly responsible for the readings of the play that insist on seeing Eman's sacrifice as unproblematically affirmative of communal ideals. It is possible to argue that Eman was not sacrificing himself for the community at all, but rather for Ifada. From the very beginning, his kindly responses to the dumb boy and the close relationship between the two are meant to signal a certain warmth which cannot be ignored in interpreting Eman's later actions on behalf of the boy. Eman pats the boy's head while talking with Sunma, and the boy 'grins happily' (116). His kindly concerns are even expanded to include kindly words to Ifada about the evening's masquerade and advice about Ifada making his own mask. This contrasts sharply with Sunma's attitude towards the boy, which is full of some inexplicable venom. The contrast is in itself significant, partly because Sunma's attitudes towards the boy derive from her inarticulable anxiety at the awareness of Ifada's potential role of sacrificial carrier. She knows this because, being native to the village, she is fully aware of the dangers that lie in store for sojourners. It is an anxiety which is signalled in a sublimated form in her frantic requests with which the play opens for Eman to leave the village by the last lorry. The stridency behind what she voices about Ifada in 'the sight of him fills me with revulsion' (117) is only a marker of the inarticulate intuition of the liminal danger associated with the boy. For Eman, however, matters are quite straightforward and he only sees the boy as a human in need of love and affection.

When Ifada escapes back to the house in abject terror, it is Eman who insists that the boy be given refuge. And when he is finally taken away the stage directions are instructive in representing Eman's feelings:

> *They go off, taking Ifada with them, limp and silent. The only sign of life is that he strains his neck to keep his eyes on Eman till the very moment that he disappears from sight. Eman remains where they left him, staring after the group.* (130)

It cannot be that, given the biography we have examined, Eman would long remain indifferent to the plight of the dumb boy. He could not restrain himself from taking the place of the voiceless boy made a victim of thoughtless traditional forces. The next time we see Eman, he is dressed as a carrier, but has broken away and is being pursued by the villagers.

In fact, the play seems to offer various hints and suggestions that show that Eman is a sacrifice for Ifada and not the villagers. Early in the play a Girl comes in pulling an effigy tied to a string. This effigy is supposed to be the carrier of an ailment with which she is afflicted. Significantly, however, it is Ifada who is invited to play with the effigy and therefore is contaminated by its supposed potencies. The specific game they play is supposed to act as a pre-figuration of the purificatory rituals of the community in general. Ifada takes the role of the village and beats the effigy with a stick, thus playing out what the villagers do to their own sacrificial carriers when they stone and abuse them. But by taking on the role of the village in this game, Ifada takes on the role of the entity that needs cleansing in the context of the game they play. It is also significant that Eman lends the girl his own 'buba' to wear on the effigy, thus associating himself with the effigy in the very visual representation of the effigy's clothes. And it must not be forgotten that both Ifada and Eman are sojourners in this land and so according to the laws of the land are both regarded as potential sacrifice. In this way, and on a discursively symbolic level, the play suggests that Ifada and Eman are equivalent and reversible in terms of the way in which their host community perceive them. In this case it is Eman who sacrifices himself for his dumb friend because it is he who speaks for those without voice. Ifada represents the highest call of a voiceless moral imperative, and Eman cannot long remain indifferent.

The play is completely silent as to the precise reasons for Eman's self-surrender to become a sacrificial carrier, so that an interpretation that suggests he did it in recognition of a pre-destined role stands on the same footing as that which would suggest that he did it for wider ethical reasons. And it seems to me that the balance is tipped away from the social to the ethical if we take account of the layered meanings that the play has associated Eman with and which we have explored. It seems, then, that Soyinka has deliberately woven a structure of indeterminacy into the play in relation to the idea of determinism and the sacrificial rituals to help place the whole notion of tragic agency at issue. The play acts as a qualification to the confident assertion of a coincidence between the values of the individual and those of the community much evident in his later elaboration of tragic agency in 'The Fourth Stage'.

The notion of sacrifice and its significance finds multiple focalization, with Eman's father a captive to one, the community a captive to another, and Eman in his actions gesturing towards a third. The question becomes: 'What is the ethical basis of one's actions and of the traditional rituals in which one is called to participate?' and not merely 'What is one's destiny and how will it be articulated?'[14] That Eman suddenly changes his mind about going through with the rituals and runs away is significant in this respect. Clearly, the realization of the scale of his moral commitment becomes unnerving, and he has to flee. Running away becomes a process of pain and self-discovery, because it is on the run that the flashbacks bring to his mind the basis of his former actions and their relationship to his present predicament. It is tempting to see the chase as expressive of the chaos of the chthonic realm that Ogun is reputed to pass through on the path to earth, but it is also important not to forget that it is not for Eman alone that the chase becomes a liberating process. The frenetic chase is also an important process of self-discovery for the community as a whole. For in the chase the possibility of *not* being able to get a carrier-sacrifice for their purificatory rituals forces the community to examine the basis of their rituals, even if subliminally. When they finally have Eman hanging from a tree, their guilt is a correct cathartic outcome of the chase that points towards a possible liberation.

The ritual of the sacrificial carrier can no longer mean the same thing in this particular dramatic instance because of the disruptive processes that have been involved in securing it. Therefore, the emotions associated with purificatory rituals are replaced by those of guilt and self-doubt, and the total meaning of the purificatory rituals takes on a problematic status to the community. The drama presents a series of dichotomies: the contradictions inherent in a belief in determinism and the articulation of free will; the contradictions involved in traditional rituals and their often authoritarian foundations; the gap between the appearance of purification and the reality of it; and, finally, the problematic space between rituals and the feelings that they are supposed to generate in those who participate in them.

Certain elements of *The Strong Breed* place it at an earlier conceptual juncture in Soyinka's exploration of the notion of tragic agency, not only in terms of its having been published earlier in his career but also in terms of the specific emphasis of the tragic conception informing it. A thing to note is the extent to which the play ties itself to the question of rite of passage in various forms within its dramatic structure. Eman's father represents one aspect of rite of passage, being the willing and self-resigned symbol of the community's pollution. Eman's interrupted puberty rites is another figuration, while a third one is captured in the village's concern with a purificatory ritual to aid in the passage from the old year to the new. All these seem to be grounded on a conception of the affective danger that is inherent in the liminal phase of passage. What was noted earlier about the perceived danger inherent in the crossing of boundaries and in in-between states seems to be an implicit motivation of the play's dramatic structure. The play's closeness to a specific affectivity of the liminal status is perhaps what leads it to explore scenes of hectic physical activity involving running across the stage, heckling, quarrelling, a near coming-to-blows and descriptions of violence in the language of the characters. It is as if the play needs to exorcise the sense of affective danger by placing the audience in a crucible of hectic activity preparatory to the problematic catharsis at its close.

The next thing to note is the sparseness of spectacle, drumming and dancing in the play. Unlike most of Soyinka's drama, *The Strong Breed* has a sparse structure of background cultural colouring. In some sense, this helps to drain the play of potential vitality in order to make it a starker examination of the moral and ethical issues it touches upon. Compared with the culturally exuberant tone of *A Dance of the Forest* produced only a year earlier, *The Strong Breed* seems to lean more towards cultural critique than celebratory affirmation. This may be linked to the focus on the empty mechanics of ritual that Soyinka places at the centre of this play. But the question of the difference between celebratory affirmation and a near-sceptical cultural critique also relates to the question of tragic agency in relation to social being in a national context. E. M. Birbalsingh has noted that Soyinka develops a 'faith in self-sacrifice' throughout his career.

However, in plays like *The Strong Breed*, *The Road* and *Madmen and Specialists* the coherence in his conception of the matter 'is temporarily disfigured by encroaching pessimism' (Birbalsingh 1982: 209). He sees the pessimism put to rest in *Death and the King's Horseman*. It is possible to agree with the first part of Birbalsingh's assertions without acquiescing to the second which implies an unproblematic evolution in a writer's work from thematic incoherence to conceptual completeness. It is rather more the case that there is a continual pendulum movement involving both ruptures and continuities in which different aspects of a scheme or of various schemes are emphasized for different purposes. The indeterminacy built into the structure of *The Strong Breed* may be taken to signal an uneasiness in Soyinka's conceptions of heroic vocation not only in relation to traditional culture but to Nigeria as well. The structure of indeterminacy in relation to indigenous culture reflects simultaneously an ambiguity in relation to Nigerian socio-political realities. In this sense, the plays Birbalsingh mentions as well as the explicitly political *Kongi's Harvest* are all explorations of the grounds of possibility for articulating a heroic vocation within the Nigerian socio-political space. This is not something to assert as an infallible perspective, but considering the disillusionment that attended his country's attainment of Independence in 1960 and the rapid exposure of political schisms which culminated in the Biafra War in 1966, it is difficult to escape the feeling that his plays of the period express an uneasiness with the meaning of the political space in general.[15] *Death and the King's Horseman* expresses aspects of this cultural critique, but this time it is not only in terms of the relationships between individual heroic vocation and traditional realities, but also between traditional culture and the historical processes of the world in general.

Several of the pre-suppositions on which 'The Fourth Stage' rests are relevant to the framework of *Death and the King's Horseman*[16] especially those to do with the nature of the abyss and the efficacy of bridging rituals. In contrast to the situation in *The Strong Breed*, both the community and the key figure in the ritual suicide share the same attitudes towards the ritual of self-sacrifice. The play outlines the events leading up to a frustrated ritual suicide which involves Elesin, the guardian of the dead king's stables. The events in the play are also placed within the context of colonial realities in which Yoruba culture is under the domination of a clumsy British administration. The ritual suicide, enjoined upon the keeper of the king's stables 40 days after the king's death, is not only to give the king a companion into the other world, but is also a way of affirming a sense of cosmos for the culture in general. When Praise-Singer affirms to Elesin that their world 'was never wrenched from its true course' (10), he affirms it in the confidence that stability is due to attending to the rituals of the ancestors. This affirmation is made to Elesin to keep him in constant awareness of how important it is for him not to fail in the ritual suicide. The preparations for the ritual are both psychological as well as physical, and the music and drumming that follow Elesin on his every appearance are meant to groom him psychologically for the ritual of transition. In the crucial dance at the end of Act III in which Elesin enters a trance-state, it is noticeable how images of passage dominate the exchanges between Praise-Singer, representing the voice of the dead king, and Elesin himself.

> PRAISE-SINGER: If you cannot come, I said, swear
> You'll tell my favourite horse. I shall
> Ride through the gates alone.
> …
>
> PRAISE-SINGER: If you cannot come Elesin, tell my dog
> I cannot stay the keeper too long
> At the gate. (42)

It is interesting to note that the king suggests his dog as replacement for Elesin in case he fails. Dogs are animals specially dedicated to Ogun, and part of Ogun rituals involves the dismembering of a dog to symbolize his own dismemberment in the abyss of transition. By such subtle suggestions, the abyss of transition through which Ogun journeyed is recalled for Elesin, further emphasizing the importance of success in the ritual for the culture.

Elesin Oba fails in his attempt at ritual suicide and explanations for this failure vary. They range from those that centre on conflicts in his mind to those that assert the failure derives from his being a product of a faulty ruling class (see, for instance, Katrak, 99; Adebayo Williams 1993). The intervention of the white man is seen as only an instrument that precipitates a crisis which tests Elesin's preparedness for death. Valid though these interpretations are, it seems fruitful to relate Elesin's predicament to the notion of the ambiguity in the state of transition as well as to the factors in his character and the culture at large. In *Horseman*, the phase of transition harbours a liminal danger that is refracted differentially for the community and for Elsesin. The state of transition as conceived in *Horseman* is figured in a series of ambiguous descriptions silhouetted in the language of the play. It is figured in the background of the major concerns of the play, but in such a way as to challenge the culture's very conception of transitional abyss at that historical moment.

It is useful to turn to Victor Turner again, but this time to recall aspects of his notions of rituals of transition to help us grasp the ambiguous nature of the transitional state. Turner argues that the liminal phase of transition is one of conceptual anti-structure and ambiguity. Conceptually ambiguous, the phase of transition is ritualized in ways that draw upon expressive symbols of cross-identities and the blurring and merging of distinctions (Victor Turner 1982: 26). Typical images of this conceptual state are:

> androgynes, theriomorphic figures, at once animals and men and women, angels, mermaids, centaurs, human-headed lions, monstrous creatures that combine nature and culture. (1990: 11)

The common denominator of all these images is that they combine aspects of nature with those of culture which are not available on an everyday experiential level. In the liminality of transition, culture is in a 'subjunctive mood' a state of 'as if', 'maybe' and 'perhaps' (1982: 82–4). Thus the state of transition is governed by a coupling of contradictory identities and impulses. In Turner's emphasis on a sense of ambiguity and category confusion as definitive of the liminal state, he shifts its axis away from the notion of affective danger which was its dominant characterization in Van Gennep's formulations. Turner's notion of acute ambiguity inherent in liminal status is appropriate for understanding *Horseman* both in terms of the play's action as well as in its relationship to a historical moment in the traditional culture's encounter with the West.

At several points in the play, there are hints that the ritual suicide and the state of transition are perceived in an ambiguous light. This is most usually expressed in images coupling death with sensuality, or, masculine with feminine essence. Elesin is the first to signal this perception of the ritual suicide:

> This night I'll lay my head upon their lap and go to sleep. This night I'll touch feet with their feet in a dance that is no longer of this earth. But the smell of their flesh, their sweat, the smell of indigo on their cloth, this is the last air I wish to breathe as I go to meet my great forebears. (10)

Elesin is speaking with Praise-Singer about the market women. Considering that this is the night of transition for him, it is highly suggestive that he expresses a sense of the passage of transition in terms of sensuality, of sleeping in the lap of women and of dancing in their embrace. That this coupling may well be due to his being an inveterate womanizer we cannot dismiss, but the coupling of death with sensuality is continually elaborated in the play by other characters and events. When Iyaloja, after some reluctance, agrees to surrender her own son's betrothed for Elesin's enjoyment, she does this because she perceives the fertile possibilities to be derived from the coupling of the transitionally positioned Elesin with the young bride. The form in which she expresses her intuitions of fertile possibilities is significant:

> Oh you who fill the home from hearth to threshold with the voices of children, you who now bestride the hidden gulf and pause to draw the

right foot across and into the resting-home of the great forebears, it is good that your loins be drained into the earth we know, that your last strength be ploughed back into the womb that gave you being. (22)

The sense of liminality is signalled by the sense of Elesin's state of transition putting him astride the two worlds. This sense is further deepened by the suggestion of equivalence between sex, birth and death captured most forcefully in the image of ploughing back into the womb. The linking of disparate elements is given a more startling expression when Iyaloja says later that 'now we must go prepare your bridal chamber. Then these same hands will lay your shrouds' (23). That this stage of the action is at the market-place in the twilight of evening adds even further suggestiveness to the unfolding events, for Yoruba culture holds the marketplace itself to be a special location. Its significance lies even deeper in an inclusive idea of sacred space which also extends to *orita* (crossroads), the favoured locale for ritual sacrifice; it is a liminal arena where the spirit world and the real world meet. A proverb in the language affirms that 'the world is a market and heaven is home' showing how important the market-place is in the culture's conception of cosmos.

Ambiguities in the state of liminality are signalled even through non-verbal cues. The music that surrounds the moment of ritual suicide is difficult to decipher. It is unclear to those who hear it from afar whether the drums are sounding the wedding or the death of a great chief. Joseph can only answer Jane Pilkings's question as to whether the drumming they hear is 'connected with dying or anything of that nature' with exasperation:

Madam, this is what I am trying to say: I am not sure. It sounds like the death of a great chief and then, it sounds like the wedding of a great chief. It really mix me up. (30)

Yet the sense of liminality does not remain solely at the level of language or non-verbal cues. It impinges on the very psyche of Elesin himself, generating important consequences for the community and for the general sense of the play. All the hopes of his people converge on Elesin at the moment of his ritual suicide. He himself has long prepared for this moment partly by virtue of his position at court. Being the guardian of the king's stables, he knows that the ritual suicide is part of his occupation. As has already been noted, what the play depicts in the exchanges between him and Praise-Singer and in the singing and drumming that constantly accompany him are only dramatic manifestations of a deeper cultural process of preparation. Elesin's character, however, marks him out as a curiously problematic figure for the onerous cultural task given him. His immense vitality is noted in stage directions, and both Iyaloja and Praise-Singer fill out his background of courage and heroic deeds through the praise names they chant of him. Not only is he 'husband of the multitudes', he is one whose 'stride disdains to falter though an adder reared/suddenly on his path', a man who, chancing on the calabash of honour, drained it to its last drop thinking it was palm-wine (14–15). Another aspect of his character may be grasped from his rapid changes of mood. These frequently serve to interrupt the flow of the action and to turn it in new directions.

When Elesin first emerges on stage, his retinue has to struggle to keep up with him. The exchanges between him and Praise-Singer centre on the realities of the other world and the implications of the coming ritual suicide.

> PRAISE-SINGER: In their time the great wars came and went, the little wars came and went; the white slavers came and went, they took away the heart of our race, they bore away the mind and muscle of our race. The city fell and was rebuilt; the city fell and our people trudged through mountain and forest to found a new home but – Elesin Oba do you hear me?
>
> ELESIN: I hear your voice Olohun-iyo. (10)

Praise-Singer is reminding Elesin of some important aspects of Oyo history. The reference to the collapse of the city walls and the migration in search of a new township certainly have historical resonances in Oyo history (see Samuel Johnson's *The History*, 159–61). The flow of these historical concerns is suddenly interrupted by Elesin when he introduces the song of the Not-I bird. In a partly humorous way showing ordinary people's attitudes to Death, the song is important because it signals Elesin's unbounded confidence in the face of the coming ritual. Unlike all the other characters depicted in the song of the Not-I bird, Elesin 'unrolled his mat of welcome' for the Not-I bird to see. He affirms confidently after the song:

> I am master of my Fate. When the hour comes
> Watch me dance along the narrowing path
> Glazed by the soles of my great precursors.
> My soul is eager. I shall not turn aside. (14)

By this time Iyaloja and the market women have come on stage and join the exchanges on Elesin's preparation for the crucial ritual. After a while, the flow of concerns is again interrupted by Elesin's sudden 'Stop! Enough of that' (15). This leads to much puzzlement for everyone around and is relieved only when he imperiously requests to be draped in rich cloths. The women happily provide these. The apparent resolution of his sudden anger is celebrated by drumming, dancing and the clucking of the market women. The theme of the singing at this stage is the pride they have in him and their preparedness to shower him with material blessings as a token of their respect:

> WOMEN: For a while we truly feared
> Our hands had wrenched the world adrift
> In emptiness.

> IYALOJA: Richly, richly, robe him richly
> The cloth of honour is *alari*
> *Sanyan* is the band of friendship
> Boa-skin makes slippers of esteem. (17)

Not long after this the flow of the action is interrupted yet again when Elesin spots a beautiful girl off-stage, who later 'comes along the passage through which Elesin made his entry' (18). The variety of the interruptions to the action, and the fact that they all derive from Elesin seem designed to tell us something about his character. Dan Izevbaye (1981) notes that the range of these interruptions shows Elesin in a state of 'spiritual paralysis' which he does not move from even till the point of the failed ritual suicide.[17] However, Izevbaye leaves his highly suggestive perceptions unelaborated. One can only surmise that what he describes as Elesin's spiritual paralysis derives from the horseman's love of material things, so that it is this material love that finally frustrates the ritual. Yet, perhaps it is better to argue that Elesin's rapid changes of mood derive from his having entered an emotionally charged phase grounded on conceptual liminality. Clearly impetuous, Elesin is at a heightened state of irritability because of the burden of duty imposed on him as a figure of transition. He is depicted as having a shifting focus of concentration whose correlatives are his intense vitality and the metaphorical fervour of his speech.

By the time of the interruption of the ritual by the white man, Elesin is caught within the grasp of multiple realities which deepen any psychological weaknesses of his character. The precise moment of the ritual is also the moment at which he is at the threshold of liminality. His psyche is exposed to all the ambiguities deriving from that state. Two different strands of significance can directly be extracted from Elesin's own reflections about the reasons for his failure. He confesses to his young bride that his attachment to her is one reason for his failure. But it is what he tells Iyaloja when she comes to chide him on ignoring earlier warnings she gave him that shows the enigmatic nature of the state of transition and the overwhelming contradictions that overcome his sense of purpose. It is worth quoting at length:

What were warnings beside the moist contact of living earth between my fingers? What were warnings beside the renewal of famished embers

lodged eternally in the heart of man? But even that, even if it over-
whelmed one with a thousandfold temptations to linger a little while, a
man could overcome it. It is when the alien hand pollutes the source of
will, when a stranger force of violence shatters the mind's calm resolution,
this is when a man is made to commit the awful treachery of relief, commit
in his thought the unspeakable blasphemy of seeing the hand of the gods
in this alien rupture of his world.

... My will was squelched in the spittle of an alien race, and all because
I had committed this blasphemy of thought – that there might be the hand
of the gods in a stranger's intervention. (69)

His attraction to the young bride and the attractions of the flesh are
only one side of the story, possibly the lesser part. His language at this
point wanders over a wide range of metaphors to help him organize
the sense of futility with which he is afflicted. There are references to
earth and to dying embers; suggestions of a deep well in 'source of
will' whose disturbance is hinted at not only in the 'polluting hand'
but is also manifested in the word 'shattering' as if the passivity of
insidious pollution has to be replaced with a verb closer to a sense of
systemic violence. The whole meditation ends on allusions to
mastication in the words 'squelched' and 'spittle' as a means of
figuring the sense of his being a victim of the whiteman's predatori-
ness. Clearly, he is highly disturbed, and the range of metaphors in
his language at this point reflects the problematic nature of the
experience and the difficulties of interpretation imposed on his conceptual resources. At another level, however, the unhappy coalescing
in his mind of the white man with the hand of his gods signals the
ambiguous nature of the area of liminality, an area that impinges on
his consciousness acutely because of his positioning in the ritual of
transition. Already charged with ambiguous significations, the area
of transition is the space of inversions and ironic transformations for
him. At the point when Elesin would presumably have focused all his
psychic energies on the aspirations of his community and the duty
imposed by ancestral deities, he enters into a zone of liminality in
which all the significations of his culture can simultaneously be
affirmed and erased as if in a part-jest part-serious play of arbitrariness. When the white man intrudes, he is fused in Elesin's mind with
the only notion of Power he has been brought up to revere, and that is
the power of his deities. This moment is particularly tragic precisely
because he is alone in the intuition of liminality brought on by the
state of transition. It is an intuition which he is unable to verbalize,
and even if he were able to, would not be understood because of the
terrible consequences that his failure harbours for the community.

At the point when Elesin fails in the ritual suicide, an overwhelming sense of doom washes over the community. His failure is a
mark of the discomposition of cosmos for them, and part of this

discomposition is captured in the filial inversions that attend the meeting between Olunde and his father. The moment is a charged one. Elesin storms onto the stage pursued by Pilkings and his guards. Olunde is already on stage with Jane Pilkings, and Elesin nearly runs into the statuesque figure of his shocked son. He stops dead. This is what transpires between them:

> (For several moments they hold the same position. ELESIN moves a few steps forward, almost as if he is still in doubt.)

> ELESIN: (He moves his head, inspecting him from side to side.) Olunde! (He collapses slowly at OLUNDE'S feet.) Oh son, don't let the sight of your father turn you blind!

> OLUNDE: (He moves for the first time since he heard his voice, brings his head slowly down to look on him): I have no father, eater of leftovers.

> (He walks slowly down the way his father had run. Light fades out on ELESIN, sobbing into the ground). (61)

The father's bewilderment and the son's frozen shock are captured in their different reactions. The most important part of the scene is Elesin's collapse at the feet of his son, gesturing to an involuntary prostration. In Yoruba culture it is young people who prostrate to their elders and sons to fathers, not vice versa. For a father to prostrate or fall before his son is a mark of role inversion and deeply shocking. Olunde's reference to his father as an 'eater of leftovers' is picked up later by Iyaloja when she continually refers to Elesin's preference for second best when his culture had offered him their choicest:

> You have betrayed us. We fed you sweetmeats such as we hoped awaited you on the other side. But you said No, I must eat the world's left-overs. We said you were the hunter who brought the quarry down, to you belonged the vital portions of the game. No, you said, I am the hunter's dog and I shall eat the entrails of the game and the faeces of the hunter. (68)

It is interesting to note that here the dog suffers a negative reputation, removing it from the respectable ambit of Ogun associations that was hinted at earlier on in the play. The implied inversions that Elesin's failure is presumed to have unleashed are presumably stopped when Olunde takes his father's place in sacrificing himself for the community. Olunde's name means 'my lord (or deliverer) has come', thus bringing a restorative and messianic import to his death. Be that as it may, his ritual suicide raises a number of serious problems. If Elesin's death at a specific time of night was crucial for bridging the abyss of transition and to ensure continuity for the culture, is this effort on Olunde's part not belated and futile even if to a degree restorative? What does it mean for the culture's self-conception that they have to find a substitute for the ritual suicide outside the parameters established by hallowed ritual practice? What does this say about the play's attitude to its cultural material?

Derrida's notion of the conceptual ambiguities of the supplement may be used as a means of understanding the significance of Olunde's self-sacrifice. Derrida points out how a supplement, added on to another item as a means of completing it, simultaneously problematizes both its meanings of 'to add' and 'to complete'. As he points out, the supplement 'produces no relief, its place is assigned in the structure by the mark of an emptiness' (Derrida 1976: 415). Clearly, Olunde is a 'supplement' to fill the emptiness marked by the failure of his father. But his gesture is an ambiguous statement of the problematic status of the ritual he completes. In supplementing or completing a ritual that has already failed in the terms laid out by the culture, his supplementarity is the hint of new models of agency for the culture. This mode derives partly from within the culture itself. The essence of Ogun, which is an implicit assumption underlying the ritual suicide, is shown to be present in unexpected folds within the culture. Thus when Olunde offers himself, he is affirming the availability of an Ogun-essence which does not lie solely with those like his father or those explicitly prepared for directly carrying the onus of transitional crossing. Yet, significantly, Olunde has been prepared for this moment by having travelled abroad and, by these travels, acquiring a sense of the relativity of all cultural values. This makes him set his own cultural values against Western ones, and despite the strenuous efforts of his educational background and his medical vocation, he finds that his own cultural values are as efficacious as those of any other culture. Whatever rituals have prepared him for this moment are not those which the play demonstrated as attending his father, but rather the rituals of self-discovery outside the parameters of his own culture. In a sense, his journey abroad was a journey through an abyss of transition perhaps as profound as any his own culture could provide for him. In this way, the essence of the transitional process involves both a proximity to and distance from his own cultural values. What Olunde's supplementarity suggests is the injection of a new mode of understanding into the sense of tragic agency by virtue of the culture's necessary insertion into new relations in the world. His sacrificial gesture, then, is a simultaneous relativization *and* affirmation of the traditional mode of tragic agency. And, though this is not fully elaborated in the play, it is gestured to suggestively in Olunde's characterization and the supreme restorative sacrifice he makes for his community.

In certain ways, the inversions that attend the cultural rituals are an extension of the effects of language which sustain the dramatic framework of the play. David Richards makes the interesting point that the language of the play, loaded as he shows it is with translated Yoruba proverbs, expresses a 'transmutation or commutation' between transition and proverb, enabling 'the former to be constantly present in the rich verbal texture of the play, because proverbs approach most closely the poetic expression of creative paradox which is the dominant metaphysic' (Richards 1984: 94). Thus, the play prepares for the inversions on several levels simultaneously. On the level of action, we see Elesin failing and being replaced by his son. This is supported by a more subtle level of signification where the dense texture of proverb usage is itself the slippery foundation for articulating the culture's self-awareness. Yet, this slipperiness is not open-ended, as Richards points out. It closes on an affirmation of communal values, no matter how problematic. It must be noted that even if the question of tragic agency is put in partial limbo by Elesin's failure, the final focus of the play is the young Bride. The play's last words are those of Iyaloja as she intones to her: 'Now forget the dead, forget even the living. Turn your mind only to the unborn.' Here, there is a recuperation of cultural values for the play despite the problematic exploration of tragic heroic vocation.

The ambiguities of the state of transition which reflect upon the consciousness of Elesin and are also manifested in the need for supplementary ritual ideals are paralleled by the historical socio-political realities within which the traditional culture is shown to be caught. One dimension of colonialism was that it placed colonized cultures in the curious position of having to mediate traditional verities while absorbing the values of a dominating Western culture. The play itself in its totality is located at such a critical conjuncture. When the Pilkingses wear the *egungun* costumes they show a gross representation of the fusion of various realities. By putting on the costumes, they re-incarnate ancestral realities in the idiom of colonial power, thus extending the notion of the liminality of transition into the space of socio-political relations. It is interesting that Soyinka takes pains to prevent the play from being viewed in terms of clash of cultures in his preface to the play, because that theme is a dimension of the play that subtends the whole notion of transition in very important ways.

Death and the King's Horseman is Soyinka's first creative engagement with the question of colonialism. In this play, however, the contact of the two cultures is shown to harbour problems for both of them in terms of the conceptually shifting historical terrain on which each of them stands. Though the British administration is clearly in control, there is an uneasy sense in which that control is itself a reflection of powerlessness. For despite all his control over the means of force, Pilkings is constantly hedged in by the limitations of a lack of complete knowledge of the culture he is in charge of. Part of the dialectic of power/powerlessness is captured in the uneasy relationships he has with Amusa and John, aide-de-camp and domestic help respectively. These two could be taken to represent extensions of his bureaucratic and domestic domains. In relation to both of these, it is evident that he needs to negotiate his position of power very carefully in order not to antagonize them and thereby make the grounds of his bureaucratic machinery questionable. This generates a measure of anxiety and frustration for him. The slippery dimensions of his authority are made evident in the discussions he has with his wife as to what course of action to take into the report of the imminent ritual suicide. To teasing from his wife about the blustering attitude he has adopted towards the matter, he replies, shouting testily:

> And suppose after all it's only a wedding. I'd look a proper fool if I interrupted a chief on his honeymoon, wouldn't I? (Resumes his angry stride, slows down.) Ah well, who can tell what those chiefs actually do on their honeymoon anyway? (He takes up the pad and scribbles rapidly on it.) Joseph! Joseph! Joseph! (Some moments later JOSEPH puts in a sulky appearance.) Did you hear me call you? Why the hell didn't you answer? (31)

We must recall that he had mildly insulted Joseph's religious sentiments earlier on, so that the sulkiness is a sign of silent protest. Later on in the action he makes a reluctant apology to Joseph over the insult. His frustration at not being able to grasp the real meaning of the reported ritual, and the problematic negotiation of authority in relation to his househelp are all signalled in the play.

At another, more humorous level, this anxiety and frustration over the proper grounds of authority is ironically expressed on Pilkings's behalf by Amusa when he goes to the Oba's palace to investigate the ritual suicide. He is confronted by young girls at the market-place who ridicule and mock his authority. There are decidedly rebellious remarks from these women and girls and the encounter produces a lot of sexual innuendoes suggesting a threat of castration for Amusa. This part of the action ends with Amusa in ignominious flight from the young girls who threaten to pull down his shorts to see what 'authority' he carries in them. At this level of action there is a mild questioning of the basis of the British administration's authority.

All the hints about the problematic status of colonial authority become even more significant when joined to the specific state of Western civilization depicted in the play. Inklings of decline are captured in the rusty 'Britannia' played by an equally rusty brass band at the Residency in Act IV. The stage directions tell us that the Residency itself is 'redolent of the tawdry decadence of a far-flung but key imperial frontier' (45). Even more significant is the fact that the over-extended empire produces illusions to justify its war campaigns. Olunde's mention of death and disillusionment among British youth called to the front is meant to foreground the desperation with which the imperial centre attempted to maintain a sense of grandeur amidst the carnage of the Second World War. Echoes of the war raging in the background are also historically relevant as marking the demise of the Empire because of the rapid changes that occurred after the war. But it is important to note that all these considerations of the decline of colonial power are only hinted at and worked into the conceptual background with which the British, as representatives of different cultural values, are depicted in the play.

Despite the richness with which Yoruba culture is depicted in spectacle, dance and language, the culture also comes with a specific historical baggage that marks it as in decline. We must recall that the ritual suicide is in the context of the political organization of Oyo. Historically, Oyo itself was a large empire and some of its political rituals were common across Yorubaland. In the play, the political dimensions of the ritual suicide are submerged under considerations of the continuity of the culture. The ritual suicide is supposed to be an affirmation of the continuity of a great cultural as well as political history, something figured partly in the hierarchy of which Elesin is a representative. However, the great Oyo empire had been in decline by the beginning of the eighteenth century and, by the period in which the play is set, had been completely superseded by fresh realities that called for reassessment of its former glory. The interrupted ritual, then, becomes the grammar of the discomposition of the cultural grandeur of the Yorubas within the ambit of new political realities.

We can see how useful the notions of transition and of liminality become for grasping the historico-political dimensions of the play. The play itself is pushed to the threshold of ambiguities at various levels even as it explores the question of transitional rituals in Yoruba culture. It shows the lapse of the efficacy of the traditional culture because of the larger historical and political realities on the one hand and the weaknesses of the human self on the other as they conjoin to usurp the glory of cultural aspirations. It enters into a dialogue with the notion of tragedy and heroic vocation elaborated by Soyinka in his essay by foregrounding and problematizing various thematic dimensions of the notions of liminality and transition.

In contrast to *The Strong Breed*, *Death and the King's Horseman* is positioned not only in relation to indigenous culture but also in relation to the outside world. It is not idle to point out that this play, along with the adaptation of *The Bacchae of Euripides* as well as *Myth, Literature and the African World* were all produced during Soyinka's period of exile at Churchill College, Cambridge in 1974–5. A sense of nostalgia for his culture is coupled with a strong urge to stress its vitality. This seems to have been particularly necessary because of the difficult context in which an Africanist literary discourse had to be articulated in the Cambridge of those days. African literature was consigned to the Department of Social Anthropology, and Soyinka himself notes his uneasiness at the state of affairs in the preface to *Myth*. It is clear that the condition of exile provided a particularly rich opportunity for him to define his culture in relation to Western cosmopolitan realities. In relation to the strategic formation we have been tracing so far, however, his explorations of Yoruba culture have always expressed a confidence in its ability to contribute meaning-fully to world culture. Soyinka's career expresses a peculiar trajectory involving several things: a celebration of his culture coupled with a steady socio-political critique; an exuberant re-writing of Yoruba mythological discourse for the projection of a confident heroic vocation; a continual elaboration of aspects of his culture in his plays and other writings; and, finally, the assertion of Ogun as tutelary deity for progressives all over the world, be they Greek playwrights, political activists or nationalists. His is a key phase of the strategic formation.

Notes

1 Wole Soyinka, 'The Fourth Stage', in *Myth, Literature and the African World* (Cambridge: Cambridge University Press, 1976): 140–60. The book is a compilation of a lecture course he gave while in Cambridge from 1974–5 and the essay is published as an appendix to these lectures. The essay was first published in a festschrift for G. Wilson Knight in 1969. However, due to various cross-references between this essay and the rest of the lectures in the book the whole collection represents an organic whole. I shall be drawing from various parts of *Myth* while focusing attention centrally on this particular essay.

2 Every Soyinka play can yield perspectives on his use of the indigenous cultural matrix. In fact the point can be made that plays like *A Dance of the Forests*, *The Road* and *Kongi's Harvest* might produce more problematic insights as to his relationship to traditional resources. My choice of *The Strong Breed* and *Death and the King's Horseman* is only in order further to ground another level of my argument which is that the indigenous resources lead to different perspectives on tropes of liminality. It has to be said that critics are far from fully exhausting the potential meanings of Soyinka's plays and that there is much research yet to be done to fully assess his contribution to African and world literature.

3 Lévi-Strauss, *From Honey to Ashes*, trans. John and Doreen Weightman (1966; London: Jonathan Cape, 1973): 354.

4 The collocation of the triad of 'sign, symbol and agency' is Toni Morrison's in *Playing in the Dark* (London: Picador, 1993): 39. She employs this phrase in her discussion of the processes by which a subsumed and unacknowledged racial difference is used to elaborate a specific 'white' identity in American literature. The important thing is her pointer to subliminal significations which nonetheless have

important consequences for identity formation.

5 Friedrich Nietzsche, *The Birth of Tragedy and The Genealogy of Morals*, translated by Francis Golffing (New York: Doubleday, 1956): 19, 30–1, 50, 56.

6 It is important to note that Obatala is seen to be the same as Orisa-nla, the god of creation. See, for instance, Idowu (1962): 71 and J. O. Awolalu (1979): 21–2. In Soyinka's theorizing, however, the two deities are treated as distinct and separate. Only once does he suggest that they are the same deity (16). At other times he refers to Obatala as a 'syncretic successor to Orisa-nla' (145, 152). There is an implied hierarchization between the two in Soyinka's theory, with Orisa-nla obviously being the more powerful of the two. Following his typology, I shall be referring to the two deities as separate and distinct in discussing his theory.

7 For the significance of the *babaláwo* in Yoruba culture, see William Bascom's classic *Ifa Divination: Communication Between Gods and Men* (Bloomington: Indiana University Press, 1969).

8 Harry Garuba, 'Frontiers, Men and Gods: Wole Soyinka's Ogun and the Myth of the American Frontier', manuscript; published in *American Studies Association Journal of Nigeria* 1.2 (1992).

9 Wole Soyinka, 'The Writer: Child at the Frontier', *The Cambridge Review*, No. 114 (1993): 58. This special issue of *The Cambridge Review*, entitled 'Two African Voices: Childhood, Colonialism and Creativity' is particularly interesting for also having an essay by Chinua Achebe in which he reflects on his early socialization into a British education and the place this had in his growing universe.

10 Karin Barber has pointed out to me in private communication that the Ogun myth, and indeed myths about other Yoruba gods in general, are undergoing continual elaboration at the level of popular theatre and culture. She cites the examples of *Ere Ogun*, a play by the Lere Paimo Theatre Group which focuses on another myth of Ogun in which Oya defects from him. She also mentions a play by Ladejo Okedeji on Shango. This suggests that Soyinka's uses of Yoruba myths are an aspect of a larger discursive manoeuvre continually going on in the culture.

11 This can be taken in the sense in which Roman Jakobson defines the term 'poetic' in his typology of discursive modes from the various permutations of the communicative elements that lie between addresser and addressee. See his 'Linguistics and Poetics', and 'The Metaphoric and Metonymic Poles' in *Modern Criticism and Theory*, edited by David Lodge (London: Longman, 1988): 32–57 and 57–61 respectively; also David Lodge, *The Modes of Modern Writing* (London: Routledge, 1977): 73–124.

12 *The Strong Breed*, in *Collected Plays Vol. 2* (Oxford: Oxford University Press, 1973): 113–46. All page references given in parentheses in the text are to this edition. An early and shorter version of the play was produced by Soyinka for a film, *Culture in Transition* in 1961 and the play we now have was first published in 1964. See James Gibbs, *Wole Soyinka* (London: Macmillan, 1986): 6.

13 Olusegun Oladipo, 'Predestination in Yoruba Thought: A Philosopher's Interpretation', manuscript; published in *Orita* No. 24 (1992).

14 Some critics see Eman as the articulation of a Christ-cum-Ogun figure in their various sacrificial contexts. But it is possible also to see him in the light of Sophocles's Oedipus as well as in that of the previous two, because of his resistance to his putative destiny. And like Sophocles's *Oedipus Rex*, *The Strong Breed* harbours an interesting conjuncture of ambivalences which might relate to the interface between an older traditional and communally held world-view and another leaning more towards the expression of individual freedom. It would be interesting to compare the two plays in this light. For opinions on the issue of the religious connotations, see Ogunba, 115 and Eldred Jones, *The Writing of Wole Soyinka* (London: Heinemann, 1973): 49–50.

15 For an extended examination of Soyinka's 'political unconscious' as may be gleaned from his autobiographies, see Ato Quayson, 'Wole Soyinka's autobiographies as

political unconscious', *Journal of Commonwealth Literature* 31.2 (1996): 19–32.

16 *Death and the King's Horseman*, (London: Methuen, 1975). Page references given in parentheses in the main text are to this edition; title abbreviated to *Horseman*.

17 The reasons for such a spiritual paralysis could of course lie elsewhere. Tejumola Olaniyan presents a highly intriguing interpretation. Describing Elesin as a 'consumate sybarite', he argues that the problem with him is his transposition of *language* away from a register of action (which it should be in a truly Ogunian state) and into one of hedonistic inaction (Olaniyan 1995: 50–5). The implication of such an interpretation is a completely new one in understandings of *Death and the King's Horseman*. For, it means that Elesin's flaw lies partly in his self-delusion by means of an improperly attuned language; one improperly linked to the full apprehension of communal expectations and tragedy that the play so subtly explores.

5
Narrative Through a Prism
of Indigenous Beliefs

Examples from Ben Okri's
Short Stories

With Ben Okri, the literary strategic formation we have been tracing enters a phase of simultaneous continuity with, as well as differentiation from, the work already elaborated in this study. An important point of departure is the fact that unlike Johnson, Tutuola and Soyinka, Okri is not Yoruba. He was born to Urhobo parents. Despite not being a Yoruba, there are many ways in which his work not only articulates the same conceptual resource-base, but, indeed, various aspects of what might be seen as a Yoruba belief system. This is perhaps traceable to several factors to do with the development of a broadly Nigerian consciousness in the eyes of the younger generation of Nigerians not only with the spread of education but also with increasing numbers of them in a diasporic existence outside the country. Local ethnic boundaries become irrelevant when identity requires definition outside the boundaries where the parameters of ethnicity acquired specificity.

The circumstances of Okri's growing up may be taken to have generated a sense of the interpenetration of cultures. Brought to London in 1961 at the age of three to join his lawyer father, he started school in one of the mixed race areas of London. He was sent back to Nigeria in 1966 where he continued his education at Ibadan and Ikenne before finally being sent to Urhobo College at Warri for his secondary education. He spent the rest of his adolescence in Lagos, a city which, like most capitals, is a place of continuing splintering and re-aggregation of identities. What seems to have finally led to his invocation of indigenous resources was his second sojourn in London from the early eighties, perhaps as a means of negotiating a sense of identity in a metropolitan diasporic environment. The earlier writers offered a set of indigenous concepts and a way of organizing reality which he was happy to draw upon in his own quest for identity and an appropriate mode of literary expression. Okri's work freely evokes elements of the work of the earlier writers while turning his resources to new uses. There is growing critical consensus that the best way to understand his work is by setting it against the work of Tutuola and Soyinka (see Chidi Okonkwo 1991; Kole Omotoso 1993). In the literary career of Ben Okri, the question of a literary tradition in Nigerian writing as the strategic filiation with a specific discursive field irrespective of ethnic identity becomes a fruitful one to pursue.

Like most African writers, Okri's quest for indigenous resources by which to organize his narratives came after his experiments with Western forms of realism. *Flowers and Shadows* (1980) and *The Landscapes Within* (1981) largely pursue a Western paradigm of realism, even though there is a sense that in the second novel a gradual breaking with that mode is in the offing. With the short stories an indigenous resource-base is joined to an impulse towards experimenting with several motifs and symbols from Western mythology and literature. An important clue to Okri's attitudes to an indigenous discursive field in Nigerian literature is given in his review of Amos Tutuola's *The Witch Herbalist of the Remote Town*:

> Amos Tutuola is a writer who straddles twilights. His fictional world is a haunting terrain; the quests he describes demand from his protagonists the necessities of energy and imagination … *The Witch Herbalist of the Remote Town* is a fascinating and thoroughly enjoyable book. One which I suspect will provide generations of artists with inspiration. (Okri 1983: 429–30)

His postulation that Amos Tutuola will provide inspiration to generations of artists is particularly interesting because it echoes a sentiment that was often voiced at the beginning of Tutuola's career. Most early commentators on Tutuola saw his work as something epochal for African literature and there were many speculations as to the effect his work would have on future literary production on the continent.[1] This particular sentiment ebbed as Tutuola's career progressed, and so it is significant that Okri re-invokes that sentiment in the same tones as was evident on Tutuola's first discovery. It would not be farfetched to surmise that this sense of wonder is a marker of Okri's own discovery of the potential in Tutuola's storytelling for new directions in narrative discourse. It cannot be an idle coincidence that *Incidents at the Shrine* and *Stars of the New Curfew*, published in 1987 and 1988 respectively, reproduce several aspects of the narrative schema of Tutuola's storytelling, though with significant refocalizations.

Both collections are also noteworthy for the ways in which the contours of setting, especially that of the city, are conceptually re-mapped. The city is postulated as having a hallucinatory experiential effect on characters. Of the fourteen stories in the two collections, eleven have the city as the dominant context. In several of them, such as 'Stars of the New Curfew', 'Incidents at the Shrine', and 'Worlds That Flourish', there is a dual movement between the city and the forest or village and the trajectory of the characters' movement traces an increasing entry into the world of the esoteric whose strongest expression seems to lie outside the city. This trajectory is not to suggest a simple dichotomy between city and forest and real and esoteric, a dichotomy which was dominant in Tutuola's mode of storytelling. Instead, there is always the sense that the reality of the city itself is interwoven with esoteric significance so that the dichotomizing gesture is increasingly problematized. As a means of delineating the problematization of the dichotomy between city/real and non-city, forest, village/esoteric, I would like in this chapter to examine two short stories, each set predominantly in one of the two domains. 'When the Lights Return' and 'What the Tapster Saw' will be used for this exercise. 'When the Lights Return' is representative of many of the stories set wholly or partly in the city which postulate of a sense of unreality that washes over the lives of the central characters in the stories, receding to leave them and us readers with a re-adjusted attitude to reality. 'What the Tapster Saw', on the other hand, is peculiar in that it is the only story in both collections narrated wholly from the perspective of the forest and the mythopoeic. Between these two stories, the central features of Okri's schema are set out to be further elaborated in his later writing such as in *The Famished Road* and *Songs of Enchantment*.

This chapter will focus on his short stories and the ways in which he focalizes elements of narrative through popular belief systems to do with the relationship between the real world and that of spirits. We shall pay particular attention to the function of mythopoeia in organizing equivalence between the City and the Forest as related grounds for the emergence of the esoteric in his narrative scheme. The gradual transformation of the dichotomy between City and Forest as symbolic axes affiliated to realist and non-realist modes of representation will also be explored in preparation for an extended analysis of the later works.

The plot of 'When the Lights Return' seems quite simple. Ede, a singer, falls out with his girlfriend Maria after her refusal to allow him to complete their love-making which was interrupted by a sudden blackout. Her persistence in refusing him her body after the blackout angers him and leads him to treat her rudely. Several weeks pass before he decides to pay her a visit. Much of the story is taken up with his journey on foot through the 'urban jungle' of Lagos. The couple achieve an uneasy reconciliation while she is on her sick bed, but he has to leave when she sinks into a delirious state. On his way back home he is informed of her death, and, inexplicably, gets entangled with some market-woman's wares. Street justice is swift and brutal. He is pronounced a thief and lynched to death.

The narration of events in the story is identified closely with Ede's own field of perception, suggesting that Ede's experiences and development throughout the narrative are what the story is about. Nevertheless, a number of things deriving from other aspects of the narrative ensure that this conclusion cannot be easily settled on. The structure of narrative events, in terms of the relationship between one segment of the action and the next moving in a largely straightforward temporal sequence, is crossed by a series of repeated motifs which disturb the simple linearity of temporal sequence by returning us to tropes that resist divulging their full meanings even till the very end of the story. In a sense, this stratum of motifs institutes a dual movement of identification with and distancing from the central character as a means of placing the narrative's mode of representation at issue. It serves to problematize our relationship to character and to the narrative events in order to bring the whole question of representation to the foreground. Before discussing the narrative's structure, however, it is useful to attempt an outline of the central characters.

That Ede is a chauvinist is not in doubt. This emerges quite strongly from his mistreatment of Maria. He is quick to blame her for the failure of his concert. He is also more interested in what she signifies for his own sexual appetites than for herself as person. Even though at a previous meeting Maria has told him she is unwell, when they next meet 'after a week's lack of contact' he reaches out first and foremost for her body: 'Without asking how she was, or whether she was feeling better, he locked the door and began to kiss her' (148). Yet what seems to be more significant in terms of his relationship to unfolding events is the relatively naive thinking he exhibits both when in conversation with Maria as well as when alone. When he visits Maria at home, his attempt to absolve himself from blame is quickly exposed for its shallowness by Maria:

> 'What can I do with your sorrow? I might have died while you stayed away.'
> 'Look, don't be too hard on me.'
> 'Why not?'
> 'You don't know how much I've suffered getting here today.'
> 'So what? I make that journey everyday. Every single day. On my way back from work. You're not the only one who suffers, you know.' (168)

Clearly, his naiveté is part of his general chauvinism and self-centredness. Yet matters are not that simple. One problem Ede has which remains largely unrecognized by him is that he does not *know* Maria, and, indeed, given the nature of his character, cannot grasp her significance. His frustrated question to her at the beginning of the story on her refusal to continue love-making, 'Why are you so strange all of a sudden,' is ironic because it is not only her body that she withholds but the very meaning of her personality. His ruminations on her character become even more ironic because he partially hits at the truth but not quite:

> She was the most challenging woman he had ever met. She always eluded him somehow, as if she were enveloped in a haze, slightly beyond comprehension. It made him hungry to think of her. (161)

What Ede perceives as her 'elusiveness', which seems to him to be merely an aspect of her coy femininity, is in fact a function of something else more ambiguous. Maria's character is defined within a trope of liminality. Her characterization is attended by ambiguities and category confusion and though she seems to be an ordinary girl, she is shown to have a quasi-esoteric status. There is a convergence in Maria's characterization of two impulses; on the one hand she is frail and sickly and therefore figures as a victim of ill-health who requires care and attention. But, on the other, there is her inhabiting of other subjectivities which points to an esoteric status beyond her immediate circumstances. For Ede, the problem is that he cannnot discern the convergence of the dual articulation of her character precisely because he lacks compassion. Perhaps, with greater tenderness and understanding, he might have got a key into her liminality and therefore not become a victim of its hallucinatory potential. By the failure of compassion he becomes a victim of the 'Other' Maria, the one that he has never known because of not appreciating her emotional needs.

And yet there is an additional level of significance to Maria's characterization which can only be decoded by a recourse to popular notions of spirituality and witchcraft. This level of significance is as important for the structure of the narrative as for the thematization of her relationship to Ede. The precise mode of recuperating the significance of Maria for the narrative requires a grasp of indigenous spiritual beliefs. Maria's character seems to be a tissue of beliefs to do with witchcraft and spirit possession. The notion of the person in most African cultures involves a belief in the person's spiritual and physical being. Yoruba belief, for instance, holds that there is a concentration of *aṣé* or vital force in both men and women. In women this is seen to create extraordinary potential 'that can manifest itself in both negative and positive ways' and are well documented (Margaret Drewal 1992: 177). A person can either become a victim of another's spiritual machinations or can themselves project such forces. In the second case they are witches. Maria's characterization relies on the mutual balancing of a notion of her as being a victim of spiritual attacks with that of her as projecting vital force outwards like a witch. Her multiplication onto the faces of animals in particular gives her kinship with witches in popular belief. Raymond Prince (1961), writing in the early sixties on 'The Yoruba Image of the Witch', describes witchcraft beliefs among Yorubas he questioned. One of the commonest beliefs was that the witch could transform herself into birds and animals, especially at night. This is further elaborated by Hallen and Sodipo (1986) in their more extensive philosophical analysis of witchcraft.

The ambivalence with which Maria's spiritual condition is defined in the narrative is significant because we are not allowed to take a simple moral position in relation to her. The essence of her being is shown to splinter across several aspects of the life of the city. She is seen on the faces of beggars, animals and even as part of massed crowds struggling to get along. Though on the one hand this may be read as punitive manifestations of her *aṣẹ* to Ede, the fact that they are encountered in his journey across the city makes the cityscape itself the centre of hallucinatory potential. There is a subtle merging of two aspects of narrative normally treated distinctly in the dominant protocols of realism: the level of characterization and the level of setting. This is achieved by grounding characterization on a decentred notion of subjectivity in which the essence of a character can be detached and projected outwards to influence the environment. The fusion of the two levels is assisted by the fact that Okri relies on indigenous notions of spiritual vitality of the person but inscribes this potential as being a potential of setting as well as character. He suggests that the source of potentially disruptive vital force, or, indeed, witchcraft, is no longer seated solely in the breasts of social misfits or 'evil' people, but is rather lodged in the details of squalid urban existence. He thus focalizes not just character but also setting through the prism of indigenous beliefs. We shall see in the next chapter how he expands this indigenous basis of his narrative protocol for *The Famished Road* and the different attitudes that are called for in relation to Madame Koto, whose characterization is based on the notion of witchcraft, and in relation to the setting of the novel as it is pervaded by the arbitrary manifestation of the spiritual essence of all things.

This brings us to an important motif which is repeated persistently and which accrues different shades of meaning as the story unfolds. This motif is that of Maria's face. At a rough count, her face, or parts of it, is referred to no less than 16 times throughout the story. Here are some examples:

1) With the microphone in his hand he stared into the haze of darkness. Her eyes glowed like that of a cat. (147)

2) [S]he looked so beautiful and her eyes were so sad that he forgot all about his petty irritations. (148)

3) Maria's body burned beside him. He got up and lit a candle. Maria's face was pale. Her lips trembled. Sweat broke out on her forehead. (150)

4) When he saw her face he was surprised that it had changed to the colour of alabaster. (153)

5) She laughed. Then he saw her clearly. Flowers grew from her ears. When her head moved he noticed that bats had matted themselves tightly to her hair. (154)

6) On the face of one of the beggar-girls he saw the face of Maria. (157)

7) Further on Ede was surprised to see Maria sleepwalking ... He pursued her, touched her on the shoulders, and when she turned to face him he could have fainted. It wasn't her. It was a blind woman with milky eyes. (158)

8) Then he began to see Maria everywhere. She transformed into an owl that was flying away. She became a cat. She turned into a dog that followed him barking. He saw her dark eyes in the eyes of chickens and goats. Dogs looked at him mournfully. He got the curious feeling that she was watching him from all the eyes of the animals, old men, and children. (177)

The variety of 'faces' that Maria is given throughout the narrative shows she is a value to be recuperated through great effort, something which Ede is clearly ill-equipped for. Some of the references to her face seem quite casual, such as that in No. 2, which is clearly a factor of Ede's amorous feelings at that moment. No. 1 is particularly interesting because she is linked to a cat. In esoteric lore, cats are frequently seen to be liminal figures, possessing knowledge of the other world. This factor of her liminality, brought in so early in the narrative, is returned to time and again in other references to her face such as that in No. 5. The image of sweat on her forehead is recalled again by Ede when he is thinking about her (156). Oddly enough, the reference to her paleness being like alabaster recalls to mind Othello's reference to Desdemona's skin as being like 'monumental alabaster' and it seems designed to link Maria to a genealogy of misunderstood and tragic heroines. The reference to alabaster is made in the first dream Ede has of her and it would not be unduly farfetched to suggest that the latent content of the dream invokes a residue of the figure of the long-suffering and pure Desdemona as a means of lending resonance to Maria's peculiar condition.

Ede fails to recognize the true nature of Maria's liminality, despite the fact that on his journey to her, various encounters enforce Maria's strange capacity for insinuating her presence in other selves, such as is suggested in Nos. 6 and 7. The interesting thing about Ede is that he refuses to reflect on his encounters. In a way, the variations on Maria's face are meant to show the difficulty in limiting her to a single meaning. She seems to be an ordinary girl at first, but becomes progressively strange as the narrative unfolds, till she is seen as multiplying and inhabiting the whole universe. For Ede, the moment when the full force of her liminality is brought to him is the precise moment of his death when the market women lynch him. When he trips and falls in the market, Maria stands over him. The shape she takes is a final affirmation of her liminal status: 'Then she disappeared and in her place was a midget-girl, with an old body, a young face, and a weird growth of beard' (179). This strange creature, combining signs of youth and old age, the masculine and the feminine, is the final incarnation of the liminal in a form designed to breed anxiety. When Ede dies, it is partly in atonement for not being able to step outside himself to recognize Maria's problematic status.

The motif of Maria's 'face' is not alone in being repeated throughout the text. Another, residing at a more dispersed discursive level, enters the frame of the story tangentially and lends meaning in terms of its partial inscription. This motif is that of the Orphic quest for a loved one. Ede is a singer. As already observed, Maria is a thoroughly liminal figure, even though she seems an ordinary person at the beginning of the narrative. At several key moments she hints at a consciousness of liminality and invokes the Orpheus motif. Parting from the angry Ede at the beginning of the story, she warns: 'And if you really love me, and if later you want to talk to me, you would have to wake me up from death. Can you do that?' (152). Characteristically, Ede can only respond with baffled silence. This casual reference to waking from the dead is re-invoked in a dream Ede later has of Maria in which she walks 'upside down, in a world of mirrors, naked':

'Why are you walking like that?' he asked.
'Sing for me,' she said.
'Why?'
'Delay what I'm going through.'
'I can't sing till the lights return.' (154)

That she is walking upside-down in a world of mirrors is a signal of her entry into the Other world. And, as we might recall, it is Orpheus's music that induces Persephone to grant him permission to take Eurydice along with him back to earth on condition he does not look back at her. In 'When the Lights Return', however, it is not easy to establish a straightforward one-to-one relationship between this couple and the Greek one. Not only is Ede's singing not spontaneous, being linked as it is to a capitalist commercialism, he cannot sing without the aid of technology, as we can glean from his reference to lights. In that sense, unlike Orpheus, who inspired even the beasts and plants and had a symbiotic relationship with nature, Ede's talent is tied inextricably to the uncertain conditions of urban dispossession. And since the urban condition is a function of arbitrary political, economic and institutional structures, he cannot recuperate a voice adequate to the task of alleviating Maria's condition. This is confirmed later in the story when Maria asks him to sing for her on a walk. He launches into a heartfelt song which embraces a concern with the disillusionment of the dispossessed as well as his love for Maria. However, he quickly slips into trying to outdo 'the record shops and the bellowing hawkers' in loudness. It is as if he returns to concerns with urban competitiveness and his place in it, forgetting the initial purpose for singing which was to salve Maria's disturbed spirit. When Maria tries to stop him and he refuses, she asks derisively, 'Or do you think you are Orpheus?'(173). Clearly, he shows himself incapable of stepping into the mould of the mythical singer. We must note, however, that at all times it is Maria who is responsible for invoking the Orpheus motif. Ede seems to remain unaware of its true significance. It is as if they operate with different significatory systems, with him continually unable to grasp the resonances of the hints she drops. But it also points to the impossibility of that type of heroism given the condition of urban dispossession and the fact that talent here is closely tied to commercial impulses. We should note also, that Maria's enunciation of the Orphic motif institutes a convergence between her and the discursive strategies of the text. This points to some disruption to the hitherto restrained manner in which the text has inscribed the overarching structure of motifs. The text generally abjures metanarrative commentary and almost surrenders the task of making meaning completely to the reader. With this convergence, however, the reader's efforts become redundant because the text offers an explicit key for decoding the allusions to the Orpheus myth which it has hitherto inscribed in a vague and allusive manner. Not only does this moment show a sudden distancing of the narrator from Ede's perspective, it also suggests a momentary portentousness when the text announces its intention of regulating the procedure for decoding its meaning.[2]

The partial homology with Orpheus's quest is also elaborated in relation to the journey Ede undertakes to visit Maria. As has already been noted, he is singularly incapable of interpreting the symbols that confront him. For him all the encounters he has with bullying soldiers, irrepressible beggars and crowds of people are merely 'obstacles' that slow him down in his goal of reaching Maria's place. Several signals are offered to show that this walk through the urban streets is a walk through some sort of hell. The very first images that confront him when he steps out of his home are significant in this respect. It is necessary to quote the relevant passage at some length:

The street had been waiting for him.
    In a patch of wasteland, in front of the houses, people were burning piles of rubbish and years of hoarded junk. It was the latest act of desperation. Ede had seen how the long absence of electricity had begun

to generate new tensions. The twigs of the fire flared up and brightened the hungry faces of the children. Ede looked over the marshland with its high grasses and its solitary stunted tree. At the edge of the marshland there was a school building whose compound was also an abattoir. Ede watched the restless goats that were tied to the school wall. Then he saw that the fire had begun to burn the stunted tree. The animals fought against the ropes. The tree had no leaves and at night he had often seen roosters curled up, asleep, on the bare branches.

Ede passed the fire and the burning tree. The crowd watched the consummation in silence. There were solitary candle-lights at the house fronts, as if the city were keeping vigil. (155)

The language of the passage is interesting in the way in which it strings together various images while avoiding the imposition of a pattern of subordination between them as they fall into Ede's field of perception. The first thing to note is the telescoping of the time that it takes Ede to see all these things. There are no explicit indications of his movement as the passage unfolds. The first sentence which locates the action 'in front of the homes' can be said to be in the close-to-medium-distance. The sentence that follows registers Ede's impression or rather comprehension of the long-term effects of the lack of electricity on the people in the neighbourhood. This impression, like all others in the passage, is registered as a precise impingement on a present moment of consciousness. There is no attempt to indicate the stages by which these present tensions have been arrived at. The impression itself seems to be a discrete object that has floated into the field of perception; the word 'seen', folding into itself a notion of awareness as well as sight helps register this impression. The sentence after that also serves to register a present impression, which is the looks on the faces of the children. However, and without any warning, Ede ceases to focus on the reflection of the fire on the faces of the children and shifts his vision 'over the marshland'. This immediately puts the field of perception in the middle-to-long distance. Again, the impressions are registered of elements in the distance, the 'high grasses', the 'solitary stunted tree', and the 'abattoir', ending on the only indication of action in the passage in the hectic activity of the restless goats tied to the abattoir. In a way, the straining of the goats contrasts with the static description of the people which came earlier on in the passage. The people were not differentiated in terms of their faces or their actions and are linked only in relation to the act of 'burning' which in itself seems more stative than dynamic. Then, and with equal suddenness, he sees that the fire has began to burn the stunted tree, as if the fire takes on the character of the people mentioned earlier and hijacks the action of 'burning'. Two sentences later we are told 'Ede passed the fire and the burning tree.' At which point did he move physically from close-distance to the far-distance implied by the position of the stunted tree? It is difficult to tell, and that difficulty resides in the relative lack of sequence markers in the passage.

In fact, each item in Ede's field of perception is registered as happening simultaneously, described as each falls into his line of vision. Apart from the sentence in which the fire burning the stunted tree is noted which opens with 'then', there are no adverbials of time or sequence throughout the passage. That sentence, lodged as it is in a general descriptive field that does not register sequentiality, makes the fire stand out, giving it greater prominence in the passage. An implicit pattern of equivalence is woven into Ede's field of vision because his eyes seem to flit from one thing to the other without any attempt to register their relationship to each other. Furthermore, in terms of the linguistic structure of the passage, the items are joined paratactically without any attempt to subordinate any single item to another. Even within the pattern of subordination available in the sentences themselves, the impulse of the subordinate clauses is mainly accretive, giving more information about the main clause. This can be seen in the following sentences from the passage:

Ede looked at the marshland *with its high grasses and its solitary stunted tree.*

At the Edge of the marshland was a school building *whose compound was also an abattoir.*

Ede watched the restless goats *that were tied to the school wall.*

All three sentences show an accretive impulse towards added information with the second and third settling on relative clauses while the first has a prepositional phrase acting as an adjectival. With the dominant sentence structure being accretive and taking account of the description of items as a series of discrete entities falling in the field of perception, the passage foregrounds a notion of equivalence between the items. T. J. Cribb (1992) has noted that Okri seems to move from the sense of a largely Renaissance and Western conception of perspectival space and psychology in the early novels to a different one in the short stories which is more fractured because it is based on a different structure of feeling. He elaborates this point in relation to Omovo, the artist-protagonist in *The Landscapes Within*, showing how he frequently struggles to find objective correlatives from the external world to organize his own artistic perceptions and the frequent failure of that effort because of the intrusion of disruptive spatio-temporal co-ordinates into his mental visions. The structure of the passage we have examined suggests a peculiarly fractured quality to Ede's perspectives. His field of vision seems to be splintered and the meanings of the items that fall into his experiential plane are not digested into a coherent syntax of meaning by which he can define his relation to unfolding events. This characteristic becomes a defining part of his relationship to the urban environment and it is noticeable that despite the various hallucinatory manifestations of Maria across his journey, he does not once pause to reflect on any of the strange occurrences. In this narrative whatever meaning there is to be gleaned from the unfolding events does not come from Ede but, rather, from the overarching pattern of symbolism which in this passage has a sense of the quasi-apocalyptic.

The word 'wasteland' is almost meant to recall Eliot's poem, and though the landscape described here has a different material significance from the images in Eliot's poem, they seem to be a parallel invocation of the same sense of spiritual aridity. The people, as has already been noted, are not individualized and they all seem to submit to the dominant force of the fire. A notion of apocalypse is subtly introduced in the image of the goats tied to the abattoir and particularly in their frantic straining against the ropes.[3] When the fire is shown to burn the stunted tree, there is a suggestion that all things seem somehow potentially at the mercy of the fire. The sense of apocalypse is further extended in the phrase 'as if the city were keeping a vigil' with all the suggestions of the Second Coming that this implies. However, the apocalyptic quality of the end of time is shown to be part of the texture of urban existence and is of a piece with the intersubjective weaving of Maria's vital force with features of the urban environment.[4] The strange apocalyptic and hallucinatory quality of the environment is confirmed later during his journey in a most dramatic way by the 'dead' man on the rubbish heap who 'resurrects' to a give a message simultaneously cryptic and clear:

'First they shat on us. Now we shit on ourselves.'
…
'REVOLT!' (163)

An important aspect of Okri's handling of this section is that the obviously charged social criticism is never made explicit in terms of narratorial commentary. The criticism emerges within the strict ambit of realist description selected for its symbolic resonance. It is obvious that, given the nature of this infernal urban environment, the heroism proper to the Orphic hero is not available to a character like Ede, trapped as he is in the very forms of self-centredness which is the motive ground of the institutions presiding over the squalor of urban infrastructure. In a sense, the Orpheus story is partially evoked to suggest the impossibility of its recuperation within such a debilitating environment. The partial invocation of the Orphic motif joins the tapestry of other literary allusions from Shakespeare, the Bible and Eliot to invoke simultaneously a residual sense of grandeur and to suggest the difficulty of achieving that grandeur in the context of the squalor and dispossession that dominate the story. This explanation would tie the meaning of the story down to one of literary nostalgia, and gives a limited purchase on what it signifies. It seems, rather, that these literary allusions form part of a larger scheme of the suggestive, the esoteric, the liminal and the extra-rational as a means of articulating forces that exceed the putatively rational agencies that preside over the urban environment in the form of electricity and social amenity boards. These social amenity boards, like the structure of the state that backs them, are normally constituted as the centres of absolute power over the lives of people. By placing the urban environment in a suggestive grid of allusions both literary and esoteric, the text problematizes the type of rationality that motivates these structures of dominance in the first place.

The trajectory of the urban environment's irrationality is partly traceable within the symbolic structure of lights-on/rationality, order and blackout/irrationality, chaos. The pattern of light and darkness links directly to the faulty electricity supply. On one level it is an indictment of the institutional structures that preside over the ordinary people's lives. As always, the mismanagement of electricity supplies is viewed by ordinary people with great suspicion as to real motives. The vast range of interpretations offered by a woman from whom Ede stops to buy a snack all point to the rabid suspicions that ordinary people have for the institutions that govern their lives (162). But the pattern of faulty electricity supplies is also linked to a symbolic scheme of chaos and beauty organizing the narrative. We must note how the blackout is described early in the narrative:

> Then it happened again, suddenly, without warning, invading their lives. Everyday, once, twice, often unaccountably, the lights went, plunging everything into darkness, releasing an obsessional tide of heat and sweat and incomprehension. (150)

The darkness is seen as possessing an insidious quality, invading people's lives quietly. It is clearly an arbitrary presence coming upon them suddenly and triggering all sorts of chaotic effects. The chaotic potential of the blackout is partly figured in Maria's sudden change in sexual mood, as if the darkness fractures libido. Part of the symbolic scheme of the narrative is meant to outline the main proposition stated in the quotation just cited, namely, that the blackout releases 'an obsessional tide of heat, sweat, and incomprehension'. Shortly after this blackout, Ede loses his temper with what he believes to be Maria's unnecessary coyness and begins raining insults on her. The mood is universal, however, because 'outside, he heard others shouting as well: some at their wives, some at their children, others seemed to shout at the air, as if to register the existence of their protest' (151).

This blackout stretches for three weeks and the bulk of events occur at night under the dominance of the blackout. Thus, the various apocalyptic images that are inscribed as part of the geography of urban streets seem linked to the incomprehensibilities of the blackout and of darkness. Lights-on, the opposite of the blackouts, is a time of beauty and of the release of libidinal energies. Maria's attempt at love-making is launched when the lights are on, but is terminated when they go out. Again, when the lights come on much later in the narrative, there is a spontaneous shout of ecstatic voices greeting its return. The return of lights has a decisive effect on the mood of the city as well as on Ede:

> The houses, the stalls with electric bulbs, the shops, all suddenly lit up. It was as if the city had woken from sleep. Ede joined in the cheering. He felt as if a burden had fallen from him. He felt freed from a mysterious pestilence. (178)

Despite the apparent binary opposition between blackout and lights-on, with all the suggested load of evil and good that the two harbour, the narrative as a whole prevents us from settling on an easy manichean typology of symbolism. Part of this is achieved by the fact that the whole story is staged at night, suggesting that the potential obsessional tide unleashed by the blackout is co-extensive with something transcendental and difficult to grasp. This is particularly pertinent because there is a persistent recuperation of esoteric moments by the narrative, suggesting that there are more incomprehensibilities that lie beyond the ambit of human perception and, by implication, beyond the boundaries that light bulbs can illuminate. The simple typology is further rendered problematic by the persistent references to lit candles and lanterns, forcing us to keep in view the continual interaction of dotted lights amidst engulfing darkness. Certainly, the references to the burning stunted tree and to 'solitary candle-lights at the house fronts' are meant to keep this dimension permanently in mind.

Most significant, however, is the fact that the simple manichean underpinnings of the relationship between blackout/potential chaos and lights-on/potential order and beauty are completely subverted at the end of the story when the coming of lights heralds a process of general madness that finally leads to Ede being submitted to irrational crowd justice. Until that point the crowds are figured as passive spectators or audiences. The very opening of the narrative has an audience shouting for their money when the lights go out during Ede's concert. Crowds occupy a largely passive and peripheral position in Ede's field of vision and any time they are mentioned they are either watching something, struggling to get along, or just waiting for something to happen. The shifting of the crowds from the periphery to the centre and their sharp and sudden metamorphosis links directly to the ironic movement in the structuring of the images of light and darkness overarching the narrative as a whole. Their menacing metamorphosis is linked to Maria's re-emergence as a multiplied presence. She is inextricably interfused with the crowd:

> He tried to stop, *but the crowd pushed him on* ... Jostled and pushed, wherever he looked he saw as if in a multiplying mirror, Maria disappearing and passing out of focus. (178, italics added)

For once, the crowd overrides his own will. The fractured images of Maria which featured in his earlier dream of her are now a pervasive part of the crowd that pushes him on. Is this linkage to suggest that the crowd is dead or dying? However this is interpreted, what is clear is the esoteric charge that gets linked to this hitherto passive aspect of the daily background to urban existence. In any case, the menacing character that the crowd now takes on does not diminish even with the coming on of the lights which occurs a few moments after his experience of being pushed on by them. The lights define a new quality, and the crowd dissolves into a hysterical movement, 'their faces defined in new energies'. The crowd's hysteria defines the arena in which he is to die because in trying to break free from them he is inexorably driven to fall, in a curious process that leads to his lynching and death. With hysteria under the aegis of light, the whole manichean symbolic edifice is subverted to suggest that even the seeming anchors of symbolic typologies are not available in a realism devoted to outlining the contours of urban squalor and dispossession. The narrative's refusal to allow even this comfort partly serves to ironize Ede's complacency as well as ours as readers. It links well with the serialization of repeated motifs which traverse the sequential unfolding of the story. The motifs constitute pockets of resistance to easy interpretation lodged within the realist mode of narration.

But what does all this tell us about Okri's narrative style and his later writing in *The Famished Road* and *Songs of Enchantment*? Perhaps the single most important thing is the problematization of realist modes of narration. Though most of his stories are grounded on the harsh realities of urban ghettos, tracing the contours of dispossession which are the heritage of its denizens, Okri suggests that realism is inadequate to the task. Yet it seems important not to depart completely from the realist mode because of the need to force a recognition of the contexts which anchor the stories. In many of the short stories, his solution is to push realist description to the very edge of its symbolic potential partly by repeating motifs to form a sort of symbolic refrain gesturing towards other levels of the text. This is the case in 'When the Lights Return' and 'Laughter Beneath the Bridge'.

Also significant is his interweaving of the esoteric with the real, usually in the form of hallucinatory impingements on the perceptions of the characters. We see this technique particularly in 'Worlds That Flourish' and in 'In the Shadow of War'. But, unlike in the later novels, the focus for organizing the narrative is centred in the real and not the other-worldly. The other-worldly is seen periodically to wash over the real, receding, yet leaving it changed. This centering is experimented with all through the short stories. But in stories like 'Stars of the New Curfew' and 'Incidents at the Shrine' there is a sense that the esoteric threatens to completely overcome the real. In 'What the Tapster Saw' to which we turn next, the centre of the story is shifted dramatically from the very beginning and resides dominantly in the world of mythopoeia.

'What the Tapster Saw' begins with what may be construed as a folktale opening, immediately setting the tone for what is to follow: 'There was once an excellent tapster who enjoyed climbing palm-trees as much as the tapping of their wines' (183). This folktale opening accomplishes several things at once. It raises our expectations of a specific mode of narrative, a mythical mode instead of a realist one, by invoking at the very start the stories of Amos Tutuola. By mentioning 'tapster' and 'palm-wine' it immediately invokes Tutuola's own story, *The Palm-Wine Drinkard and his Tapster in the Deads' Town*. However, though this invocation places 'What the Tapster Saw' within the same generic field as Tutuola's book, the narrative that follows is careful to show that it is not merely a variation of the folktale genre but an important re-evaluation and test of its boundaries.

This emerges from a simultaneous proximity to and distancing from the Tutuola type of story. Like most folktale narratives, Tutuola's stories normally start from a real world setting of village or family life before proceeding through an initial crisis to enter into the realm of the ghostly. The realm of the ghostly or esoteric is normally one of ambiguities and category confusion where people can turn into trees, birds and even canoes. 'What the Tapster Saw' abridges the Tutuolan opening sequence by launching straight into the moment of crisis. The tapster here has a bad dream of falling off a tree and so decides to consult Tabasco, a renowned herbalist friend. Moreover, the abridgement is problematized by making indeterminate the specific moment of the crossing of the liminal boundary into the realm of the esoteric. The narrative introduces several liminal boundaries, making it difficult for us to locate the precise point of entry into the esoteric realm. The boundary could be at the first mention of the tapster's dream of falling from a tree and dying (183). Or, it could be when he goes to consult his friend Tabasco. This seems quite plausible because of the nature of the apparently pointless tale his friend decides to tell him which speaks of hunters shooting antelopes which turn into women (ibid.). But we cannot be sure because the tapster is described as having fallen asleep again *after* his visit to the herbalist and a heavy draught of palm-wine (184). Things are further complicated by the fact that we are later given an explicit liminal boundary in an Oil Company sign that he encounters 'the next morning' on his way to tap palm-trees:

> He had been riding for some time when he came to a signboard which read: DELTA COMPANY: THIS AREA IS BEING DRILLED. TRESPASSERS IN DANGER. (184)

The notions of trespassing and of danger can be construed as explicit signs of a threshold, possibly into the esoteric realm. There is corroboration in the strange things that confront him immediately after the signboard: thick cobwebs and the intoxicating smell of green bark. Yet the narrative introduces another potential threshold in the fact that he falls from the tree he attempts to climb, 'the first time he had fallen in thirty years', and on waking feels no pain. His being goes through a substantial metamorphosis marked by the fact that 'fireflies darted into his nose and ears and re-emerged from his eyes with their lights undimmed' (185). He also feels 'unbelievably light and airy'. He seems to have finally entered the esoteric realm, but what are we to make of the next Oil Company signboard which is a variation of the first one: DELTA OIL COMPANY: TRESPASSERS WILL BE PROSECUTED (ibid.)?

What is to be made of this series of potential thresholds? As was mentioned earlier, the opening manoeuvre of the folktale is not only foreshortened but also fused with the next stage. It seems that, in addition, the abridgement of the opening manoeuvre also involves the multiplication of the threshold stage as if to suggest that it is something no longer to be taken for granted in narrating the folktale. The question of which is the precise point of entry is never resolved even till the end of the story when the tapster wakes up on Tabasco's couch, because each of the potential thresholds we have enumerated could serve as triggering the process that finally lands him on the couch. And it must also not be forgotten that he wakes up on the couch after being dead for 'seven days', a fact which suggests that the experiences in the esoteric realm relate to a life after death, a concern also discernible in Tutuola's stories. But the question persists: When exactly does the tapster enter the esoteric realm?

The factor of undecidability involved in attempting to locate the precise point of entry into the esoteric realm is in fact part of a larger scheme governing the story. Unlike in 'When the Lights Return' the contours of this one are extremely difficult to delineate because of the persistent re-inscription of key moments such as that of the liminal threshold. By this type of manoeuvre the narrative frustrates any expectations of temporal sequence and enforces the need for continual re-adjustment on the part of the reader. And the narrative is so exuberant in throwing up surreal images in a more or less arbitrary relationship to one another that it forces a sense of provisionality onto any interpretative engagement with it.

In many ways, the realm of the esoteric is substantially different from that of Tutuola's folktale universe. In Tutuolan versions, the hero is normally one of titanic heroic stature who, by encounters with monstrous spirits, has his stature continually re-affirmed. Even in a narrative like *My Life in the Bush of Ghosts*, in which the little boy is initially merely a victim of the variety of ghosts he encounters, there is a gradual acquisition of prowess which serves the hero well in his final encounters in the Bush of Ghosts. The esoteric realm of 'What the Tapster Saw' is also populated by strange figures, but in this case the protagonist is decidedly not a titanic figure. He is more of a passive victim of esoteric circumstances. Things are very strange in this esoteric realm. The mark he makes on a tree trunk erupts into a fully festered wound. The river he encounters is viscous and almost still, breaking into a transparent luminousness when a multicoloured snake slithers into it. He also encounters three strange turtles with eyes of glass. One of them has the face of Tabasco. They perform all sorts of seemingly arbitrary actions such as urinating, laughing and discussing matters gravely 'like scholars without a text' (192). The point is to mark the qualitative difference between this environment and that which the tapster has left to enter it. However, what these creatures say and do is not as disconcerting as what *happens* to the tapster.

There is a structure of surreal arbitrariness in the things that happen to him. The distinguishing feature of all the strange happenings is the potential interpenetration of the qualities of various natural phenomena. This potential interpenetration is often inscribed on his own body. It is not insignificant that at one of the thresholds to the esoteric realm fireflies enter his nose and emerge out of his eyes with lights undiminished. At another point, he feels the substance of his being dissolve and at yet another he sees himself multiply all around (186). It is as if to suggest to him his basic atomic foundations, something which he shares in common with all beings in the universe. In this context, his copulation with a nameless creature is meant to register, in a somewhat anxiety-generating way, his closeness to animal and bird nature.

One particular happening, which coagulates into a regular feature of his experiences, is the knocking he frequently receives on his head on thinking 'inappropriate' thoughts. The knocks come only when he reacts negatively to the things in the esoteric realm. Once he is knocked when he thinks the look on the Tabasco turtle's face is 'positively fiendish' and laughs (186). When he counts the eggs resulting from his copulation with the strange creature, he screams and, again, is rewarded with a 'laughter like death' that roars from the sun, crashing on him, shaking him and leaving 'large and empty spaces in his head' (187). And when he abuses the place in desperation he is again rewarded with several knocks. It is clear, then, that a mode of censorship goes on in relation to his thoughts, but it is in the general direction of rectifying the value-system with which he enters the esoteric realm. The censoring knocks suggest the inappropriateness of bringing into the esoteric realm the same scale of expectations as to the possibilities for action in the real world. The knocks he receives are meant to force him into re-organizing his value system to be able to accommodate the arbitrariness and grotesqueness of the esoteric realm without implicitly setting it against the values of the world he departs. They are meant to suggest that coherence lies within the arbitrary structure of incoherence. The series of knocks has a significant effect on his attitudes because he 'learns patience':

> He learned to watch the sky, and he saw that it wasn't so different from the skies of his drunkenness. He learned not to listen to the birth groaning within the eggs. He also learned that when he kept still everything reflected his stillness. (187)

This phase of stillness ushers in a new segment of the narrative in which he roams in this new world while several visions unfold before him. The visions themselves are a tissue of images of political chaos such as wars and also of a quasi-apocalypse (188, 189). This section seems to be the residue of a simultaneous national as well as universal memory. The images of undetonated bombs and the execution of armed robbers and politicians are surely reminiscent of the situation in Nigeria, but these images are later linked to quasi-apocalyptic images heralded by that of 'an old man who had died in a sitting position while reading a bible upside-down' (189). Apparently, the tapster's process of education is not yet complete because he relapses into impatience and is afflicted with more knocks. Later, a voice comes to run him through a number of gnomic sayings, such as 'even the good things in life eventually poison you,' and 'the wind blows back to us what we have blown away' (191). It is only when he says a weary 'thank you' that the voice leaves him. By this time it seems his education is more or less complete because he is instituted in the process of returning to the real world which culminates in his waking up on Tabasco's couch.

The story is different from the Tutuola type in that the normal paradigm of rite of passage which leads to an affirmation of the titanic stature of the hero is abrogated here. Rather, he undergoes an open-ended learning process whose full value can only remain conjectural since the story ends just when he wakes up from his 'adventures'. The Tutuolan narratives would have attempted to reinsert the hero into society and to demonstrate the value of the adventures. Not here. In the ending as in the beginning, the manoeuvres of the Tutuolan type of narrative are aborted to make way for open-ended interpretations. It is as if the story plays with the devices of the folktale to show how artificial they are in the first place.

Okri's short stories represent an important move towards filiating narrative form to indigenous belief systems. This is done at several levels simultaneously. The short stories represent a testing of the limits of various genres with a view to locating an appropriate mode for engaging with the bewildering reality of Nigeria. The range of experiments in the stories find concentrated expression in *The Famished Road* and *Songs of Enchantment* and though they can be discussed fruitfully on their own, we cannot draw conclusions as to their full significance without turning to the novels.[5]

Notes

1 This is particularly evident in the essays collected in Lindfors, ed. already cited, especially the essays by Gerald Moore, Harold Collins and Paul Neumarkt.

2 Okri's use of the Orpheus motif in this story operates at a double level of intertextuality since Soyinka had already deployed the story in his novel *Season of Anomy* (1973) in presenting the collective tragedy that had befallen Nigeria in 1966 and after. The fact is given away in the names of his characters Ofeyi and Iriyise. It is of interest to note that Okri adheres more closely to the classical version of the original myth, especially the ending in which Orpheus is torn to pieces by Thracian Maenads. For a discussion of Soyinka's use of the myth, see Abdulrazak Gurnah, 'The Fiction of Wole Soyinka', in Adewale Maja-Pearce, ed. (1994: 72–9).

3 There seem to be echoes here of the biblical Parable of the Sheep and Goats, Matthew, Chapter 25: verses 31–3.

4 The idea of an 'overloading' of space, in which space ceases being homogenous and itself seems to carry the significance of a character is quite common in magical realist writing. But it is important to note the subtle differences between different schemes of magical realism. For a contrastive analysis of the effects of Okri's writing, with particular reference to 'When the Lights Return' and that of Kojo Laing's *Search Sweet Country*, see Ato Quayson, 'Esoteric Webwork as Nervous System: Reading the Fantastic in Ben Okri's Writing', in Abdulrazak Gurnah, ed. (1995).

5 Okri has published other work after the esoteric novels. *Astonishing the Gods* is only partially in the tradition he sets up in *The Famished Road* and *Songs of Enchantment*. Is is more muted in style and extremely elegant in its use of the quest motif. *Dangerous Love*, on the other hand, is a re-writing of *The Landscapes Within* and becomes a simultaneous return to the earlier mode of realism with which he began his writing as well as to a post-Biafra Nigeria in which creativity and romance have to contend with the darker social forces of corruption and disillusionment that have started to dominate Nigerian life. I focus mainly on the esoteric novels to align the esoteric tendency in his work to the mythopoeisis we have seen operating in the work of the other writers in this study.

6

Harvesting
the Folkloric Intuition

The Famished Road

There is a growing critical consensus that Okri's work operates within the same tradition of writing as Tutuola's and Soyinka's.[1] *The Famished Road* operates in this tradition of writing in an even fuller and more suggestive way than the short stories. In this work Okri produces what might be termed new mythopoeic discourse with the invocation of myths, folklore and other aspects of indigenous beliefs. Particularly interesting is the range of esoteric passages in the novel and the variety of ways in which they are connected to events in the putative real world of the story.[2] But, because the novel is yet to accrue critical research, the precise terms by which to relate it to the literary tradition remain vague. The novel represents a vast arena of interdiscursivity not only with earlier literary works but also with various indigenous beliefs to do with the relationship between the real world and the supernatural. One of the concerns of this chapter will be to trace the nature of that interdiscursivity in both directions. In addition, attention will be paid to the various ways in which these indigenous beliefs become transvaluated in the body of the narrative to hint at a validation as well as a critique of the indigenous belief system. Finally, an attempt will be made to show how Okri's work articulates a particular perception of events in post-colonial Nigeria that brings the literary tradition into a direct engagement with the ambit of the socio-political while remaining steadfastly in the realm of the mythopoeic.

The interdiscursive relationship with earlier writings is suggested from the very title of the novel. In south-western Nigeria, there are special prayers said to the road asking it not to swallow up suppliants on their journeys. In Soyinka's latest autobiography *Ibadan*, the name of his *alter ego* Maren is a contraction of such a prayer: *We nu ren n'ojo ebi n'pona*, meaning 'May you not walk when the road waits, famished' (*Ibadan*, 100). Soyinka elaborates this supplicatory attitude to the road at several places in his *Idanre* collection of poems. Such a supplication is lodged in the poem 'Death in the Dawn', which directly invokes the prayer that lies behind the name Maren:

> The right foot for joy, the left, dread
> And the mother prayed, Child
> May you never walk
> When the road waits, famished (*Idanre*, 11)

The notion of the famished road is re-echoed in the Ogun praise-poem 'Idanre' and there is even a direct reference to the road's hidden belly: 'And the monolith of man searches still/ A blind hunger in the road's hidden belly' (*Idanre*, 69). As a symbol, the road is highly suggestive and Soyinka elaborates it even further in *The Road*, a play which centres on the relationships between various people from the underclass and the road in both its technological and metaphysical significatory dimensions.

In Okri's novel, the famished road has multivalent significance. On the one hand it has an umbilical connection to the genesis of creation itself as hinted in the very first sentence of the novel: 'In the beginning there was a river. The river became a road and the road branched out to the whole world.' It is because it was once a river that the road remains 'always hungry'. Later in the novel, a story is told that relates the road's hunger for appeasement to its having been reduced from a ravenous god to a mere belly.[3] It is also possible to suggest another application of the symbol with reference to the human hunger for journeys and movement. It is not by accident that Azaro is persistently on the move, with an itinerary traversing both the real and spirit-worlds. But this hunger for movement is also a hunger for completion and meaning, something which the novel suggests is extremely difficult to reach. For one thing, given its genealogy, the road is unending. Furthermore, it always has two and possibly four sides to it, all of which manifest themselves at different times: its two side edges, its surface and its belly. Thus in *The Famished Road*, the road itself is hungry as well as transferring its existential hunger to humans. It ensures that closure and completion remain highly problematic even though constantly desired. With his title, Okri makes an important ritual gesture towards the literary tradition he is elaborating as well as to the indigenous traditions and beliefs. From the very outset he pays homage to both.

Another important symbol of dominant interest in the novel is that of the *abiku*. The *abiku* phenomenon refers to a child in an unending cycle of births, deaths and re-births. The belief in the *abiku* phenomenon is widespread in southern Nigeria with the name 'abiku' being shared by the Yorubas and Ijos while the Igbos refer to them as *ogbanje.*[4] The concept of *abiku* is what may be described as a 'constellar concept' because it embraces various beliefs about predestination, re-incarnation and the relationship between the real world and that of spirits. However, in terms of the rituals that are geared towards appeasing the *abiku*, the concept also implies a belief in the inscrut-ability and irrationality of the Unknown. It is of the utmost impor-tance to be able to locate where the *abiku* child hides the charms that link it to its spirit companions on the other side for the proper rites to be carried out to snap that connection. Until that is done, the *abiku's* parents, and, indeed, the community at large, are at the mercy of the disruptive and arbitrary cycle of births, deaths and re-births of the spirit-child. Chidi Maduka (1987) points out that in fact the word *ogbanje* in the Igbo language is used to denote a person who acts in a weird, capricious, callous and even sadistic way.

The phenomenon itself has exercised the imagination of Nigerian writers from different backgrounds. Soyinka (a Yoruba), Clark-Bekederemo (an Ijo) write poems directly addressing the *abiku*, while Achebe (an Igbo) has a long section in *Things Fall Apart* devoted to the tracking of the hidden charms of Ezinma, one of Okonkwo's children who was an *ogbanje*.[5] Though all three writers draw on the same set of concepts, their explorations of the significance of the phenomenon show varying emphases that signal the suggestiveness of the *abiku* concept for the literary imagination. Achebe's treatment is largely ethnographic, with a careful detailing of the belief about *ogbanje*. There is a measure of irony attached to the human efforts at coping with the *ogbanje*, signalled in Ezinma's supreme nonchalance in taking her fuming father and the rest of the village on a circuitous journey before agreeing to show them where she has buried her charms. There is therefore a measure of suspense and balance between the forces of chaos and those of order. Ezinma's charms are recovered and her connection to the spirit-world seems to be broken. As Maduka rightly suggests, Achebe resolves the conflict between order and chaos in favour of order. What must be added is that in the mode of realism Achebe operates in *Things Fall Apart*, the conflict can only be resolved in favour of order because his project is to validate the coherence of Igbo beliefs and the efficacy of the structures built by the culture as security against the irrational. This is in spite of his careful delineation of the tensions in the social fabric of the culture and in some of its beliefs, one of whose consequences is the speed with which social outcasts become bridgeheads of the invading Christian religion. The culture is shown to have a resilience that ensures its survival despite these tensions.

In Clark-Bekederemo's poem, the power of *abiku* is acknowledged. The concept is personified and Abiku is addressed in supplicatory tones. It is seen as capricious but there is a suggestion that the proper attitudes and modes of address can stem the tide of the irrational and entice Abiku to stay. In a sense, Clark espouses the same logic grounding the rituals around the phenomenon because the rituals imply that it is possible to arrest the cyclical process and please the *abiku*. With Soyinka matters take a decidedly different turn. Not only is Soyinka's poem articulated in the voice of Abiku itself, it is registered in a mocking and magisterial tone to suggest that humans are at the mercy of the irrational lodged in the Unknown. For Soyinka it is the non-conformism of the recalcitrant Abiku that fascinates him.[6] The important thing to note about Soyinka's handling, however, is the attempt to locate the organizing consciousness of the literary artefact within the realm of the spirit-world. All the ritual gestures of the real world are perceived from the vantage point of the spirit-world and declared puny and futile. This edge of irony suggests that man is wholly at the mercy of the Unknown and that, perhaps, the only way to cope is through an aesthetic empathy with that which is most feared.

Okri's handling of the concept in *The Famished Road* reproduces aspects of all three positions: in many ways it is partly ethnographic in the lavish descriptions given about rituals to do with claiming the *abiku* child for the real world; the timbre of supplication dominates the mode by which Azaro's parents address him, even though they sometimes veer from this, much to their discomfiture; and the entire human landscape is viewed through the eyes of the *abiku* child. One important difference, however, is that the context in which the real world and that of spirits is explored is not in an either/or framework as is implied by the treatment of the concept in the reflections of the earlier writers. Rather, because Azaro desires to stay in the real world while at the same time refusing to break links with that of his spirit companions, both real world and that of spirits are rendered problematically equivalent in his experience. Since the narration is in the first person, with all events being focalized through the consciousness of Azaro, the universe of action is located simultaneously within both the real world and that of spirits. The question of a suggested equivalence between the real world and that of spirits cuts across various levels of the text and is one we shall pay attention to later in the chapter. The *abiku* concept can be said to be a constellar one and its constellar status is particularly relevant to *The Famished Road* because of the range of indigenous beliefs traversed by the novel, something that will also be examined in our discussion.

The form of *The Famished Road* is radically determined by locating the narrative in Azaro's consciousness. This leads to a peculiar contradiction relating to the point in the life of Azaro when he experiences events and the later time in the narrative when he tells us the story. We are not told at which precise point in time Azaro decides to narrate his childhood, and though the narrative resides firmly in the consciousness of a child, the first intimations of a maturer sensibility are to be glimpsed in the observable contradictions between the 'I' of the narrating instance and the 'I' of the narrated events.

The impression is generated early in the narrative that Azaro is a child, possibly seven years of age:

> One of the reasons I didn't want to be born became clear to me after I had come into the world. I was still very young when in a daze I saw Dad swallowed up by a hole in the road. Another time I saw Mum dangling from the branches of a blue tree. I was seven years old when I dreamt that my hands were covered with the yellow blood of a stranger. (7)

The impression of events filtering through the mind of a child is sustained throughout the novel, but because of the adoption of a predominantly preterite tense mode of narration, the question as to whether Azaro is still a child when he narrates these events seems to be relevant. At several points the impression of a child's consciousness is undermined by the generalizing comments that Azaro makes in the course of the narrative. He often launches into confident assertions and generalizations of a gnomic and proverbial character:

> In the beginning there was a river. The river became a road and the road branched out to the whole world. And because the road was once a river it was always hungry. (3)

> The world is full of riddles that only the dead can answer. (75)

> During the harmattan we always forget the rainy season. That's why it rains so viciously on the first day, reminding us of its existence. (286)

> There are many riddles of the dead that only the living can answer. (427)

> History itself fully demonstrates how things of the world partake of the condition of the spirit-child. (487)

These seem to be the pronouncements of a mature wisdom, certainly sharing kinship with that available to the wizened narrators of folk history. If these are explained away as possibly available to the *abiku*'s uncanny sense of its community's values, then this child's mind encases a more nebulous and mature consciousness. Further evidence that this Azaro is no child (or even if he is, his narrating self inhabits a temporal plane different from the narrated self) is also perceptible from the nature of the analogies he draws in his descriptions of human nature. Once, when his mother sighs despondently, he remarks:

> Her sigh was full of despair, but at the bottom of her lungs, at the depth of her breath's expulsion, there was also hope, waiting like sleep at the end of even the most torrid day. (93)

He receives a flogging at his father's hands and likens his father's manner to 'the way a master boxer beats an inferior partner, with rage and methodical application' (324–35). His father's creditors huddle conspiratorially together 'talking in low business tones as though they were about to form a limited liability company' (54). These analogies seem much too sophisticated for a child's consciousness, and the analogy of a limited liability company clearly resides in areas of experience not available to Azaro. It is very tempting to rapidly dismiss these contradictions as deriving from the improper relationship between the implied author and his narrator, for these seem to be veritable signals of an implied author's omniscience attempting to break the limitations on it imposed by the limited perspective of a first person narrator. Appealing though this explanation seems, it is nonetheless inadequate.

Do we settle for the explanation of there being adult recall and generalization? This would have been extremely plausible if the text had not been scrupulously silent over the exact point in Azaro's life which he decides to narrate the story. There is no reference whatsoever within the text to these narrated events being related from the vantage point of adulthood. This is no *Great Expectations* or *Ibadan*. An argument too that would use Azaro's privileged access to both spirit and real worlds as an explanation of omniscience to explain away these contradictions is bound to flounder when confronted with the fact that he frequently expresses amazement at some experiences of both worlds.[7] Is this not a sure sign of an inherent limitation of awareness that would preclude the wide-ranging knowledge he is allowed to affirm in analogies and gnomic generalizations?

What these contradictions signal is the uneasy location of the perceptual modes of a communal narrator within the largely child-like consciousness of the narrator of the novel. The contradictions illustrate the problems of such a fusion very forcefully. Okri allows Azaro to take up the narration and thereby activates a folkloric paradigm available to a communally held culture from within the framework of a childlike consciousness. This position is even more plausible when we recollect that Azaro relates some of his experiences with a clear etiological emphasis, as if the reader is conceived of within the context of a communal audience requiring the same rationalizations of experience as himself.[8] The reader is thus continually socialized into a narrative situation that combines the gnomic and proverbial affirmations of communal world-views with the growing and provisional perceptions of a limited narrative perspective. This may be said to derive from Okri's drawing on mythopoeic discourses that reside pre-eminently in contexts of orality. He reproduces the oral narrator's mode of relating to the audience even as this is inscribed within a new literary domain. Azaro's consciousness is automatically and irretrievably framed by the mythopoeic paradigm it articulates. The contradictions emerge not merely because he is a child who sometimes speaks like an adult, but because he is made simultaneously to speak as himself as well as a communal intuition in which he is vitally implicated by *being* (in the sense of living the essence of) *abiku*.

It is evident that drawing on a mythopoeic framework for writing the novel puts the narrative discourse within the purview of dual organizing paradigms, one of which is grounded in orality and the other in the literary. Indeed, this simultaneous articulation of the oral-folkloric and the written-literary is also displayed in the area of the novel's organization of time and temporality. The plot of real events in the novel is a fairly uncomplicated one devoted to tracing the life of Azaro, his family, and their small compound community and the gradual changes that occur in their lives due to the growth of political activities in their area. Additionally, there is a focus on Madame Koto and the development of her career as bar owner, political sympathizer and, finally, dominant owner of capital and spiritual power in the area. This plot of events in the real world is structured around a number of temporal indices which are often vague but useful as a means of tracing the sequence of events. However, there is a constant interruption of the chronological sequence to enter into the esoteric realm.

The novel opens with a time reference evocative of myth and thoroughly a-temporal in the invocation of quasi-biblical beginnings: 'In the beginning there was a river.' Using a formulaic opening pushes the events of this opening section far beyond the realm of the events that will later follow and also beyond any recognizable time scheme. The mythical opening gives way to a more time-bound scheme of temporality in Chapter 2 where Azaro plots his early childhood. Even here his childhood is plotted in the iterative, showing isolated examples of repeated events. Thus the events are an embodiment of repeated time located within moments in the temporal flow of the narrative proper. They are a tissue of the repeated and the habitual:

> When I was very young I had a clear memory of my life stretching to other lives.... Sometimes I seemed to be living several lives at once. (7)

> As a child I could read people's minds. I could foretell their futures. Accidents happened in places I had just left. One night I was standing in the street with Mum when a voice said:
> 'Cross over.' (9)

These references to iterative incidents within a generalized time frame resolve themselves into a specific frame when the text focuses on one of the various incidents and expands it to become the trigger for the rest of the events in the narrative. A nocturnal conflagration and the ensuing riots offer such a frame. Time indices are employed to locate the incidents that ensue after the riots in relationship to that inaugural event. The conflagration and the riots occur the same night:

> On another night I was asleep when the great king stared down at me. I woke up, ran out of the room, and up the road. My parents came after me. They were dragging me back when we discovered that the compound was burning. On that night our lives changed …
>
> It was a night of fires … Three policemen … fell on us and flogged us with whips and cracked our skulls with batons … (9–10)

The narrative undertakes a massive digression shortly after this section to relate Azaro's adventures at the hands of the 'cult of women' who capture him when he is separated from his mother by the milling and riotous crowd that gathers due to the fires.[9] Azaro manages to escape the women, is later taken into custody by a policeman and his wife, and is finally rescued by his mother. He has stayed in the policeman's house for 'several days' when his mother comes for him. As a means of bridging the gap between the time of their separation during the riots and their coming together again, his mother later relates the incidents that occur after his being lost on the night of the riots, thus updating us on all the events that have transpired and also locating the mass of events in relation to the main frame of the fires and riots.

Throughout all these myriad events, no specific time indices are given. All the time indices are vague references to 'that night', 'the next morning', 'during that time' and so on. Subsequently, the narrative makes concessions to temporality by referring to a sequence of days such as 'Saturday' and 'Sunday' as a frame for the occurrence of certain events.[10] It is clear that the narrative imposes a framework of temporality on the narrated events rather reluctantly, for, as it progresses temporal indices become less and less prominent. The central operation of the narrative in this respect is to recall significant events that come to mind without necessarily noting time's passage. This mode of organization has a telling effect on overall plot structure, rendering it loosely episodic not only because of the massive esoteric digressions, but also because of the marked absence of temporal indices.

There is an even more complex implication of the relative paucity of temporal indices in the text. Because we are not given an indication of what period of time each event spans, it is difficult if not impossible to define the relative duration of each event. Narratologists have mapped out how duration is grasped by the reader, linking it to the relationship between the clock time consumed in reading a passage and the temporal frame given by the passage itself.[11] If three hundred years is plotted in three paragraphs, it signals a short duration and the telescoping of a long time span. The lavish description of an hour's incident in thirty pages shows a long duration, slowing down the pace of the narrative. In *The Famished Road*, however, the lack of definite temporal indices in relation to events ensures that a mode of equivalence is insinuated as definitive of the relationships between various events. In other words, no event is subordinated to another in terms of temporal duration. Thus, a homogenous sense of a-temporality, relieved only by the vaguest time indices, is spread throughout the narrative.

Yet another formal textual feature that helps enforce a sense of homogeneity is the relative absence of character recall of earlier events. At no time, for instance, do any of the characters ever refer back to the conflagration of the earlier stages of the narrative in constructing a sense of life in the ghetto. After the food poisoning brought on by the powdered milk of the Rich People's Party (130–2), no reference is made later in the narrative to this traumatic event as a means of defining the character of the party. That the Party is populated by hooligans is never forgotten, but this is continually demonstrated by the text rather than being recalled. As a third instance of this structural feature, we must note that even at the second house-party thrown by Azaro's father there is no reference whatsoever to Azaro's welcoming party which occurs much earlier in the narrative and seems to be a narrative precursor of the second one. There are also no flashbacks or what Genette calls 'anachronies' in the novel in the sense of an event appearing later in the sequence of the narrative but indicated to have occurred earlier in the story.[12] It is as if there is an effort not only to disperse a series of discrete events across time but also to enforce a sense of a continual forward narrative movement. But, at the same time, this seeming teleological narrative impulse is disturbed by the constant recurrence of extended esoteric moments that do not follow any teleological trajectory. Furthermore, there is a pervasive sense of the interpenetration of the essence of the two realms of the real and the spirit.

How are these various contradictory movements in the narrative strategy of the novel to be explained? And what effect do they ultimately have on the reader's response to the universe of the work? Perhaps the contradictions can only be explained in relation to the novel's evocation of an orality paradigm within the space of a literary one, so that there are, properly speaking, two sets of expectations that it relies on for its conduct. Joseph C. Miller (1980) offers an interesting discussion of structuring in oral traditions which can act as a basis for groping towards an explanation of Okri's erasure of temporal indices in *The Famished Road*. Miller notes that oral narrators structure their tales around clichés and that these are often grouped together in epochal sets. In societies where the state is central to social structure, oral historians commonly represent these epochs as the reign of kings. However, though the logical status of epochs seems to parallel that of years in Western history, it is misleading to infer chronology from the reign of kings because of the numerous irregularities that can be shown to inhere in the sequence of epochal sets. The important thing to note is that:

> The creation of 'epochs' by oral historians resembles 'structuring' in that narrators collect clichés (and thereby appear to associate with each other the events the clichés represent) together according to *non-temporal criteria*: cultural preferences, cosmological tenets, or the unconscious tendencies of the human memory. (Joseph Miller: 14; italics added)

Here seems to be the key to understanding the principle of association working in oral narratives. Though Miller's focus is on the significance of this structuring for deriving history from oral traditions, it seems possible to draw implications for oral narratives in general. Clichés include songs, proverbs, thematic sequences and even specific heroic tropes (Miller: 7). They are themselves important elements in an oral culture's mnemonic system. Strung together in epochs they become a textual encoding of the site of a culture's memory ready to be activated for different purposes. The stringing together of clichés in non-temporal significatory frameworks produces a paratactic structure to many oral traditions. As will be recalled from our discussion of Yoruba historiography in Chapter 2 of this study, one of Michel Doortmont's observations about Rev. Samuel Johnson's work was that it was 'a collection of not very well-connected praise songs engineered into a seemingly coherent epic.' Apart from the prominence of songs in Johnson's historiography, what this points to is the essentially paratactic movement of his work. The paratactic quality of oral narratives seems to derive directly from the fact that they are constructed as a collection of items that have been secreted in collective memory as expressive of significant cultural or social insights. These become nodal points for the organization of discourse in oral contexts and need not be tied to temporal criteria.

The same operation is discernible in folktales. Tutuola's narratives have few temporal indices. His narratives rush forward as rapid recollections of exciting encounters between heroes and spirit-figures, making them episodic and largely paratactic in structure. With Tutuola, the reliance on oral forms of narration is quite obvious and impacts on several levels of his narrative scheme. As we noted in our discussion of his work, one thing that prevents his narratives from becoming like novelistic discourse is the fact that he strings together a series of etiological and other cultural fragments while retaining their points of closure in proverbial sayings or etiological explanations. Furthermore, there are no flashbacks in Tutuola. Nor are there 'anachronies' in Genette's term. The narratives trace an inexorable forward movement. It is obvious that, unlike much novelistic discourse, Tutuola's narratives and the folktales upon which he draws do not shuffle with the notion of temporal sequence, even though they are frequently digressive. Rather than being vertical and imposing a structure of subordination between events, the digressions in oral narratives are horizontal and reside on the same lateral plane as the events or incidents in the story they depart from. Subordination is cued from a wider context of signification such as the moral difference between good and bad or from other cultural contexts of immediate material reference.

Ben Okri relies on this mode of discourse, but, because he writes in a self-consciously literary mode, he replicates the structures of oral discourse while at the same time generating literary expectations. *The Famished Road* is evidently episodic with little attempt to link events to one another in any but a sequential framework. With the frequent gnomic generalizations, proverbs and even etiological speculations, a sense of reaching for the closures of oral narratives is evoked as a means of socializing the reader into the discourses of orality. This is further deepened by the lack of all but the vaguest temporal indices and the lack of recall or of anachronies. The flow of the narrative is paratactic and episodic with Azaro moving from one incident to the other in a bewildering framework of arbitrary shifts between the real and spirit-worlds which all seem to reside on a lateral plane. However, the important thing to note about the narrative here is that these communal referents are raised as literary surrogates of what pertains in a context of orality. It is as if Okri conceptualizes the narrative in the context of a communal orality before looking for the best way of rendering that consciousness in a literary mode. The contradictions emerge because not only does he seem to conceptualize his narrative in that way, he grounds it completely within a mythopoeic paradigm by routing it through the mind of the *abiku* child.

Despite *The Famished Road's* a-historical narrative structure, the events are supposed to take place within a specific historical setting, indeterminable though it often seems to be. It is that of Nigeria at the verge of independence. The vague references to political activity are all supposed to derive from that period. Even in this putative historical grounding, history is problematized by the fact that, unlike most other references to that period, the novel inscribes a sense of disillusionment into the events. It is as if the mood of post-Independence disillusionment is transferred onto the period before Independence when the mood was supposedly more euphoric and hopeful. In this way, Okri separates the historical referents from the affective corollaries to which they are usually conjoined, suggesting that history is as much a construction as the fiction he is writing. Additionally, this splitting could also relate to his deployment of the *abiku* motif to stand for the history of his country. Since the *abiku* is caught in a cyclical web of births, deaths and re-births, it fractures history and problematizes the unity of the materiality of events and their putative affective referents. If the country is like the *abiku*, the affective status of its history is thrown into doubt precisely because it is trapped in a grid of non-progressing motion. When Okri suggests this, however, it is not to postulate an ineluctable determinism, but rather to suggest that his country has not done enough to transcend the trauma of unending underdevelopment or the nausea of confusion in its unfocused attempts to escape it. As is pointed out in the novel:

> Things that are not ready, not willing to be born or to become, *things for which adequate preparations have not been made to sustain their momentous births*, things that are not resolved, things bound up with failure and with fear of being, they all keep recurring, keep coming back, and in themselves partake of the spirit-child's condition. They keep coming and going till their time is right. History itself demonstrates how things of the world partake of the condition of the spirit-child. (487; italics added)

The pointer to improper preparations for momentous births links up with Soyinka's own reminder to his nation of the cyclicality of political irresponsibility in *A Dance of the Forests*, a play commissioned specifically to mark Nigeria's Independence celebrations in 1960. The nation is partly figured in that play as a half-bodied child, alluding suggestively to an *abiku* condition and also to the fact that the country's nation-status is not something to be taken for granted in euphoric celebrations of a new birth. By splitting history from its affective referents 30 years later, Okri gives the allusion an even more disturbing slant by showing that the cyclicality is one that becomes endemic if not recognized for what it is.

This takes us to what promises to be the most contentious aspect of the novel, that is the 'spirit' or 'esoteric' passages, their relationship to the passages of realism and the implications these have for the meaning of the work. The narrative is constructed out of a dense weaving of esoteric and reality passages, but a close examination reveals several manners of weaving and differing relationships between the two.

It has already been noted that the nocturnal conflagration and the ensuing riots of the first night provide the initial impetus for the flow of all the narrative events in general. More importantly, the incidents of that night provide a take-off point for the first of numerous digressions into spirit passages. In the confusion of the riots, Azaro is separated from his mother and begins wandering belatedly in search of her. He is suddenly kidnapped by several women 'smelling of bitter herbs' who carry him off to a strange island in the middle of a river along with a wounded woman they pick up on the way. After being warned by a 'cat with jewelled eyes' about the threat to his life continued stay on the island would bring him, Azaro decides to escape in a canoe and does so accompanied by the wounded woman. The events of this digression run pell-mell for four pages to the end of Chapter Three (11–14). But at the opening of Chapter Four (15), Azaro materializes under a lorry:

> That night, I slept under a lorry. In the morning I wandered up and down the streets of the city.

We must pause to examine the relationship of this digression to the first narrative of the conflagration and riots. The esoteric digression seems to have rejoined the first narrative almost at the same point from which it departed. It is still night and since there are no other time indices we have no way of knowing whether it is a different night from that of the riots. At least we know that the events of the 'cult of women' digression all take place at night so we can venture to imagine this reference to be to the same night but in a different part of the city. If that is granted, then it means that what the digression has accomplished is a filling of the interstices between two discrete moments in the narrative with a myriad of esoteric events. This seems plausible also because the incidents of the first narrative do not have any relationship whatsoever with those of the esoteric digression. What this particular form of linkage suggests is that the spirit-world remains a vital life operating *between* the arena of real events. And yet it is not a betweenness that interferes with the space or temporality of the real world. The only direct link between the esoteric events of these passages and those of the reality plane is that they are both experienced through the consciousness of Azaro.

Another digression follows after that of the cult of women, and it also offers insight into another method of interweaving the esoteric and reality passages. Azaro's emerging from underneath the lorry in the morning to resume his wanderings becomes a subsidiary frame for the pursuit of yet another esoteric digression within the narrative. He arrives at a marketplace, gets a loaf of bread from a man with a 'severe face' and 'four fingers' and continues his wandering in the market. Looking at the people who have come to the market, he realizes most of them are strange spirits who have also come to buy and sell:

> I shut my eyes and when I opened them again I saw people who walked backwards, a dwarf who got about on two fingers, men upside-down with baskets of fish on their feet, women who had breasts on their backs,

babies strapped to their chests, and beautiful children with three arms. (15)

He gets a momentary scare when some of these strange creatures discover he can see them, and runs off to another part of the market. He decides out of curiosity to follow some of the strange creatures when they are departing to their homes and settles on a 'baby spirit' which leads him into a clearing in the forest, apparently the beginning of an expressway. Trees have been levelled, and at places the earth is red, but what fascinates Azaro most is a 'gash' in the earth. As he stares at the gash, he hears a sharp noise, as of something sundering, shuts his eyes in horror, and discovers on opening them that he is somewhere else. Azaro is in the belly of the Road! He is quizzed by an irate giant turtle as to his presence and purpose there, but, dissatisfied with his answers, the turtle lumbers away leaving him to cry himself to sleep on 'the white earth of the land'. It is when he wakes up that the esoteric narrative rejoins the previous narrative frame, and that is what is of interest to us here:

> When I woke up, I found myself in a pit from which sand was excavated for the building of the road. I climbed out and fled through the forest. (17)

The rest of the narrative is located within the reality plane. The 'belly of the earth' is in fact an excavated sand pit. In the switch from the esoteric to the real in which the same space is simultaneously within both realms, the narrative suggests that Azaro (and by implication the rest of nature and existence) is in a continually shifting space, and partly at the mercy of those arbitrary shifts. It is interesting that, unlike the first type of digression in which he has to escape the esoteric realm through his own effort, in this case the change occurs without regard to his own volition.[13] A second impression that this particular method of weaving the esoteric with the real suggests is that in the narrative, reality and the spirit-world relate to each other in a kaleidoscopically shifting relationship in which the same phenomenon takes on different accents and hues depending on its location on the reality-esoteric axis at any one moment.[14]

In both these instances, Azaro is alone in experiencing the dual realities and the two planes do not interfere with one another. They seem to be strictly dichotomized. At other times, however, the dichotomy is blurred when Azaro, though ostensibly sharing the same experiences with other characters, perceives aspects of the experience from which the other characters are excluded. This sometimes leads to comic situations, as is the case when in Madame Koto's bar with his father he falls off his seat in reaction to the violent sneezing of a 'three-headed spirit'. His father does not see the three-headed spirit, and, imagining his son has fallen off due to the sneezing of one of the bar girls, rounds on him scathingly:

'What is wrong with you?' Dad said.
'Nothing.'
'A woman sneezes and it blows you away? Are you not a man?' (298)

Only Azaro has the dubious privilege of perceiving the dualities in the experience.[15] In such sections the two planes coalesce in subtle ways that differentiate the manner of construction of these sections from the other sections examined.

Another form of linkage, which this time establishes a calibration of perspectives between the two realms, is offered in the section in which Azaro travels to the underworld in the company of the three-headed spirit.[16] He decides to depart to the underworld in violent reaction to being flogged by his father. In this particular digression the narrative is orientated towards both planes simultaneously, but it is mainly focalized from the vantage point of the esoteric plane. All the human gestures that occur in the reality plane are simultaneously correlated with the events in the esoteric zone in terms of the action of elemental forces. When Azaro's father crouches beside him, his breathing 'manifests itself as a strong wind in the world in which I was travelling' (327); and when his mother sheds tears over his prostrate body, these become 'rainfall which wiped away most of the labours of the people' in the spirit realm (331). Our perceptions have to undergo frenetic shifts getting to the end of the section because the gestures of his parents and those of the herbalist brought to revive him all take shape within his dream-journey as a frantic struggle between his three-headed spirit guide and an old woman with the feet of a lioness:

> The weapon of the old woman with the feet of a lioness had become golden-red. One of the heads of the spirit had rolled onto the river of mirrors and its eyes stared at the eternity of reflections in a bad-tempered astonishment ... Dad's knife, full of reflections, was lifted above me, as if I was to be the sacrificial victim of my own birth. I screamed. The knife in Dad's hand descended swiftly, slashed the air twice. The herbalist released a piercing cry. The old woman struck the spirit at the same moment, with a mighty swipe of her weapon. Dad slashed the chicken's throat. The old woman severed the spirit's last head. The spirit fought vainly in the canoe as the chicken twitched. Its blood dripped on my forehead ... (339)

The strength of this section lies in the rapid translation of events in one plane into events on the other thus calling on us to orientate ourselves to both planes simultaneously. The section also becomes a masterly literary adumbration of the relationship between dream-work and sensory stimuli, permitting us to perceive the dreamwork and its external stimulus frame interacting continually one with the other.[17] This, however, is no ordinary dream because it requires an adjustment in attitudes about the relationship between the real world and that of spirits. A form of equivalence is hinted at in the calibration of events between the two worlds. In this episode the mundane world exerts power over the spirit-world. Seeing that the episode is about the beliefs and practices of traditional medicine, it can also be read as an endorsement of indigenous medical practice which attaches great importance to the physical as well as the spiritual prognosis of disease. From the point of view of Azaro's position, however, the episode further emphasizes his powerlessness in the face of the relationships between spirit and real worlds because he is totally at the mercy firstly of the three-headed spirit and then of the herbalist for his entry and exit from the spirit-world. He is the victim of forces beyond him.

In this section as in other sections in which the distinction between the esoteric and the real are deliberately blurred, the narrative suggests that in its universe of discourse it is difficult to differentiate the one from the other. And because these coalesced sections are juxtaposed with other methods of weaving the esoteric with the real, the narrative works to undermine any easy conclusions that may be arrived at from an examination of any one method of interweaving. The novel's formal strategy may be related to other elements of the narrative to show that an important interest of the story is to demonstrate the fantasy inherent in any experience of real life. In the particular destitution, impoverishment and brutality in which the people in the novel are caught, the realities of existence are frequently tinged with an eerie light. It is instructive to remember that at a crucial stage in the narrative when thugs attack the ghetto and spread mayhem, the events of the night are described in highly poeticized images to bring out the essential 'ghostliness' of the experience;[18] the brutalities seem so unreal that in spite of the fact that several people lose their lives the people later begin to think they 'had collectively dreamt the fevers of that night' (183). We see then that the narrative insists on the essential 'ghostliness' of reality not only in terms of its formal strategies of esoteric weaving but also in terms of the delineation of squalor and destitution, these being the new seats of hallucination.

Certain implications derive from the specific interweaving of the reality and esoteric planes in *The Famished Road*. In the narrative shifts from the reality plane to the esoteric plane in which the same space is simultaneously located within both realms, there is a suggestion that Azaro, and by implication the rest of nature and existence in general, is in a continually shifting conceptual space and partly at the mercy of those shifts. This affects the general notion of time and space and therefore the liminal thresholds and transitions that operated in Tutuola's narratives. Liminal thresholds are no longer conceived of as medial points within a process of transition from one status to another of perhaps greater significance. Those processes of transition are normally marked by acts of volition in the narrative space of the indigenous folktale, and, within a larger cultural context, by acts of ritual self-preparation. The possibility of accessing the spirit-world through ritual acts of volition or self-will is frustrated within the narrative of *The Famished Road*. And this is mainly because the shifts from one experiential plane to the other are no longer within the control of the central characters. Unlike what we saw operating in Tutuola's narratives, the spaces of reality and of the spirit-world are no longer demarcated so that men can move from one to the other through their own volition. The logic of arbitrary shifts seems to take precedence over the volitional acts of the central characters.

The nature and scope of the spirit-world of the novel further establish the similarities and contrasts between Okri's mythopoesis and Tutuola's by suggesting a dispersal and re-distribution of the anxiety-generating potential lodged wholly in the ghostly realm in the work of the earlier writer. The esoteric in Okri has a wide-ranging scope and incorporates several elements that are not wholly reducible to any single cosmogony, though that of Southern Nigeria remains the central impulse. It is difficult to escape the impression of biblical echoes in the opening lines of the novel. And it is also notice-able that the denizens of the spirit realm of *abikus* have a king who has undergone several incarnations on earth in the shape of good and holy men and thus automatically establishes kinship with the leading figures of world religions:

> Our king was a wonderful personage who sometimes appeared in the form of a great cat. He had a red beard and eyes of greenish sapphire. He had been born uncountable times and was a legend in all worlds, known by a hundred different names. (3)

The *abikus'* spirit-world can only be described as celestial. They play with 'faunas, the fairies, and the beautiful beings'. 'Tender sibyls, benign sprites and the serene presences' of their ancestors are always with them. The children's spirits make vows to return to the enchanted existence 'in fields of flowers and in the sweet-tasting moonlight' of that world (4). This world's kinship to paradise is unmistakable. Interestingly, Okri veers significantly from the tissue of beliefs to do with the *abiku* phenomenon in suggesting that Ade, another *abiku*, had previous incarnations as a 'murderer in Rome, a poetess in Spain, a falconer among the Aztecs, a whore in Sudan, a priestess in old Kenya, a one-eyed white ship captain who believed in God and wrote beautiful hymns and who made his fortune capturing slaves in the Gold Coast' (481). Clearly, the *abiku* concept is partially filiated to con-ceptions of the afterlife not wholly African. The multiple dimension-ality of afterlife remains as a potential in the narrative and is not developed as a coherent dimension of the *abiku* phenomenon.

When he comes into the real world, the spirits Azaro encounters come in a variety of categories. Some are spirits who have 'borrowed' parts of the human body but not the human body's symmetry. Thus, they frequently appear incongruous. At Madame Koto's bar spirits enter who have misshapen heads 'like tubers of yam', or eyes not properly co-ordinated. Azaro is often amazed at their deformities. Another set are thoroughly grotesque in their constitution. Such are the three-headed spirit and a spirit Azaro encounters in the forest described as 'a creature ugly and magnificent like a pre-historic dragon, with the body of an elephant and the face of a warthog' (247). Many of these spirits are dangerous and seek to kidnap him to enhance their own potencies.[19]

Yet at various other times it is humans who take on the manifestations of spirits, thus problematizing the distinction between humans and spirits. In the two instances when Azaro encounters lunatics, there is the suggestion that they share a curious kinship with the grotesqueness of spirit figures. Witness the description of the first lunatic whom Azaro meets at the market-place and who expresses an uncanny interest in a piece of bread he is holding:

> There was a man standing near me. I noticed him because of his smell. He wore a dirty, tattered shirt. His hair was reddish. Flies were noisy around his ears. His private parts showed through his underpants. His legs were covered in sores. The flies around his face made him look as if he had four eyes. I stared at him out of curiosity. He made a violent motion, scattering the flies, and I noticed that his two eyes rolled around as if in an extraordinary effort to see themselves. (17)

The impression that this lunatic's eyes have undergone multiplication because of a swarm of flies is unsettling enough, but what is even more distressing is that his eyes, much like the flies that surround them, cannot keep still. A second lunatic is encountered in front of Madam Koto's bar. His description is also striking:

> He had on only a pair of sad-looking underpants. His hair was rough and covered in a red liquid and bits of rubbish. He had a big sore on his back and a small one on his ear. Flies swarmed around him and he kept twitching. Every now and then he broke into a titter.
> ... He had one eye higher than another. His mouth looked like a festering wound. He twitched, stamped, laughed, and suddenly ran into the bar. (84)

Once again we should take note of the odd nature of this man's eyes. And his mouth itself is like a festering wound, referring as much to its raw look as to the overpowering stench of putrefaction that can be thought to emanate from such a mouth.

To grasp the true significance of the relationship between these lunatics and the other grotesque spirit figures in the formal strategy of the novel, it is necessary to turn again to Tutuola's handling of the folktale form and the ways in which *The Famished Road* simultaneously evokes and differentiates its mythopoeic discourse from it. As was noted earlier, in Tutuola's narratives there is a clear boundary between the real world and that of spirits with the suggestion that it is the crossing into the world of spirits that triggers the experience of the esoteric and the anxiety-generating forces inherent in nature figured in the form of grotesque spirits. In this novel, however, the boundary is progressively erased with a redistribution of the grotesque among figures in both the reality as well as in the spirit plane. Whereas in Tutuola's narratives the anxiety-generating forces are encoded as dominantly inherent in the 'Other', here there is a suggestion that real world existence, especially in the context of squalor and dispossession, shares in the absurdity of that other. Thus the dichotomizing gestures of mythopoeia are turned towards showing reality in a new light.

The refocusing of the nature of the spirit-world ramifies at other levels. The specific nature of the spirits in *The Famished Road* also implies alterations to the notion of heroic vocation that dominated the form of the folktale as exercised by Tutuola. In terms of the heroic vocation of the central protagonist, Azaro, there is a decided diminution of the hero here in relation to the spirit encounters. In the dominant discourse of mythopoeia, the protagonist is usually an articulation of titanic grandeur and heroic energy. Azaro has none of these characteristics. He partially subsists within the mythopoeic framework by having access to the spirit-world but no longer is this access volitional and part of an epic quest. Since entry into the spirit-world is purely arbitrary and not due to conscious choice, the esoteric adventures that Azaro undergoes seem purely fortuitous. It is Azaro's unfortunate existential condition that he must perceive the dual aspects of reality whether he likes it or not. And, unlike the heroes of Tutuola's novels, Azaro remains utterly powerless against the spiritual forces he encounters; he retains crucial human limitations right through to the end.

There is a strategic refocusing on heroic energy in the novel away from the central mythopoeic domain to be re-inscribed in the arena of real world actions. The diminution in the stature of the mythopoeic protagonist in the novel is accompanied by a displacement of the heroic potential onto the character of Azaro's Dad, also known in the novel as Black Tyger.[20] That Dad has titanic stature is left in no doubt. He is continually referred to either as a giant or a titan (see pages 28, 34 and 94). From the very beginning Black Tyger is portrayed as a man full of energy burdened by the struggles imposed by an impoverished existence. He carries this burden with much grumbling and is not beyond outbursts of domestic violence. But at the same time there are suggestions that his struggle against poverty borders on a titanic struggle with elemental forces that would destroy man's soul. An Ogun genealogy is posited behind this titanic stature and he is filiated to the god of war in several subtle ways. Black Tyger's own father was a priest of the God of Roads and he was supposed to have succeeded him but left to pursue a boxing career. Dad is further linked to an Ogun essence by his telling of the story of the 'King of the Road', the only full length etiological story in the novel.[21] Significantly too, he is shown to be a good hunter, suggested in his trapping of the wild boar early in the narrative. He is also a great lover of palm-wine, the favourite drink of Ogun himself. Given the array of such references and the fact that he has a ferocious fighting energy, he seems almost to fall directly in line with the essence of Ogun as defined in indigenous Yoruba discourse. These references are, however, linked to another set of references that encode Black Tyger as Shango-like as well, hinting at the necessity for justice and suggesting a gradual shift in tutelary references to make them more appropriate to the concerns of the dispossessed in the novel.

At several points Dad is linked to a gentle or dark wind by which he 'materializes':

[A] gentle wind came into the room and turned into a dark figure, towering but bowed ... The figure was Dad. (199)

Then the wind blew a man to the front door. He stood outside, visible behind the strips of curtain. He came in and looked round and two of the women rushed to him and led him to a seat. It was Dad. (296)

Dad's being somehow linked to the elements is further deepened by his continual association with thunder and lightning. This becomes most evident when he is angry; it is demonstrated when he comes home one evening to discover his creditors have seized his boots and centre table in his absence:

He growled like an enraged lion, drew himself up to his fullest titanic height, stormed out of the room, and began raging down the passage so loudly that it seemed as though thunder had descended amongst us. (96)

In another incident at Madame Koto's bar, the association is made even more explicitly in a fight he has with thugs. One of the thugs rounds on Black Tyger and is bragging about the powers stored in his amulet:

'So what do you want to do?' the man asked, fingering his amulet. 'Do you know this thing I have here, eh? If you touch me you will fall down seven times and then ...'

The braggart is not allowed to complete his sentence. Something fantastic happens:

> Suddenly – it seemed like a flash of lightning was lost in the bar – Dad had hit him in the face. It happened very fast. The next moment the bar door was wide open and the man had disappeared. We heard him groaning outside in the dark. The lightning vanished back into Dad's fist. (301)

The associations with thunder and lightning subtly inscribe a Shango essence which is further grounded in the fact that Dad is a stickler for justice. This is evident from his inarticulate but determined opposition to the Party of the Rich. He opposes them even at the risk of falling foul of his landlord and of endangering his family. It is as if, despite the problematization of the heroic stature of the folklore hero as signalled in the diminished potential of Azaro, the narrative incorporates an index of grandeur and heroic stature by linking Black Tyger to deity references. However, the way this is done shows that the mythopoeia is eclectic to accommodate the complexities of real world existence. There is a subtle shift from allegiance to the particularities of a single deity. This represents a strategic elaboration of what Soyinka does in his persistent invocation of Ogun. Okri reaches for the eclecticism inherent in polytheistic cultic dispensations and in this reproduces the temper of indigenous attitudes to the gods. The eclectic temper of Okri's inscription of multiple deitic qualities can also be said to mark a sense of the hybridity which is a function of the multicultural environments in which he grew up. The filiation to the indigenous resource-base, then, is a strategic filiation to its hybrid and eclectic potential as much as to its specific motifs and images.

If it is postulated that, unlike Azaro's, Black Tyger's development defines the trajectory of a rite of passage, then it is important to trace the specific mode by which his experiences may be said to constitute a rite of passage that contrasts with the a-teleological experiences of his son. There seem to be three phases in his development. The first phase involves his struggles for existence amidst the squalor and dispossession of the ghetto. He has to take up all sorts of jobs to make ends meet, including porterage at the lorry park as well as surreptitious latrine carrying.[22] This phase is often punctuated by his expressions of bewilderment at the harsh ways of the world. The second phase involves a definition of his relationship to politics, notably in his fierce onslaught against the Party of the Rich despite dire consequences for himself. The third phase is the most complicated because it involves the affirmation of his titanic stature in various fights, yet the consequences of exercising this potential are shown to be highly problematic for the definition of an appropriate social role for himself.

Confirmation of his titanic stature starts with his fight against the spirit of Yellow Jaguar, a boxer whose body felt like a tree and who had a mighty voice, 'speaking with the power of darkness' (356). His defeat of Yellow Jaguar is succeeded by a period of serious illness in which he lingers in 'a curious state of shock, between agony and amnesia' (359). Interestingly, he is said to become like 'the biggest newborn baby in the world (ibid.). The suggestion of a potential re-birth is, however, not picked up by the text, because in terms of the development of Black Tyger's character, the defeat of Yellow Jaguar only serves to make him self-centred and swelled up in the belief in his invulnerability. After his recovery, he moves further and further into a definition of a social role based on strength and violence. The value of his ferocious strength is problematically affirmed in his battle with Green Leopard, a huge thug who had been menacing the streets and was now on the payroll of the Party of the Rich. Again he accomplishes an impressive victory over his enemy (395–42). At this point, however, new realities make themselves felt which test Dad in other directions.

Earlier on, during a training session at one of his secret bases prior to the encounter with Green Leopard, he undergoes an epiphanic experience when a strange old man 'carrying something invisible' on his head comes to test his charitable impulses. Crucially, he passes the test and the old man tells him how lucky he is to have passed. It is an important experience for him as he later tells his son: 'I am beginning to see things for the first time. This world is not what it seems. There are mysterious forces everywhere. We are living in a world of riddles' (388). The encounter introduces a second aspect to his quest for an appropriate social role and his development after the bout with Green Leopard fuses these two dimensions. Black Tyger progresses in the direction of charitable impulse even as his titanic stature is affirmed through fights. He enters into a phase of idealism in which he desires to create a socialist utopia in which, among other things 'everyone must learn music and mathematics and at least five world languages, and in which every citizen must be completely aware of what is going on in the world, be versed in tribal, national, con-tinental and international events, history, poetry and science' (409). In terms of his quest for a mode of social existence this idealism is important because it leads him to attempt to organize his neighbour-hood into a greater awareness of their surroundings, even though his initial efforts at neighbourhood cleaning attract only derision and insults. Secondly, the idealist drive moves him to contemplate hijacking the machinery of politics as a means of enabling the achievement of his utopian ideals. These efforts are shown to be cranky and severely limited because of the seriously debilitating structure of underprivilege of which he is clearly a victim. All this phase of idealism gives him is a devoted constituency of deformed beggars who gatecrash a party he organizes and become permanent appendages of his political plans.

The constituency of beggars becomes the objective test of the charitable impulses we noted earlier. Not only are the beggars a rather trying group, the attitude that other people in the neighbourhood adopt towards them is decidedly different from Black Tyger's. In fact, it is precisely in relation to these beggars that he has his final titanic fight. His decisive intervention to avert the nasty fate that would surely have befallen them at Madame Koto's party finally joins up the two movements in his characterization, one towards violence and the other towards charitableness (467–71). Black Tyger enters this fight precisely because he espouses the cause of the dispossessed represented by the beggars. It is the first time he fights not to make money for himself but in a principled defence of others. When bets are collected during this last fight he insists he wants the money to build a university for the beggars, thus adding the provision of social welfare to that of social justice.

Black Tyger is no richer at the end than he was at the beginning of the novel, but his character undergoes a decided enrichment in terms of the definition of a form of social existence appropriate to the condition of the dispossessed. The vast 're-dreaming' of the world he has in the delirious aftermath of his last fight might be construed as unduly homiletic in tone, but the point is that it marks the achievement of a prophetic and humanist mode of understanding the world for him. Thus it can be said that, unlike Azaro, Black Tyger's experiences constitute a rite of passage in the terms often reserved for the heroes of mythopoeia. What this strategy achieves is the problematization of the heroic vocation in the Tutuola type of narrative to suggest that it is the processes of real life existence that must define the heroic vocation and that this vocation depends on the resources of the real world as well as that of spirits.

The deflection of heroic energy from Azaro onto his father might be read as unsatisfactory in terms of the implicit validation of a masculine mode of heroism. That seems to be a valid point considering Mum's relative self-effacement in the text. Hers is a harried and difficult existence. In relation to the characterization of Madame Koto, however, there is a partial challenge to any notion of heroism being a masculine preserve. The indigenous resource-base for Madame Koto's characterization renders her a massive challenge to a masculinist notion of heroism, though, it must be said, a notable ambivalence attaches to her character which undermines her as a potential centre of heroic significations.

Madame Koto is shown to be highly resourceful, independent and ambitious. When she is first introduced to the narrative, her credentials are rapidly established by her wrestling with a drunken customer who tries to make trouble after being defeated at draughts in her bar by Dad. At several other points, she takes decisive action against recalcitrant customers as well as Azaro. She shows a strong dissatisfaction with the conditions of squalor and deprivation she has to bear and, as she expresses it to Azaro, her dreams are to one day escape the cycle of poverty to become a rich and influential person (251). The nature of her dissatisfaction with her circumstances is not much different from the nature of dissatisfaction of all poor people. Dad frequently expresses such dissatisfactions, though his ambitions are shown to be substantially different from hers. Significantly, however, the narrative poses Madame Koto's dissatisfaction as a problem linked to witchcraft. Three different perspectives are given into her potential witchcraft and all three serve to pass judgement on her. The first perspective is offered by the rumours that circulate about her. Much of the knowledge about Madame Koto's character is woven out of rumours from the very beginning. When she throws out the recalcitrant drunken customer, her legend, 'which would sprout a thousand hallucinations', is born. Born of stories and rumours, it would in time 'become some of the most extravagant realities of our lives' (37). The subtle and gradual concretization of rumours into reality is implied in this statement but we are not sure whether it is meant that the rumours would later have the status of fact or whether it is her actions that would confirm some of the worst rumours about her. The narrative itself leans towards the second rather than the first explanation.

The rumour mill turns out an elaborate and coherent under-standing of Madame Koto's character based entirely on beliefs in witchcraft:

> They said of Madame Koto that she had buried three husbands and seven children and that she was a witch who ate her babies when they were still in her womb. They said she was the real reason why the children in the area didn't grow, why they were always ill, why the men never got promotions, and why the women in the area suffered miscarriages. They said she was a bewitcher of husbands and seducer of young boys and poisoner of children. They said she had a charmed beard and that she plucked one hair out every day and dropped it into the palm-wine she sold … and that she belonged to a secret society that flies about in the air when the moon is out. (100–1)

Each item in this barrage of rumours is a direct affirmation of the belief that she is a witch. If they are isolated, they fall into three distinct sets of beliefs about witchcraft: the first set asserts that she is incapable of marriage and is a destroyer of fertility, suggested in her burying of several spouses and her destroying of children in the womb. This set of assertions is tied to a popular belief that all women are potentially vessels of fertility or their opposite. As soon as a woman either fails to marry or have children she is seen as the inverse of fertility. The second set of assertions relates to the witch's carnal status. They are believed to have strong sexual urges. These urges are believed not to be exercised within the ambit of the socially permissible because of the witch's natural predilection for transgressing the socially acceptable. The third set links women's enterprise to esoteric power. The assertion that her beard is charmed and is used to sell palm-wine is a clear linking of her commercial success to negative power (see Hallen and Sodipo 1986: 102–7). The tissue of popular beliefs asserted by the rumours are variously affirmed by the narrative. Though Madame Koto is not shown to be wanton, she is surrounded in the later parts of the narrative by prostitutes. That she is pregnant with three *abiku* children she refuses to give birth to is a clear sign of the inversion of fertility. And we are left in no doubt that juju is behind her commercial enterprise and that she immerses herself in dubious spiritual practices.[23]

It is evident that Okri defines Madame Koto in an ambivalent light. On a purely sociological reading, this serves as a literary inscription of some of the ambivalent attitudes to strong-willed and successful women in Nigerian society. Southern Nigerian women are generally noted to be highly independent in spirit. Yoruba women are noted to be vigorous traders and have a highly independent disposition. However, they have to operate within a predominantly patriarchal social structure. Because of their perceived independence, a process of demonization of women is inscribed in Yoruba culture along with a great respect for their resourcefulness. The first level of this process involves linking the marketplace, the very seat of women's commercial activities, to Eshu, the god of mischief. Even more importantly, the commercial progress women make is seen as linked to witchcraft, something generally believed to be an immense threat to society. The witch is said to prosper through her dominion in the world of spirits. But, as Judith Hoch-Smith (1978: 265) points out, this demonization of women's power symbolizes 'the struggle between the sexes for power on many levels: sexual, social, political, the derogatory female image being related to the normative ethos of the patrilineage.'

Madame Koto is posited as a potential centre of heroic energy in parallel with Black Tyger, and we are meant to admire her. She frequently has him drink palm-wine without charge and shows numerous kindnesses to his family. It is she who rushes to bring Mum herbal medicine when she lies ill and at the verge of death, and her warmth towards Azaro is unmistakeable. However, there is a dichotomy between Black Tyger's heroic potential and hers because of the different directions in which their filiation to the spirit-world leads them. Whereas he moves to greater social conscience, she

moves towards self-interest. The narrative suggests there are sociological reasons to rationalize the exercise of her particular options.
Being a trader and owning some capital in the form of the palm-wine
bar gives her a distinctly more privileged status than the rest of the
neighbourhood and defines her primary motivations. Because of her
ownership of capital it is not difficult for her to drift towards The
Party of the Rich as a means of consolidating her class position.
Unfortunately, the narrative suggests that that consolidation goes
hand-in-hand with the negative use of spiritual power, thus justify-
ing the worst popular suspicions held about her. With this trajectory,
Okri joins a potential sociologically based stereotype to the
moralizing predilection of mythopoeia to inscribe Madame Koto as
the obverse of Good. Though the ambivalence with which she is
defined prevents the text from plunging into a full-blown manichean
typology, all doubt as to her status in Okri's mythopoeic schema are
removed in *Songs of Enchantment*, where the mythopoeisis takes a
decided plunge into the moralism of indigenous myth and folktale
and the central conflict in the novel is between the forces of Good,
championed by Dad, and those of Evil, spearheaded by the Jackal-
Headed masquerade and Madame Koto. In *The Famished Road*,
though the potential moralism of mythopoeia is not entered into, the
narrative nonetheless leaves its inherent masculinism intact because
the energetic character of Madame Koto is not allowed to disrupt the
articulation of Black Tyger as the legitimate inheritor of the heroic
vocation of mythopoeia. Basing her characterization on indigenous
beliefs of witchcraft has a decidedly different effect from what we
saw operating in relation to Maria in 'When the Lights Return'.
Whereas in the short story the text allowed a moral ambivalence to
Maria's characterization, here the balance tips against Madame Koto.
The stereotype of the witch gains greater intensity as it is progressively transposed onto the implicit moralism of the later novels.

How do we relate Okri's literary practice to the literary formation?
How does it articulate particular stresses in Nigerian society and
culture in general? What does it signal about potential directions in
literary production in his country?

Ben Okri grew up in the period after Independence when the
coherence of the Nigerian nation-state was in doubt. The country had
entered into a period of rapid disillusionment with the constitution of
the country and by 1966 it had erupted into a full-scale secession bid
by the Igbos. For Okri's generation the unfolding events had a drastic
effect. By the time of the Biafra war, Okri was only seven years old
and at school in Minna. 'Laughter Beneath the Bridge', a story set in a
time of war and centering on the experiences of a young boy, tells
something about the bafflement that must have afflicted any person

of his age at the time. The effect of the war was to shake the foundations of the sense of national unity in the minds of both old and young. Another and perhaps more profound effect on those close to the theatre of war was the shock of seeing and hearing about the death and putrefaction of human bodies all the time. It can be conjectured that in such conditions stories about spirits and their relationship to the real world would take a greater urgency.

Another process which was to have a decisive effect on Okri's generation was the gradual but sure emergence of graft and corruption as a dominant feature of national life. Older Nigerian writers such as Soyinka and Achebe had already attempted to engage with the emerging problems in works like *The Interpreters* and *A Man of the People*, both of which express a growing dissatisfaction with the rise in corrupt tendencies in Nigeria. The stories that circulated in the seventies and eighties about embezzlements in the country have literary treatment in Okri's 'Disparities', a story that tells of the pauperized existence of the narrator in the knowledge that a Nigerian state official had 'forgotten' a quarter of a million pounds in the back of a cab in London. Okri had a particularly bitter taste of the effects of the corruption due to growing up in the ghettos of Lagos where social amenities were always uncertain and people were forever at the mercy of their landlords. In fact, his first bid at writing was to relate in fictional form some of the problems in the ghettos of Lagos (see Jane Wilkinson 1992: 77–9). What the corruption did to the psyche of many young Nigerians was to give them a permanent distrust of received ideas from authority figures. But more important for an analysis of Okri's work is that the state of corruption made it impossible to write about events with the rationalism of prevailing protocols of realism. He gives an inkling of his preoccupations in answer to the question as to whether he was thinking of a possible new way of writing when working on *The Landscapes Within*:

> I wasn't, no. But I've come to realize you can't write about Nigeria truthfully without a sense of violence. To be serene is to lie. Relations in Nigeria are violent relations. It's the way it is, for historical and all sorts of other reasons ... [I]n an atmosphere of chaos art *has* to disturb something. For art to be very cool, very clear – which, in relation to chaos, is a negative kind of disturbance – or it has to be more chaotic, more violent than the chaos around. Put that on one side. Now think of the fact that for anything new, for something good to come about, for it to reach a level of art, you have to liberate it from old kinds of perception, which is a kind of destruction. An old way of seeing things has to be destroyed for the new one to be born. (in Wilkinson: 81)

It is interesting that these concerns were on his mind as early as his second novel published in 1981. *The Landscapes Within* tells of the ennui of the artist-protagonist Omovo in his search for objective

147

correlatives in the social landscape to help organize his artistic impressions. That novel is unsettling enough in many ways, but Okri's sense of liberating his art form from older perceptions cannot be said to really take off till the short stories. It is evident from his answer that he sought a way of engaging with the irrational logic of Nigerian life from the very start. Biodun Jeyifo (1986) traces an extensive genealogy in African writing for this type of dissatisfaction. He points out that Nigerian works like Achebe's *A Man of the People* and Soyinka's *The Interpreters* along with works by other African writers such as Ayi Kwei Armah's *Fragments*, Ngugi's *Petals of Blood* and Dambudzo Marechera's *The House of Hunger* share the same dissatisfactions:

> In all these works, in varying levels of technical self-assurance and competence, the narrative and stylistic organization of the material is informed by a *problematic* which assumes that the work of fiction can no longer complacently proffer a fictional 'reality' axiomatically at variance with the socio-historical reality of alienation, degradation, chaos and instability for the vast majority of its living generations.
>
> It is neccessary to clarify that what is implied here in the aesthetics of these novels, as in all the previously published works now intertextually 'revised', is not merely a thematic exploration of social malaise but the insinuation of this sense of social disjuncture into the very form and structure of these novels.

For Okri, the problem is tackled by harnessing all levels of his narrative to indigenous forms of knowledge centering on beliefs in the intercourse between the world of spirits and that of living beings. The particular form of his harnessing poses new questions about protocols of representation which are yet to be answered. Harry Garuba (1993) comes closest to providing a new terminology for discussing Okri's later work when he refers to it as dominated by 'animist realism'.[24] Unfortunately, he leaves this highly suggestive term unexplained thereby allowing it to be drafted into other frames of analysis without being defined.[25]

Animism is the belief in a spiritual vitality lying behind all natural objects. It formed the basis of conceptions of African culture by early Western anthropologists and has come under serious attack by Africanist philosophers and scholars.[26] Animist realism would be realism constructed with such a belief as its basic tenet. It would not have the same semantic field as that of anthropological usage, though it would borrow something of that conception. *The Famished Road* and *Songs of Enchantment* imply a belief in such an animist realism. The impression that all things from trees to photographs have a potential spiritual vitality is inescapable on reading the novels. The literary expression of such animism is clearly meant to stand as a surrogate for indigenous beliefs in spirits, but it should be read more as a literary defamiliarization of indigenous beliefs than a true replica o such beliefs in reality. Okri's postulation of a universally pervasive animism can only be read as a magnification of certain indigenous beliefs for the purpose of problematizing the relationship between reality and the other-worldy in literature. It is, as Eileen Julien (1992) holds, the negotiation of an aesthetic problem, in this case to do with the dominant protocols of realism. All the different aspects of realist narrative such as character and setting are based on the implicit belief in the knowability of the real as it unfolds its meaning in linear time. To postulate realism based on a pervasive animism is to fracture that basis of belief by suggesting that not only is the real decentered because of its permanent interplay with the esoteric, but that neither is reducible to the other. Standard realism, then, promotes a view of reality which is inadequate to engaging with the problematic fusion of the real with the other-wordly (see Hawley 1995; Ogunsanwo 1995).

Okri's animist realism has important implications for the direction of the literary expression of indigenous beliefs as well as for the relationships that are established with readers. The first problem lies in the suggestion that *every* narrative detail has potential symbolic value. Since such an animist generalization suggests that any item is capable of manifesting an intrinsic 'spiritual' potential at any given time, the implication is that a reader requires a much greater alertness to the potential symbolic value of all narrative elements. This can easily lead to reader fatigue, particularly in the context of long novels that eschew explicit teleological patterning. In a way, it enforces a regime of constant reader participation in constructing the meanings of the text while at the same time ensuring that the reader cannot completely enter the process of creation because there are not enough cues for predicting the precise moment of the articulation of the spiritual behind things. The problem is much less pronounced in the context of the short stories, not only because of their length but also because Okri avoids infusing animism into all the narrative levels of the text. It is decidedly different in *The Famished Road* and in *Songs of Enchantment* where the narrative agency is taken over by a spirit figure. How are we to know the principles by which an *abiku* decodes the spirit potential of things?

In another sense, the animist realism implies a quasi-religious attitude to reality. It is difficult not to think that Okri's enterprise has affinities with what we noted to be the case with Tutuola and Fagunwa: that the gradual dominance of a world religion generates a sense of attraction to the more frightening aspects of indigenous religion and its practices. Since this is done with recourse to the mythopoeisis of indigenous culture, and myths harbour an implicit moralism necessary for the socialization of the community, it is not difficult for the deflected religious feeling to find a fairly coherent discourse that can challenge the dominant form of Christian religious expression while at the same time replicating the grand and generalizing tendencies of the world religion.

The implied interface between different modes of belief, between orality and literacy and between modernity and an indigenous resource-base are well attested to in Okri's writing. The resources of the indigenous conceptual system are refracted at several levels simultaneously and their strategic invocation is in order to problematize not only received modes of narrative representation but also the indigenous resource-base itself. Okri projects the folkloric intuition earlier exercised by Tutuola onto a new plane of significance. By setting much of his work in the urban ghettoes and producing a sense of the fluid interchange of various subjectivities, he captures in his own peculiar way a conundrum of the modern African condition. For, in entering into the modern world, the present-day African activates different processes of socialization that combine ritual gestures towards indigenous beliefs with an acceptance of a more Western paradigm imbibed through education and the media. The issue can be said to be most acute precisely at the level of ghetto existence, since the denizens of the ghettoes are never fully integrated into dominant social and economic structures and reside problematically at the liminal interstices, often eking out an existence from what has been called the informal or parallel economy in Africa. It seems, however, that Okri arrives at this important intuition through his own placement at another conjuncture of increasing importance in the constitution of identity for the Nigerian and, indeed, the African; that is the condition of exile or residence in the diaspora where the need to negotiate multiple identities becomes most acute. Though he had first-hand experience of life in the ghettoes of Lagos and so shared in their liminal conceptions, it is residence in a Western capital that heightens the sense of liminality. That he can draw on the indigenous resource-base already activated by Johnson, Tutuola and Soyinka goes to show the versatility of the resource-base and its applicability to fresh problems and experiences.

Notes

1 It is curious to note that Okri does not seem to have been influenced by the work of J. P. Clark-Bekederemo, whose Ijo people share the same area as Okri's own ethnic group. Clark-Bekederemo has also attempted to give a national dimension to the mythology of his own people, through his play *The Raft* and especially in his dramatic version of the Ijo oral epic *Ozidi*. It is evident that Okri is drawn to the Yoruba system as actualized by Soyinka and others rather than to the Ijo/Urhobo closer to his own ethnic origins. For a discussion of Clark-Bekederemo and the multiple dimensions of the Ozidi saga, see Dan Izevbaye, 'J. P. Clark-Bekederemo and the Ijo Literary Tradition', *Research in African Literatures* 25.1 (1994): 1–21. I wish

to thank Prof. Abiola Irele for bringing this point to my notice in private communication.

2 I have drawn up a list of these 'esoteric' passages with their relevant page numbers in an attached Appendix. I shall discuss these passages with reference to the numbers I give them in the Appendix.

3 No. 27.

4 The belief is by no means limited to these ethnic groups. Edos, Efiks and Kalabari peoples all have different names for the same concept.

5 Wole Soyinka, 'Abiku' in *Idanre*: 28–30; J. P. Clark-Bekederemo (then J. P. Clark) 'Abiku' in *A Reed in the Tide* (London: Longman, 1965): 5; Chinua Achebe, *Things Fall Apart* (1958; London: Heinemann, 1986): 53–61.

6 Maduka suggests that the Abiku's non-conformism gets woven into Soyinka's definition of a heroic vocation in his later writings. It seems Soyinka is always attracted to rebels and non-conformists, something which accords well with his own political temperament; this is regularly illustrated in *Ibadan*. See Maduka, 27; also Quayson, 'Soyinka's autobiographies as political unconscious' already cited and Obi Maduakor (1993).

7 A typical example occurs in the first few pages, when, in reaction to the various strange images that he perceives, he laments in bewilderment, 'I had no idea whether these images belonged to this life, or to the previous one, or to one that was yet to come …' page 7; see also 291 for an expression of a desire to escape the bewildering esoteric visions.

8 Examples of etiological explanations of some of his experiences: 'That was the first time I realized it wasn't just humans who came to the marketplaces of the world', 16. See also page 136 for an explanation of spirit rationale for 'borrowing' parts of the human body.

9 The word 'digression' in this context is somewhat clumsy since it insinuates a normative scale with the events of the putative real-world of the novel being the point from which the esoteric digresses. This is inescapable because it is only the texture of real-world events that remains recognizable and to which we are always returned after forays into the esoteric. However, the novel ensures that all such notions of priority remain provisional and I stick to the word only as a means of imposing an organizational perspective on the discussion.

10 The events that occur from Azaro's homecoming party on page 41 to the end of Book 1, page 71 take about four days, but it is impossible to be sure. Again, Chapters 5 and 6 contain references to the Rich People's Party's milk distribution on a Saturday evening; on Sunday all the neighbourhood people react to food poisoning. After that there is an abandonement of this temporal framework, with Chapter 7 opening on page 133 with a vague 'The next time I went to Madame Koto's bar …'

11 Gerard Genette gives the most exhaustive analysis of the relationship between narrative time and clock time, and it is his model I draw upon here. See his *Narrative Discourse*, trans. Jane E. Lewin (London: Blackwell, 1980): 86–112; also Meir Steinberg, *Expositional Modes and Temporal Ordering in Fiction* (Baltimore: Johns Hopkins University Press, 1978): 236–305.

12 Genette, 35–6; and for an excellent discussion relating to Chinua Achebe's *Things Fall Apart* see Majorie Winters, 'An Objective Approach to Achebe's Style', *Research in African Literatures* 12.1 (1981): 55–86.

13 For other digressions that are rejoined to the mainframe through some act of volition on Azaro's part see Nos. 13, 17, 18, 20 and 26.

14 For digressions which rejoin the first frame through arbitrary shifts on the reality-esoteric axis see Nos. 2, 5, 21, 29, 31 and 40. No. 29 is particularly interesting because in this one Azaro poses the question to himself as to how he will escape the nightmare of the esoteric. When he is finally returned to the real world he comments on how everything around him takes on a disconcerting significance.

15 This is in fact the most common situation. For other comic situations arising from the differences in perception see also No. 24 and pages 40, 62, 253 and 354.

16 No. 34.

17 It is generally believed that the process of naturalizing sensory stimuli within dreams is a mechanism to ensure the continuance of sleep. This dates from Freud and *The Interpretation of Dreams*. Though it falls outside the ambit of this study, the psychology implied by Azaro's esoteric experiences would be interesting to research.

18 No. 22.

19 See, for example, Nos. 17, 21 and 32.

20 He is referred to simply as 'Dad' by his son, but with the progress of the narrative and the increasing affirmation of his violent energies, he is called 'Black Tyger'. I shall be using the two names interchangeably as a signal of the novel's own multiple usage.

21 No. 27.

22 The references to porterage are widespread, but for a particularly poignant description of what this involves see pp. 144–9. 'Masquerades' in *Incidents at the Shrine* is the best guide to what psychological stress the carrying of latrine involves. The particular stress for Dad is depicted in pp. 199–201 of *The Famished Road*.

23 Two of the esoteric digressions deal directly with the question of Madame Koto's involvement with juju. See Nos. 20 and 29.

24 Harry Garuba, 'Ben Okri: Animist Realism and the Famished Genre', *The Guardian* (Lagos) 13 March 1993.

25 The pages of *The Guardian* of Lagos have been the most active in grappling with the writing of Ben Okri along with those of other younger writers. For an attempt to define Okri's work in relation to Gestalt psychology and taking into account Garuba's new terminology, see John Otu, 'Beyond Surrealism: A Gestalt Perspective', *The Guardian* (Lagos) 10 April 1993.

26 The most controversial of these seems to have been Fr. Placide Tempels's *Bantu Philosophy*. For critical evaluations of Tempels as well as of that type of anthropology in general see the works of Paulin Hountondji, Valentin Mudimbe and Christopher Miller earlier cited.

Appendix
'Esoteric' Passages in *The Famished Road*

In drawing up a table of the passages that relate to excursions into the spirit-world, I generally ignore those of less than a dozen lines. The esoteric sections are described from their take-off point; brief contextual indices are given either as lines from the text or as general descriptions. Tales related by different characters in the course of the narrative are given in brackets. These share many characteristics with the esoteric passages in the main narrative, but are mainly differentiated by being related by characters other than Azaro.

Description	*Page Numbers*
1 'In the Beginning.' Description of the abode of spirit companions from which Azaro emerges into the real world.	1–3
2 Fragmentary encounters with spirit companions in childhood.	7–9
3 Conflagration, police brutalities, riots. Azaro abducted by cult of women to strange island.	10–14
4 Escapes from cult of women. Strays into marketplace, sees strange spirit-visitors to the market and follows a baby-spirit out of market into the forest.	15–17
5 Escapes from mad man who chases him for loaf of bread. Is overwhelmed by voices of spirit companions, collapses.	18

34 In reaction to being flogged, refuses food and descends   325–9
   into spirit-world with three-headed spirit first seen at
   Madame Koto's. Events in underworld journey
   simultaneously correlated with gestures of parents and
   others in the real world.

35 Father's fight with spirit of Yellow Jaguar.   354–8

36 Herbalist woman, running into forest in pursuit of   405
   Azaro's father, turns into a bird.

37 At Madame Koto's. Crippled beggars enter;   431–2
   he perceives one of them to be a spirit. Spirit tries to
   lure him.

38 At Madame Koto's. Father falls asleep and Azaro sees   436–7
   astral form of changing colours above his father's body.
   (Father wakes up and tells him dream of 'The Continent
   of the Hanging Man').

39 At Madame Koto's party, sees duiker tied to tent pole   456–8
   and is drawn into duiker consciousness.
   Adventures therefrom.

40 Perceives that some of the people at Madame Koto's   459–61
   party are half human, half animal. Midget dances him
   into new realm.

41 Still at Madame Koto's party, re-enters duiker   464
   consciousness briefly and 'perceives' *abiku* children in
   Madame Koto's stomach.

42 At home. Father is in delirious slumber after another   478
   fight; Azaro gets entangled in mother's dream while
   she attempts to reach her husband's slumbering spirit
   in sleep.

43 At home. Staying awake to protect father's spirit   482–4
   while he slumbers. (Mother's tale of white man
   who seeks road out of Africa, and his metamorphosis
   into Yoruba).

44 Relates his father's massive re-dreaming of the world's   492–7
   history and destiny; intersperses it with own musings
   about Madame Koto's spirit and reflections on the
   nature of politics.

7

Conclusions & Reflections

Methods, Means & Meanings

If there is something basically enabling and positive in the undoing of disciplinary boundaries, authoritative privileges and canonical sources and modes of presentation, it may nevertheless be too easy to celebrate this new fluidity, this new scope for exhilarating tresspass ... It remains important to argue about the effectiveness of different disciplinary technologies; about the politics of analytical strategies; about the appropriateness of particular theoretical languages.

Nicholas Thomas
Colonialism's Culture

Writing in English makes the writers discussed here mediators of conjunctural realities in their culture's meeting with the rest of the world. This way of viewing their work has its dangers not the least of which is the implied valorization of work done in Europhone languages as against those written in local ones. It is a danger Karin Barber identifies as lying behind most studies of African literature today. It is seen partly in the evolutionary paradigm in which orality is postulated as enabling written literature but is passed over quickly to make way for the analysis of literary texts. Even in landmark contributions of post-colonial theory such as *The Empire Writes Back,* this valorization of the Europhone and the literary is implied in the idea that contests with the metropolitan centre were secreted in writing and that it was in Europhone literature that 'writing back' constituted the supreme challenge to the centre. This, Barber (1995) notes, brackets out the efficacy and vitality of contexts of orality in expressing opposition to domination during the colonial period and after.

These are important considerations. However, it is possible to argue that the context of orality or of writing in non-Europhone languages persists in a status of subordinacy in contemporary theory precisely because of the limited audiences that such a literature reaches given the limited geographical spread of local languages and the dynamics of international publishing. The filiation of Europhone African writing with contexts of orality can then be read as a useful way of making indigenous cultures gain access to a wider audience by making it necessary to engage with knowledge of such cultures for the sake of uncovering the various levels of meanings of the literary texts. The work of the writers in this book is particularly appropriate for discussing this dimension of Europhone African literature because of the sheer density of indigenous references that make it impossible for an outsider not to have the sense of encountering the discourses of a different culture. The work of Tutuola, Soyinka and Okri along with others from Nigeria can be said to have done more for a knowledge of Nigerian culture outside the boundaries of that country than any of the texts in local languages. Their works can be seen as nodal points for entry into a different sense of things, even if accessibility seems initially simple because the texts are in an English understood across the world. A recognition of this is not however to postulate African literary texts as mere mirrors or receptacles of culture. Rather, it is to recognize that every work of art has a cultural dimension which discursively interacts with other aspects of the literary text to locate it in a particular field of relevance instead of another. Altering the dominant grid of interpretation might justify its inclusion under different rubrics such as African, Commonwealth or post-colonial, but immediately the specific cultural dimension is highlighted it narrows the descriptive labels to be applied.

No literary history can avoid tackling questions of continuity and change. However, the specific dynamic that is identified in the relationship between literature and culture or society has an important effect on how continuity and change are perceived. The notion of a literary strategic formation was meant in this book to accomplish a shift from tracing a literary tradition in terms of the movement of consciousness to identifying it in terms of varying inter-discursive relationships between literature and an indigenous resource-base. The specific configuration of this strategic formation was that it demonstrated a will-to-identity expressed in exercising the option of mythopoesis and ritual instead of realism. In this light, the literary strategic formation can be said to differ from other potential literary configurations in Nigeria in which the filiation with indigenous resources subserves realist protocols of representation. However, even a shift from tracing the growth of consciousness to the delineation of a cultural praxis needs to be thoroughly historicized to be adequate to the complexity of the relations between literature, culture and society in Nigeria. I attempted to historicize the literary strategic formation firstly by slicing the tradition of writing I was discussing along a synchronic axis. The historiography of Samuel Johnson was an attempt to show that what the literary writers were doing in filiating to indigenous resources was in fact a feature of a larger impulse in the society which dated from the late nineteenth century. With Johnson, too, it was possible to show how his work articulated a cultural nationalist impulse discernible in the efforts of the cultural elite in compiling collections of ethnographic materials. Synchronicity was also implied in the chapter on Soyinka where I tried to show that his redeployment of Ogun was part of wider cultural uses of the war god for defining identity.

The dominant step in the book, however, was to follow the strategic formation along a diachronic axis, seeing the work of the writers in terms of developments from Johnson through to Okri. Historicizing the formation also called for identifying the relationships of the writers to political and historical realities, since, ultimately, they could be seen as mapping out responses to politico-historical developments in Nigeria. I attempted to indicate such a context in terms of the growth and crisis of the nation-state from the late nineteenth century to the present time. Even though the background of political events was presented in a selective and fragmentary form, my aim was to show the impossibility of understanding the strategic positionings of these writers except in relation to the wider dynamics of the Nigerian nation-state. Thus, it was possible to show that Samuel Johnson's work was a nodal point in the expression of cultural nationalism at the point when the Nigerian cultural intelligentsia was adopting a more critical stance towards colonial domination in the late nineteenth century and that Tutuola, Soyinka and Okri were all responding to new opportunities and crises in the Nigerian nation-state. The rubric of the history of the nation-state forced a re-thinking of Irele's focus on the Yoruba in his definition of a literary tradition, because of the impossibility of positing a pure ethnic basis to the work of the writers without taking account of their interrelationships within wider national realities. The work of Okri was used to problematize the notion of ethnic resources which lay behind the work of the other writers. With Okri was seen the refraction of the concepts first deployed by the Yoruba writers for the formulation of a general indigenous and not specifically Yoruba sense of things. It would have been possible to pursue this line of analysis even further by examining texts from other ethnic groups such as the Igbo. The work of Christopher Okigbo, for instance, could have furnished a rich seam for exploring an indigenous sense of things from another ethnic perspective. However, this possibility was left unpursued for the sake of focusing on a delimitable field of cultural resources to help regulate the field of reference both for the historical and literary dimensions of the study. For it is evident that the work of Tutuola, Soyinka and Okri display similarities of motifs, symbols and even tropes that make it easier to discuss them in relation to each other than in relation to a different trajectory. It is important to point out, however, that I did not set out to define an ethnic tradition but to outline a sense of indigenous resources. Okri's inclusion serves to make this point quite clearly. It is hoped that the methodology outlined here can serve the purpose of outlining a sense of indigenous resources even if the specific background is shifted within or outside Nigeria. A continental study on the lines adopted here could well include *Two Thousand Seasons; Search Sweet Country; Burning Grass; Anthills of the Savannah; Labyrinths* and *Petals of Blood* in addition to the works outlined in this study for defining the strategic filiation with indigenous resources. The important thing is that, unlike current studies of African literature, such a study would be interested in the typology of strategic filiations and not just in the question of authenticity that oral traditions lend to African writing.

My sense of a literary history was also regulated by an understanding of the micro-dynamics of the literary artefacts themselves. If I suggest that the texts examined are all responding to the pressure of external socio-political events, it is not to affirm a simple relationship of base with superstructure. Rather, the response of literature to external events is to impose a specific configuration of literary norms on the structuring of the symbolic universe. Yet it is impossible to legislate a uniform configuration of literary norms for each and every literary text. I tried to show my sense of this by paying attention to the specific details of each text. Thus it was possible to demonstrate that Okri's work responds to the crisis in Nigeria by fracturing the form of realism and abolishing the neutrality of setting. Setting is invested with an esoteric and other-worldly potential which is not subordinated to realist codes of representation. This was shown to be different from Soyinka's sense of things in which his task was to simultaneously affirm and problematize the links between individual self-sacrifice and corporate understanding. Soyinka shows the partial disarticulation of communal rituals at the moment of their focalization through individuals because of their consciousness of contradictions in either the moral code or in their sense of self identity. In Soyinka's plays this is done through dramaturgy of a highly ambiguous texture in which the vitality of indigenous culture is demonstrated in spectacle, hieratic ritual and language only to be controverted by the totality of the structure of the plays. As a means of imposing a thread of continuity on the texts studied, I isolated a particular trope of liminality and tried to show how it gets differentially refracted in the work of the writers. Highlighting this

trope, however, was also a way of foregrounding a feature of mythopoeia, which, because of the writers' reliance on that resource instead
of on protocols of realism, becomes inscribed as a dimension of the
form of the literary texts themselves.

But this trope also helps foreground an important dimension of the
literary strategic formation itself, in that the reliance on the mythopoeic potential of indigenous resources generates a particular
mythopoeic sense of things rather than a realist one. This is the sense
of an organic link between the individual and the community. This
link imposes an epochal sense to the heroic vocation of the individual. Mythopoeia normally inscribes heroes as larger-than-life and set
against potentially destructive forces that are also larger-than-life.
The organic relationships between self and community make the
hero a metonymic representation of that community in general.
Every act of the mythopoeic hero has therefore an epochal quality to
it. This quality is discernible in all three literary writers. However,
there is also a simultaneous movement away from this epochal sense
of things, especially in Soyinka's problematization of heroic vocation
in his plays and in the diminution in the vitality of the central
character Azaro in Okri's mythopoeic novels. It can be said, then, that
the literature also describes the potential dissolution of this organic-
ism even as it displays it in all its potential grandeur. This might well
be linked to the processes of modernization to which indigenous
culture has been subjected for over a century in which the affirmation
of communal values has gone hand-in-hand with the growth of
individualism and disillusionment. In a sense, the work of these
writers captures the mood of Africa's contemporary history without
being necessarily historical.

However it is conceptualized, a typology of literary forms loses its
value if it limits itself merely to the description of the individual
artistic expression and the differences between one expression and
another without integrating them into a more comprehensive and
metahistorical account of that typology. It is to this type of explanation that I turn in defining the questions of continuity and change for
concluding this book.

As was noted in Chapter 2, Johnson's *History* discursively reproduced the ethnographic forms of Yoruba historiography in subserving a sense of History that could be recuperated for contemplating
the veritable disarray into which the culture was thrown in the late
nineteenth century. In this essentially ethnographic drive, he was at
one with the impulse towards collecting proverbs, *oríkì*, Ifa divination
verses, folktales and traditional songs that dominated late nineteenth-
century cultural nationalism in Nigeria. This impulse, which we may
schematically label the collectionist impulse, was dominant until the
late thirties when Yoruba writers began imaginatively entering these

ethnographic materials for fictional purposes. Fagunwa's work was a landmark in this respect because he liberally re-worked the form of the folktale not in a collectionist mode but rather with the freedom of the literary artist. With Tutuola writing in his peculiar English, this imaginative engagement with ethnographic materials was projected onto another level by acquiring an international audience. That Tutuola brought out his earliest work at the moment when the country had entered a late phase of decolonization was itself significant because he inadvertently staked a claim for the rationality of indigenous resources in the constitution of the identity of the new state. The specific claim of the rationality of Tutuola's work was however received with a measure of scepticism if not outright derision by many of his countrymen. It was a different type of rationalism that was seen to be appropriate to the task of defining a viable identity. It was the rationality of realism that seemed adequate to the task of forging a national identity at the conjuncture of global realities. As was pointed out in Chapter 3, it is the rationalism of realism dispersed in texts as varied as newspapers, Onitsha market literature and in the earliest titles of the African Writers Series that dominated the discourses of the period.

In this period too, and stretching into the 1960s, the collectionist paradigm itself had mutated into an academic discipline. This was an important mutation of the collectionist paradigm as it ensured that it would acquire greater rigour. But in a sense, however, it also represented a partial fossilization of cultural forms because of the dominance of univocal grids of analyses deployed in dealing with them. For the Ibadan School of History, for instance, oral traditions were seen as historical texts and nothing else.[1] For Idowu, Yoruba mythology served as a source of anthropological generalizations about the culture's attitudes to the Supreme deity, while numerous other studies focused on ethnographic materials for sociological and other analyses. In all these studies the multivalent potential of orality was stilled in the service of abstracting a stable set of ideas for academic study. Such a procedure can be said to be the foundational episteme of the African University in general.

Soyinka represents an interesting conjuncture of the collectionist tendency with the literary one. Though he started his career by collecting indigenous materials, these served as an archive for his literary imagination. Furthermore, despite his respect for the essential parameters of indigenous materials (he did not attempt to create new gods, for one thing), he subjected them to creative revisions to make them yield meanings for contemporary use. He carried the potential of Yoruba mythology to a new level by re-writing its form to accommodate not only a Yoruba sense of things but a national and even continental sense of indigenous culture. His was the definition of a fresh aesthetic for ethnographic materials as well as a mode of cultural action-in-the-world. The Ogun myth served this purpose well and even the choice of the war-god was itself indicative of the distance from mere ethnographic representation that the attitudes to indigenous resources had undergone.

With Ben Okri, matters take an even more complex turn. Not only are putatively Yoruba resources appropriated by a non-Yoruba , they are transposed into a radical form that throws the status of everything into doubt not least the very coherence of the cultural materials he discursively deploys. Okri represents the indigenous resource-base comprehending its own hybridity and discursive eclecticism. Yet, in a way, he also hints at its potential discomposition. Odia Ofeimun describes Okri's work with an image that is rich in its ambiguity. To him Okri's work is like a snake eating its tail. This image might signal a dead-end, but as was pointed out to Ofeimun by Ketu Katrak in an ensuing discussion, it could well be an image of fertility, which is what it is in India.[2] That it is impossible fully to decide what the metaphorical value of Okri's work is points to an important mutation in the collectionist impulse. No longer are the cultural materials relayed in a positivist and unambiguously affirmative light.

Since in Okri's work the literary universe is itself fractured and multivalent, it means the whole world, including indigenous culture itself, is pushed to the edge of chaos. At the same time, this is counterbalanced by an utopian projection (seen in Black Tyger's re-dreaming of the world) as if to acknowledge that the fracturing of reality needs to be transcended even if momentarily. But, once that fracturing has taken place, reality cannot be re-constituted in the literary imagination in its prior epistemological coherence. Thus, it is possible to argue that with Ben Okri the filiation with indigenous resources comprehends traditional culture's potential non-being. The attitudes to the indigenous resource-base seem to have come full circle.

This change from a largely positivist paradigm to a discursively eclectic, hybrid and potentially chaotic one may be related to the growth of individualism at the conjuncture of the traumas of post-colonialism. In the late nineteenth century, it was desirable and possible to affirm a sense of coherence for indigenous culture precisely because any potential disillusionment of the individual writer was a function of the Other's oppression. Indigenous culture is posited as coherent in a programme of self-definition against the colonizing Other. With the attainment of Independence the coherence of indigenous culture is buffeted from various angles. Widespread education weakens the bonds of ethnic identification as does the growth of large urban centres attracting labour from across the country and crossing ethnic identities with the stratifications of class.

In the particular case of Nigeria, the coherence of indigenous culture is further problematized because of the terrible events unleashed by political mismanagement. The Biafra War was a key point in the political confusion of the country. It is even to some the mark of Nigeria's true beginning as a nation; the point at which, for better or worse, people decided to test or defend its political and conceptual boundaries.[3] With the aggressive affirmativeness of people who had benefited from the euphoria of the decolonization struggle, however, the nation-state could for a while be defined in terms of severe contradictions rather than of incoherence or chaos. Thus, Soyinka's work inscribes contradiction as a mode of engaging with indigenous culture without necesarily asserting its potential dissolution. This is because the sense of unreality unleashed by the acute contradictions of the nation-state is counterbalanced by the hope that the contradictions can still be resolved.

For Okri's generation, the benefit of decolonization euphoria is not available and all there is to contend with is the trauma and disillusionment of unavailable opportunities for personal fulfilment. It is a more cosmopolitan, self-conscious and disturbed sense of individualism that governs this generation. The degree of disillusionment is so high as to lead in the economic sphere to mass migrations of people to other countries, and, in the literary sphere, in the foregrounding of ambiguity and chaos in place of mere contradiction. On this account, the varying appropriations and thematizations of tradition (to return to Abiola Irele's formulation) are metonymic of wider national realities.

This explanation accounts for changes in the literary attitudes to the indigenous resource-base. Continuity in the literary strategic formation we have identified is best defined in terms of the continuing affirmation of mythopoeia rather than of realism for the definition of identity. As far back as the historiography of Samuel Johnson it is evident that history depends on the parameters of myth to problematize the boundaries between positivist history and mythology. It becomes more pronounced with the literary writers. That this derives from a conceptual opposition to what is perceived as a Western form of realism it is difficult to doubt. It is even pertinent to note in this regard that in the work of major African writers such as Achebe, Armah and Ngugi, the movement of their work has been from protocols of realist representation to those of mythopoeic experimentation. That the pursuit of these alternative models of representation is possible over a long perod of time in relation to the indigenous resources we have outlined is a credit to the vitality of those resources and their relevance in the modern world.

To outline the matter of change and continuity in Nigerian literature in this way runs the danger of affirming literary history with an implicit valorization of the present. Such an evolutionary trajectory would only serve to obscure the simultaneous articulation of all the different attitudes to indigenous resources at the present time. All the different strands we have identified subsist in the context of present-day realities. The important thing is to note that the attitudes to indigenous resources have branched out in several directions since the late nineteenth century under the pressures of varied historical processes and that the future could generate any number of configurations of different attitudes. If there is any value in tracing African literary history in this way, it is to point out the impossibility of carrying out the enterprise without a rigorous attention to the complexities and conjunctures, the means and the methods, and the meanings – of literature, history, culture and politics. African literature demands no less.

Notes

1 See, for an instance of an 'endogenous' form of historiography that emerged and was consolidated in that period, *Sources of Yoruba History*, a collection of history papers from the early sixties, edited by S. O. Biobaku (Oxford: Oxford University Press, 1973).

2 At the 20th Annual African Literature Association Conference, Accra, 25 March to 1 April 1994. The discussion itself was generated by a paper I presented on 'Literature and the Crisis of the African Nation-State', 30 March 1994.

3 This point is made by Abiola Irele in an introductory article to *The Oriki of a Grasshopper and Other Plays*, by Femi Osofisan. But it is one that is expressed in a far more problematic way in the life and writing of Ken Saro-Wiwa (e.g., *On a Darkling Plain* (1989) and *A Month and a Day* (1995)); it has also been expressed in a different way by Gabriel Gbadamosi (1994: 120ff). It seems to be a sentiment worth further investigation.

Bibliography

PRIMARY TEXTS

Rev. Samuel Johnson. *The History of the Yorubas*. Edited by O. Johnson. Lagos: CMS, 1921.

Amos Tutuola. *The Palm-Wine Drinkard*. London: Faber, 1952.
—. *My Life in the Bush of Ghosts*. London: Faber, 1954.
—. *The Brave African Huntress*. London: Faber, 1958.
—. *The Witch-Herbalist of the Remote Town*. London: Faber, 1981.
—. *The Wild Hunter in the Bush of Ghosts*. Edited with an introduction and postcript by Bernth Lindfors. Washington: Three Continents Press, 1982
—. *Pauper, Brawler and Slanderer*. London: Faber, 1987.

Wole Soyinka. *Collected Plays*, Vol. 1 (*A Dance of The Forests*, 1963; *The Swamp Dwellers*, 1964; *The Strong Breed*, 1964; *The Road*, 1965; *The Bacchae of Euripides*, 1973). Oxford: Oxford University Press, 1973.
—. Collected Plays, Vol. 2 (*The Lion and the Jewel*, 1963a; *Kongi's Harvest*, 1967; *The Trials of Brother Jero*, 1964; *Jero's Metamorphosis*, 1973; *Madmen and Specialists*, 1971). Oxford: Oxford University Press, 1974.
—. *Idanre and Other Poems*. London: Methuen, 1967.
—. *Season of Anomy*. London: Rex Collings, 1973.
—. *Death and the King's Horseman*. London: Methuen, 1975a.
—. *Ogun Abibiman*. London: Rex Collings, 1976.
—. *Ake: The Years of Childhood*. London: Rex Collings, 1981.
—. 'The Forest of a Thousand Daemons: a hunter's saga.' Translation of D. O. Fagunwa's *Ogboju-ode Ninu Igbo Irunmale*, 1968; London: Nelson, 1982.
—. *Isara: A Voyage Around Essay*. London: Methuen, 1990.
—. *Ibadan: The Penkelemes Years, A Memoir, 1946–1965*. London: Methuen, 1994.
—. 'From a Common Backcloth: A Reassessment of the African Literary Image.' *American Scholar* 32 (1963b): 387–97. Reprinted in *Art, Dialogue and Outrage*: 7-14.
—. 'Neo-Tarzanism: The Poetics of Pseudo-Tradition.' *Transition* 48 (1975b): 38–44.
—. *Myth, Literature and the African World*. Cambridge: Cambridge University Press, 1976.
—. *Art, Dialogue and Outrage: Essays on Literature and Culture*. Edited with and introduction by Biodun Jeyifo. Ibadan: New Horn Press, 1988.

Bibliography

—. Nobel Prize Banquet Speech in *Black American Literature Forum* 22.3 (1988): 447–8.
—.'The Writer: Child at the Frontier.' *The Cambridge Review* No. 114 (1993): 57–65.

Ben Okri. *Flowers and Shadows*. London: Longman, 1980.
—. *The Landcapes Within*. London: Longman, 1981.
—. *Incidents at the Shrine*. London: Vintage, 1986.
—. *Stars of the New Curfew*. London: Penguin, 1988.
—. *The Famished Road*. London: Vintage, 1991.
—. *An African Elegy*. London: Cape, 1992.
—. *Songs of Enchantment*. London: Cape, 1993.
—. *Astonishing the Gods*. London: Phoenix House, 1995.
—. *Birds of Heaven*. London: Phoenix House, 1996.
—. *Dangerous Love*. London: Phoenix House, 1996.
—. Review of Amos Tutuola's *The Witch Herbalist of the Remote Town*, *West Africa Magazine*, 14 February (1983): 429–30.

CRITICAL TEXTS

Abimbola, Wande, ed. *Yoruba Oral Tradition*. Ife: Ife University Press, 1975.
Achebe, Chinua.'The Novelist as Teacher.' *Morning Yet on Creation Day*. London: Heinemann, 1975: 42–5.
—.'Work and Play in Tutuola's Palm-Wine Drinkard' in Lindfors, ed. (1980): 256–64.
Adedeji, J. A.'The Aesthetics of Soyinka's Theatre.' *Before Our Very Eyes*. Ed. Dapo Adelugba. Ibadan: Spectrum Books, 1987: 104–31.
Afolayan, Adebisi (ed.). *Yoruba Language and Literature*. Ife: University of Ife Press, 1982.
Afigbo, A. E. 'The Social Repercussions of Colonial Rule: The New Social Structures,' in Adu Boahen, ed. (1985): 487–507.
Agiri, B. A.'Early Oyo History Reconsidered.' *History in Africa* 2 (1975): 1–16.
Ahmad, Aijaz. 'Jameson's Rhetoric of Otherness and the "National Allegory."' *Social Text* 17 (1987): 3–25.
—. *In Theory: Classes, Nations and Literatures*. London and New York: Verso, 1992.
Ajayi, J. F. Ade. 'How Yoruba Was Reduced to Writing.' *Odu* 8 (1960): 49–58.
—. 'Nineteenth-Century Origins of Nigerian Nationalism.' *Journal of the Historical Society of Nigeria* 2.2 (1962): 196–210.
—. *The Christian Missions in Nigeria 1841–1891: The Making of an Educated Elite*. London: Longman, 1965.
—.'The Aftermath of the Fall of Old Oyo.' *History of West Africa*. Eds. J. F. A. Ajayi and M. Crowder. London: Longman, 1987: 55–77.
Ajuwon, 'Bade.'Ogun's *Iremoje*: A Philosophy of Living and Dying' in Barnes, ed. (1989): 173–98.
Akintoye, S. A. *Revolution and Power in Yorubaland: 1840–1914*. London: Longman, 1971.
Anderson, Benedict. *Imagined Communities: Reflections on the Spread and Origins of Nationalism*. London and New York: Verso, 1983.
Appiah, Kwame Anthony, 'Out of Africa: Topologies of Nativism.' *Yale Journal of Criticism* 2.1 (1988): 153–78.
—. *In My Father's House: Africa in the Philosophy of Culture*. London: Methuen, 1992.
Apter, Andrew, 'Que Faire? Reconsidering Inventions of Africa.' *Critical Inquiry* 19.1 (1992a): 87–104.
—. *Black Critics and Kings: The Hermeneutics of Power in Yoruba Society*. Chicago: Chicago University Press, 1992b.
Ashcroft, Bill, Gareth Griffiths and Helen Tiffin. *The Empire Writes Back: Theory and Practice in Post-Colonial Literatures*. London: Routledge, 1989.
Awolalu, J. A. *Yoruba Beliefs and Sacrificial Rites*. London: Longman, 1979.

Bibliography

Awoniyi, T. A.'The Role and Status of the Yoruba Language in the Educational System of Western Nigeria: 1846–1971.' Ph.D diss., University of Ibadan, 1973.

Ayandele, E. A. *The Missionary Impact on Modern Nigeria, 1842–1914*. London: Longman, 1966.

Babalola, Adeboye. 'Yoruba Folktales.' *West African Review* (1962): 41-9.

—. *The Content and Form of Yoruba Ijala*. Oxford: Oxford University Press, 1966.

—. 'Yoruba Literature.' *Literatures in African Languages*. Eds B. W. Andrzejewski, S. Pilaszewicz and W. Tyloch. Cambridge: Cambridge University Press, 1985: 157–76.

—. 'A Portrait of Ogun as Reflected in Ijala Chants.' in Barnes, ed. (1989): 147–72.

Bakhtin, Mikhail. *The Dialogic Imagination*. Trans. C. Emerson and M. Holquist. Ed. M. Holquist. Austin: University of Texas Press, 1981.

Bamgbose, Ayo.'Yoruba Folktales.' *Ibadan* 27 (1969): 6–12.

Barber, Karin. 'How Man Makes God in West Africa: Yoruba Attitudes Towards the Òrìsà.' *Africa* 51.3 (1981): 724–45.

—. 'Yoruba Oríkì and Deconstructive Criticism.' *Research in African Literatures* 15.4 (1984): 497–518.

—. 'Interpreting Oríkì as History and as Literature' in Barber and de Moraes Farias, eds (1989): 13–23.

—. 'Discursive strategies in the texts of Ifá and the "Holy book of Odù" of the African Church of Orunmila' in de Moraes Farias and Barber, eds (1990a): 196–224.

—. 'Oríkì, Women and the Proliferation and Merging of Òrìsà.' *Africa* 60.3 (1990b): 313–36.

—. *I Could Speak Until Tomorrow: Oríkì, Women and the Past in a Yoruba Town*. Edinburgh: Edinburgh University Press, 1991a.

—. 'Multiple Discourses in Yoruba Literature.' *Bulletin of the John Rylands University Library of Manchester* 73.3 (1991b): 11–24.

—. 'African-language Literature and Post-Colonial Criticism.' *Research in African Literature* 26.4 (1995): 3–30.

Barber, Karin and P. F. de Moraes Farias, eds. *Discourse and its Disguises: The Interpretation of African Oral Texts*. Birmingham: Centre for West African Studies, 1989.

Barnes, Sandra T., ed. *Africa's Ogun: Old World and New*. Bloomington and Indianapolis: Indiana University Press, 1989.

—. 'Introduction: The Many Faces of Ogun' in Barnes, ed. (1989): 1–26.

Barnes, Sandra T. and P. G. Ben-Amos.'Ogun, the Empire Builder' in Barnes, ed. (1989): 39–64.

Barthes, Roland. *Image, Music, Text*. Trans. Stephen Heath. Glasgow: Fontana, 1977.

Bascom, William. *Ifa Divination: Communication Between Gods and Men*. Bloomington: Indiana University Press, 1969.

Baxandall, Michael. *Patterns of Intention: On the Historical Explanation of Pictures*. New Haven and London: Yale University Press, 1985.

Belasco, Bernard I. *The Entepreneur as Cultural Hero: Readaptation in Nigerian Economic Develpment*. New York: J. F. Bergin Publishing, 1980.

Bell, Catherine. *Ritual Theory, Ritual Practice*. Oxford: Oxford University Press, 1992.

Benjamin, Walter. *Illuminations*. Ed. with an introduction by Hannah Arendt. Trans. Harry Zohn. London: Fontana, 1973.

Bhabha, Homi K. 'Representation and the Colonial Text: A Critical Exploration of Some Forms of Mimeticism.' *The Theory of Reading*. Ed. Frank Gloversmith. Brighton: Harvester Press, 1984: 93–122.

—. *The Location of Culture*. London: Routledge, 1994.

—. ed. *Nation and Narration*. London: Routledge, 1990.

Biobaku, S. O. ed. *Sources of Yoruba History*. Oxford: Oxford University Press, 1973.

Birbalsingh, E. M.'Soyinka's *Death and the King's Horseman*.' *Présence Africaine* (1982): 202–19.

Boahen, A. Adu, ed. *UNESCO General History of Africa, Vol. VII*. London: Heinemann, 1985.

Bibliography

Bourdieu, Pierre. *Language and Symbolic Power*. Trans. Gino Raymond and Matthew Adamson. Ed. with an introduction by John B. Thompson. Cambridge: Polity Press, 1991.

—. *The Field of Cultural Production: Essays in Art and Literature*. Ed. with an introduction by Randal Johnson. Cambridge: Polity Press, 1993.

Brennan, Timothy. *Salman Rushdie and the Third World*. London: Macmillan, 1989.

Briggs, Charles L. 'Metadiscursive Practices and Scholarly Authority in Folklorists.' *Journal of American Folklore* 106 (1993): 387–434.

Calinescu, Matei. 'Orality in Literacy: Some Historical Paradoxes of Reading.' *The Yale Journal of Criticism* 6.2 (1993): 175–90.

Chinweizu, Onwuchekwa Jemie, and Ihechukwu Madubuike. *Toward the Decolonization of African Literature*. Enugu: Fourth Dimension Press, 1980.

Clark, Katerina and Michael Holquist. *Mikhail Bakhtin*. Cambridge, Mass.: Harvard University Press, 1984.

Clayton, Jay and Eric Rothstein. 'Figures in the Corpus: Theories of Influence and Intertextuality.' *Influence and Intertextuality in Literary History*. Eds Jay Clayton and Eric Rothstein. Madison: University of Wisconsin Press, 1991: 3–36.

Clifford, James and George E. Marcus. *Writing Culture: The Poetics and Politics of Ethnography*. Berkeley: California University Press, 1986.

Clifford, James. 'On Ethnographic Authority.' *Representations* 1.2 (1983): 118–46.

Cohn, Dorrit. *Transparent Minds: Narrative Models for Presenting Consciousness in Fiction*. Princeton: Princeton University Press, 1978.

Collins, Harold. *Amos Tutuola*. New York: Twayne, 1969.

—. 'Founding a National Literature: The Ghost Novels of Amos Tutuola' in Lindfors, ed. (1980): 43–54.

Comas, James.'The Presence of Theorizing/Theorizing the Present.' *Research in African Literatures* 21.1 (1990): 5–31.

Cribb, T.J. 'Transformations in the Fiction of Ben Okri.' *From Commonwealth to Postcolonial*. Ed. Anna Rutherford. Sydney: Dangaroo Press, 1992: 145–50.

Davidson, Basil. *The Black Man's Burden: Africa and the Curse of the Nation-State*. London: James Currey, 1992.

de Moraes Farias, P. F. 'Yoruba Origins Revisited by Muslims,' in de Moreas Farias and Karin Barber, eds, (1990a): 109–47.

—. 'History and Consolation: Royal Yoruba Bards Comment on Their Craft.' *History in Africa* 19 (1992): 263–97.

de Moraes Farias, P. F. and Karin Barber, eds, *Self-Assertion and Brokerage: Early Cultural Nationalism in West Africa*. Birmingham: Centre for West African Studies, 1990a.

Derrida, Jacques. *Of Grammatology*. Trans. with an introduction by Gayatri Chakravorty Spivak. Baltimore: Johns Hopkins University Press, 1976.

Dodds, E. R. *The Greeks and the Irrational*. Berkeley: University of California Press, 1951.

Doortmont, Michel R. 'Samuel Johnson and *The History of the Yorubas*: A Study in Historiography'. Unpublished MA diss., University of Birmingham, 1985.

—. 'The invention of the Yorubas: Regional and Pan-African Nationalism versus Ethnic Provincialism.' In de Moraes Farias and Barber, eds (1990): 101–8.

—. 'Recapturing the Past: Samuel Johnson and One Construction of the History of the Yoruba.' Ph.D diss., Erasmus University, Rotterdam, 1994.

Doty William, G. *Mythography: The Study of Myths and Rituals*. Alabama: University of Alabama Press, 1986.

Douglas, Mary. *Purity and Danger: An Analysis of the Concepts of Pollution and Taboo*. 1966; London: Routledge, 1992.

Drewal, Margaret. *Yoruba Ritual: Performers, Play, Agency*. Bloomington: Indiana University Press, 1992.

Eagleton, Terry. *Criticism and Ideology*. London: New Left Books, 1976.

—. *Walter Benjamin, or Towards a Revolutionary Criticism*. London: Verso, 1981.

Eboreime, Joseph O. 'Group Identities and the Changing Patterns of Alliances Among the Epie-Attissa People of Nigeria, 1890–1991.' Ph.D diss., University of Cambridge, 1992.

Ekpo, Denis. 'Towards a Post-Africanism: Contemporary African Thought and Post-Modernism.' *Textual Practice* 9.1 (1995): 121–35.

Eliade, Mircea. *Myth and Realty*. New York: Harper Row, 1963.

Eliot, T. S. 'Tradition and the Individual Talent.' *Selected Prose of T. S. Eliot*. Ed. with an introduction by Frank Kermode. 1919; London: Faber, 1975.

Ensowanne, Uzo.'The Madness of Africa(ns): Or, Anthropology's Reason.' *Cultural Critique* 17 (1990): 107–26.

Ermarth, Elizabeth Deeds. *Realism and Consensus in the English Novel*. Princeton: Princeton University Press, 1983.

Falola, Toyin and Michel Doortmont, eds. '*Iwe Itan Oyo*: A Yoruba traditional history and its author.' Edited history of Oyo by Michael Adeyemi. *Journal of African History* 30 (1989): 301–29.

Finnegan, Ruth. *Oral Literature in Africa*. Oxford: Oxford University Press, 1970.

—. 'Literacy versus Orality: the Great Divide.' *Modes of Thought*. Eds Ruth Finnegan and Robin Horton. London: Faber, 1973.

—. *Oral Poetry: Its Nature, Significance and Social Context*. Cambridge: Cambridge University Press, 1977.

—. *Literacy and Orality: Studies in the Technology of Communication*. Oxford: Blackwell, 1988.

Folayan, Kola. 'Yoruba Oral History: Some Problems and Prospects,' in Abimbola, ed. (1975): 89–114.

Foucault, Michel. *Language Counter-Memory, Practice: Selected Essays and Interviews*. Trans. Donald F. Bouchard and Sherry Simon. Ed. with an introduction by Donald F. Bouchard. Oxford: Basil Blackwell, 1973.

—. *Discipline and Punish: The Birth of the Prison*. Trans. Alan Sheridan. New York: Vintage and Random House, 1979.

—. *The History of Sexuality, Volume I: An Introduction*. Trans. Robert Hurley. New York: Vintage and Random House, 1980.

—. 'The Subject and Power.' *Michel Foucault: Beyond Structuralism and Hermeneutics*. Eds Hubert R. Dreyfus and Paul Rabinow. New York: Harvester Wheatsheaf, 1982: 208–26.

—. *The Archaeology of Knowledge*. Trans. A. M. Sheridan Smith. 1969; London: Tavistock, 1986.

—. 'What is an Author?' in Lodge, ed. (1988): 197–210.

Freund, Bill. *The Making of Contemporary Africa*. Bloomington: Indiana University Press, 1984.

Frow, John. *Marxism and Literary History*. Oxford: Basil Blackwell, 1986.

Gardiner, Michael. *The Dialogics of Critique: M. M. Bakhtin and the Theory of Ideology*. London: Routledge, 1992.

Garuba, Harry. 'Frontiers, Men and Gods: Wole Soyinka's Ogun and the Myth of the American Frontier.' Manuscript; published in *American Studies Association Journal of Nigeria* 1.2 (1992).

—. 'Ben Okri: Animist Realism and the Famished Genre.' *The Guardian* (Lagos) 13 March, 1993.

Gates, Henry Louis Jnr. *The Signifying Monkey: A Theory of Afro-American Literary Criticism*. Oxford: Oxford University Press, 1988.

Geertz, Clifford. 'Blurred Genres: The Re-configuration of Social Thought.' *Local Knowledge: Further Essays in Interpretive Anthropology*. Clifford Geertz, ed. New York: Basic Books, 1983.

Gbadamosi, Gabriel. 'Madmen and Specialists: New Nation States and the Importance of Tragic Art', in Adewale Maja-Pearce, ed. (1994): 116–27.

Genette, Gerard. *Narrative Discourse*. Trans. Jane E. Lewin. London: Blackwell, 1980.

Godelier, Maurice. *Perspectives in Marxist Anthropology*. Cambridge: Cambridge

University Press, 1977.

Goody, Jack and Ian Watt. 'The Consequences of Literacy.' *Literacy in Traditional Societies*. Ed. Jack Goody. Cambridge: Cambridge University Press, 1968: 27–68.

Gurnah, Abdulrazak. *Essays on African Writing* I. London: Heinemann, 1993.

—. 'The Fiction of Wole Soyinka', in Adewale Maja-Pearce, ed. (1994): 61–80.

—. *Essays on African Writing* II. London: Heinemann, 1995.

Gunner, Elizabeth. 'Orality and Literacy: Dialogue and Silence' in Barber and de Moraes Farias (1989): 49–56.

Halbwachs, Maurice. *On Collective Memory*. Trans. and edited with an introduction by Lewis A. Coser. Chicago: University of Chicago Press, 1992.

Hallen, Barry and J. O. Sodipo. *Knowledge, Belief, Witchcraft: Analytic Experiments in African Philosophy*. London: Ethnographica, 1986.

Harrow, Kenneth. *Thresholds of Change in African Literature: The Emergence of a Tradition*. Portsmouth, NH and London: Heinemann and James Currey, 1994.

Havelock, Eric A. *Preface to Plato*. Cambridge, Mass.: The Belknap Press of Harvard University Press, 1963.

Hawley, John C. 'Ben Okri's Spirit Child: *Abiku* Migration and Postmodernity.' *Research in African Literatures* 26.1 (1995): 30–9.

Hobsbawm, Eric J. *The Age of Capital* [1962]. London: Weidenfeld & Nicholson, 1995.

—. 'Inventing Traditions.' *The Invention of Tradition*. Eds E. Hobsbawm and Terence Ranger. Cambridge: Cambridge University Press, 1983: 1–14.

—. 'The Social Function of the Past: Some Questions.' *Past and Present* 55 (1972): 3–17.

—. *Nations and Nationalism Since 1780: Programme, Myth, Reality*. Cambridge: Cambridge University Press, 1990.

Hoch-Smith, J. 'Radical Yoruba Female Sexuality: The Witch and the Prostitute.' *Women in Ritual and Symbolic Roles*. Eds J. Hoch-Smith and Anita Spring. New York: Plenum Press, 1978: 245–67.

Holquist, Michael. *Dialogism: Bakhtin and His World*. London and New York: Routledge, 1990.

Horton, Robin. 'African Traditional Thought and Western Science.' *Africa* 37.1 (1967): 50–71; reprinted in *Patterns of Thought in Africa and the West: Essays on Magic, Religion and Science*. Cambridge: Cambridge University Press, 1993: 197–258.

Hountondji, Paulin. *African Philosophy: Myth and Reality*. Trans. Henri Evans and Jonathan Rée with an introducton by Abiola Irele. Bloomington: Indiana University Press, 1983.

Idowu, E. B. *Olodumare: God in Yoruba Belief*. London: Longman, 1962.

Innes, Lyn. 'Africa Goes Postmodern.' Review of Kenneth Harrow's *Thresholds of Change in African Literature*. *Times Literary Supplement*, 2 December 1994.

Irele, Abiola. *The African Experience in Literature and Ideology*. Bloomington: Indiana University Press, 1990a.

—. 'African Literature and the Language Question', in Irele (1990a): 43–65.

—. 'Tradition and the Yoruba Writer: D. O. Fagunwa, Amos Tutuola and Wole Soyinka', in Irele (1990a): 174–98.

—. 'The African Imagination.' *Research in African Literatures* 21.1 (1990b): 47–67.

—. 'Orality, Literacy and African Literature.' *Semper Aliquid Novi: Littérature Comparée et Littératures d'Afrique*. Eds János Riesz and Alain Ricard. Tübingen: Gunter Narr Verlag, 1990.

—. 'African Letters: The Making of a Tradition.' *The Yale Journal of Criticism* 5.1 (1995a): 69–100.

—. Introduction to *The Oriki of a Grasshopper: and other Plays* by Femi Osofisan. Washington: Howard University Press, 1995b.

Isola, Akinwumi. 'Contemporary Yoruba Literary Tradition.' *Perspectives on Nigerian Literature: 1700 to the Present, Vol.* I. Ed. Yemi Ogunbiyi. Lagos: Guardian Books, 1988: 73–84.

Izevbaye, Dan. 'Mediation in Soyinka: The Case of the King's Horseman.' *Critical*

Perspectives on Wole Soyinka. Ed. James Gibbs. London: Heinemann, 1981: 116–25.

—. 'J. P. Clark-Bekederemo and the Ijo Literary Tradition.' *Research in African Literatures* 25.1 (1994): 1–21.

Jakobson, Roman. 'Linguistics and Poetics', in Lodge, ed. (1988): 32–57.

—.'The Metaphoric and Metonymic Poles', in Lodge, ed. (1988): 57–61.

Jameson, Frederic. 'Third-World Literature in the Era of Multinational Capitalism.' *Social Text* 15 (1986): 65–88.

Jeyifo, Biodun. *The Yoruba Popular Travelling Theatre of Nigeria*. Lagos: Nigeria Magazine Publications, 1984a.

—. *The Truthful Lie*. London: New Beacon Books, 1984b.

—. 'The Voice of a Lost Generation: The Novels of Ben Okri', *The Guardian* (Lagos) 12 July, 1986.

—. 'The Nature of Things: Arrested Decolonization and Critical Theory.' *Research in African Literatures* 21.1 (1990): 33–48.

Jones, Eldred. *The Writing of Wole Soyinka*. London: Heinemann, 1973.

—. 'Myth and Modernity', in *Orature in African Literature Today, 18* (London: James Currey, 1992): 1–8.

Julien, Eileen. *African Novels and the Question of Orality*. Bloomington: Indiana University Press, 1992.

July, Robert W. *The Origins of Modern African Thought*. London: Faber, 1968.

Katrak, Ketu. *Wole Soyinka and Modern Tagedy: A Study of Dramatic Theory and Practice*. New York: Greenwood Press, 1986.

Ki-Zerbo, Joseph. General Introduction to *Unesco General History of Africa Vol. 1*. London: Heinemann and Unesco, 1981: 1–23.

Kristeva, Julia. *Desire in Language: A Semiotic Approach to Literature and Art*. Trans. Thomas Gora, Alice Jardine and Leon S. Roudiez with an introduction by Leon S. Roudiez. Oxford: Basil Blackwell, 1981.

La Pin, Deirdre. 'Story, Medium and Masque: The Idea and Art of Yoruba Storytelling.' Ph.D diss., University of Wisconsin, Madison, 1977. Three volumes.

Larsen, Stephan. *A Writer and His Gods: A Study of the Importance of Yoruba Myths and Religious Ideas to the Work of Wole Soyinka*. Ph.D Diss., Stockholm: Department of the History of Literature, 1983.

Law, Robin. 'The Heritage of Oduduwa: Traditional Historiography and Propaganda Among the Yoruba.' *Journal of African History* 4.2 (1973): 207–23.

—. 'Early Yoruba Historiography.' *History in Africa* 3 (1976): 69-89.

—. 'How Truly Traditional is Our Traditional History?' *History in Africa* 11 (1984): 195–221.

—. 'How Many Times Can History Repeat Itself?' *International Journal of African Historical Studies* 18.1 (1985): 33–51.

—. 'Constructing "A Real National History": A Comparison of Eward Blyden and Samuel Johnson', in de Moraes Farias and Barber, eds (1990): 78–100.

Le Page, R. B. and Andrée Tabouret-Keller. *Acts of Identity: Creole-based Approaches to Language and Identity*. Cambridge: Cambridge University Press, 1985.

Lévi-Strauss, Claude. *From Honey to Ashes*. Trans. John and Doreen Weightman. 1966; London: Jonathan Cape, 1973.

Lincoln, Bruce. *Discourse and the Construction of Society: Comparative Studies of Myth, Ritual and Classification*. Oxford: Oxford University Press, 1989.

Lindfors, Bernth, ed. *Critical Perspectives on Amos Tutuola*. London: Heinemann, 1980.

—. 'Amos Tutuola: Debts and Assets', in Lindfors, ed. (1980): 224–55.

Lodge, David, *The Modes of Modern Writing*. London: Routledge, 1977.

—. ed. *Modern Criticism and Theory*. London: Longman, 1988.

Lord, Albert B. *The Singer of Tales*. Cambridge, Mass.: Harvard Unviversity Press, 1960.

Lynch, Hollis R. *Edward Blyden: Pan-African Patriot, 1832-1912*. London: Oxford University Press, 1967.

Maduakor, Obi. *Wole Soyinka: An Introduction to His Writing*. New York: Garland

Publishing, 1986.

—. 'The Political Content of Wole Soyinka's Plays.' *Journal of Commonwealth Literature* 28.1 (1993): 82–96.

Maduka, Chidi. 'African Religious Beliefs and the Literary Imagination: *Ogbanje* and *Abiku* in Chinua Achebe, J. P. Clark and Wole Soyinka.' *Journal of Commonwealth Literature* 22.1 (1987): 17–30.

Maja-Pearce, Adewale (ed.). *Wole Soyinka: An Appraisal*. London: Heinemann, 1994.

Marcus, George E. and Michael M. J. Fischer. *Anthropology as Cultural Critique*. Chicago and London: University of Chicago Press, 1986.

Mbembe, Achille. 'Provisional Notes on the Post-Colony.' *Africa* 62 (1992): 3–37.

Miller, Christopher. *Theories of Africans: Francophone Literature and Anthropology in Africa*. Chicago: Chicago University Press, 1990.

Miller, Joseph C. 'Introduction: Listening for the Past in Africa.' *The African Past Speaks*. Ed. Joseph C. Miller. Kent: Dawson, 1980: 1–60.

Moore, Gerald. 'Amos Tutuola: Nigerian Visionary', in Lindfors, ed. (1980): 34–42.

Moretti, Franco. *Signs Taken for Wonders: Essays in the Sociology of Literary Forms*. Trans. Susan Fischer, David Forgacs, and David Millee. London: New Left Books, 1983.

Morrison, Toni. *Playing in the Dark*. London: Picador, 1993.

Morson, Gary Saul. *Bakhtin: Essays and Dialogues on his Work*. Chicago and London: University of Chicago Press, 1986.

Morton-Williams, P. 'An Outline of the Cosmology and Cult Organization of the Oyo Yoruba.' *Africa* 34.3 (1964): 243–61.

Mudimbe, V. Y. *The Invention of Africa: Gnosis, Philosophy and the Order of Knowledge*. London and Bloomington: James Currey and Indiana University Press, 1988.

Nietzsche, Friedrich. 'The Birth of Tragedy.' *The Birth of Tragedy and the Genealogy of Morals*. Trans. Francis Golffing. New York: Doubleday, 1956.

Obiechina, Emmanuel O. *Onitsha Market Literature*. London: Heinemann, 1972.

—. *Culture, Tradition and Society in the West African Novel*. Cambridge: Cambridge University Press, 1975.

—. 'Amos Tutuola and the Oral Tradition', in Lindfors, ed. (1980): 84–105.

Ogunba Oyin. *The Movement of Transition*. Ibadan: Ibadan University Press, 1975.

Ogundele, Wole. 'Death and the King's Horseman: A Poet's Quarrel with his Culture.' *Research in African Literatures* 25.1 (1994): 47–58.

Ogunsanwo, Olatubosun. 'Intertextuality and Post-Colonial Literature in Ben Okri's *The Famished Road.' Research in African Literatures* (1995): 40–52.

Okediji, F. Olu. 'The Sociological Aspects of Traditional Names and Titles.' *Odu* 3.1 (1966): 64–79.

Okonkwo, Chidi. 'The Quest for Order in a Changing Order.' *Cambridge Anthropology* 15.3 (1991): 41–52.

Okri, Ben. Review of Amos Tutuola's *The Witch Herbalist of the Remote Town. West Africa Magazine*, 14 February, (1983): 429–30.

Oladipo, Olusegun. 'Predestination in Yoruba Thought: A Philosopher's Interpretation'. Manuscript; published in *Orita* 24 (1992).

Olaniyan, Richard. 'Elements of Yoruba Diplomacy: An Assesssment', in Abimbola, ed. (1975): 293–332.

Olaniyan, Tejumola. *Scars of Conquest/Masks of Resistance: The Invention of Cultural Identities in African, African-American and Caribbean Drama*. New York & Oxford: Oxford University Press, 1995.

Omotoso, Kole. 'No Poor Relation.' Review of Ben Okri's *Songs of Enchantment. The Guardian* (Manchester) 23 March 1993.

Omu, Fred I. A. *Press and Politics in Nigeria, 1880-1937*. London: Longman, 1978.

—. 'The Newspaper Press in Southern Nigeria, 1800-1900.' *Studies in Southern Nigerian History*. Ed. Boniface I. Obichere. London: Frank Cass: 1982. 103–26.

Ong, Walter. *Orality and Literacy: The Technologizing of the Word*. London: Methuen, 1982.

Opoku, Asare, K. 'Religion in Africa During the Colonial Era', in Boahen, ed. (1985): 508–38.

Ortner, Sherry B. 'Theory in Anthropology since the Sixties.' *Comparative Studies in Society and History.* 26.1 (1984): 126–66.

Otu, John. 'Beyond Surrealism: A Gestalt Perspective.' *The Guardian* (Lagos) 10 April, 1993.

Owomoyela, Oyekan. 'Tortoise Tales and the Yoruba Ethos.' *Research in African Literatures* 20.2 (1989): 165–80.

Pallinder, Agneta. 'Adegboyega Edun: Black Englishman and Yoruba cultural patriot', in de Moraes Farias and Barber (1990): 11–34.

Palmer, Eustace. *The Growth of the African Novel.* London: Heinemann, 1979.

Parry, Milman. *The Making of Homeric Man: The Collected Papers of Milman Parry.* Oxford: Clarendon Press, 1971.

Peel, J. D. Y. *Aladura: Religious Movement Among the Yoruba.* London: Oxford University Press, 1968.

—. 'History, Culture and the Comparative Method: A West African Puzzle.' *Comparative Anthropology.* Ed. Ladislav Holy. Oxford: Basil Blackwell, 1987: 88–18.

—. 'The Cultural Work of Yoruba Ethnogenesis.' *History and Ethnicity.* Eds Elizabeth Tonkin, Maryon McDonald and Malcolm Chapman. London: Routledge, 1989: 198–215.

—. 'The Pastor and the *Babalawo*: The Interaction of Religions in Nineteenth-Century Yorubaland.' *Africa* 60.3 (1990): 338–69.

—. 'Historicity and Pluralism in Some Recent Studies of Yoruba Religion.' *Africa* 64.1 (1994): 150–66.

—. 'A Comparative Analysis of Ogun in Pre-Colonial Yorubaland', manuscript; to be published in Sandra T. Barnes, ed., *Africa's Ogun: Old World and New*, 2nd edition, (Bloomington: Indiana University Press).

Priebe, Richard. 'Tutuola the Riddler', in Lindfors, ed. (1980): 215–23.

—. *Myth, Realism, and the West African Writer.* Trenton, NJ: Africa World Press, 1988.

Prince, Raymond. 'The Yoruba Image of the Witch.' *Journal of Mental Science* 107 (1961): 795–805.

Propp, Vladimir. *Morphology of the Folktale.* Ed. with an introduction by Louis A. Wagner. Trans. Laurence Scott. Austin: University of Texas Press, 1971.

Quayson, Ato. 'Esoteric Webwork as Nervous System: Reading the Fantastic in Ben Okri's Writing', in Abdulrazak Gurnah, *Essays on African Writing II* (1995): 144–58.

—. 'Orality – (Theory) – Textuality: Tutuola, Okri and the Relationship of Literary Practice to Oral Traditions.' *The Pressures of the Text: Orality, Texts and the Telling of Tales.* Ed. Stewart Brown. Birmingham: Centre for West African Studies, 1995.

—. 'Contemporary Literary Theory and the Analysis of Indigenous Cultures: Three Examples on the Yoruba.' *Research in African Literatures* 26.4 (1995): 185–96.

Richards, David. 'Òwe l'esin òrò: Proverbs Like Horses in Wole Soyinka's *Death and the King's Horseman*.' *Journal of Commonwealth Literature* 13.1 (1984): 86–97.

Riffaterre, Michael. 'Intertextual Representation: On Mimesis as Interpretive Discourse.' *Critical Inquiry* 11.1 (1984): 141–62.

Rosaldo, Renato. 'Doing Oral History.' *Social Analysis* 4 (1988): 89–99.

Roudiez, Leon. Introduction to Kristeva (1981).

Sahlins, Marshall. *Islands of History.* Chicago: University of Chicago Press, 1985.

Said, Edward. *Orientalism.* London: Routledge, 1978.

—. 'Representing the Colonized: Anthropology's Interlocuters.' *Critical Inquiry* 15.2 (1989): 205–25.

Saro-Wiwa, Ken. *On a Darkling Plain.* Port Harcourt: Saros Publishers, 1989.

—. *A Month and a Day: A Detention Diary.* London: Penguin, 1995.

Smith, R. S. *Kingdoms of the Yoruba.* 3rd edition. London: James Currey, 1988.

Spivak, Gayatri Chakravorty. *The Post-Colonial Critic: Interviews, Strategies and Dialogues.* Ed. Sarah Harasym. London: Routledge, 1990.

Steinberg, Meir. *Expositional Modes and Temporal Ordering in Fiction*. Baltimore: Johns Hopkins University Press, 1978.

Street, Brian. *Literacy in Theory and Practice*. Cambridge: Cambridge University Press, 1984.

Stoler, Laura Ann. *Race and the Education of Desire: Foucault's History of Sexuality and the Colonial Order of Things*. Durham and London: Duke University Press, 1995.

Thomas, Nicholas. *Colonialism's Culture: Anthropology, Travel and Government*. Cambridge: Polity Press, 1994.

Tonkin, Elizabeth. 'Oracy and the Disguises of Literacy', in Barber and de Moraes Farias, eds (1989): 39–48.

—. 'Zik's story: autobiography as political exemplar', in de Moraes Farias and Barber, eds (1990): 35–54.

Turner, Victor. *The Forest of Symbols*. Ithaca: Cornell University Press, 1967.

—. *The Ritual Process: Structure and Anti-Structure*. London: Routledge and Kegan Paul, 1969.

—. 'Variations on a Theme of Liminality.' *Secular Ritual*. Eds Sally F. Moore and Barbara Myerhoff. Amsterdam: Van Gorcum, 1977: 36–52.

—. *From Ritual to Theatre*. New York: Performing Arts Journal Publications, 1982.

—. 'Are There Universals of Performance in Myth, Ritual and Drama?' *By Means of Performance: Intercultural Studies of Theatre and Ritual*. Eds. Richard Schechner and Willa Appel. Cambridge: Cambridge University Press, 1990: 1–18.

Van Gennep, Arnold. *The Rites of Passage*. Trans. Monika B. Vizedom and Gabriele L. Caffe, 1908: Routledge and Kegan Paul, 1960.

Vansina, Jan. *Oral Tradition*. Trans. H.M. Wright. London: Routledge & Kegan Paul, 1965.

—. *Oral Tradition as History*. 2nd edition. London: James Currey, 1985.

Viala, Alain. 'Prismatic Effects.' *Critical Inquiry* 14.3 (1988): 563–73.

Wauthier, Claude. *The Literature and Thought of Modern Africa*. London: Pall Mall Press, 1966.

Weimann, Robert. *Structure and Society in Literary History: Studies in the History and Theory of Historical Criticism*. London: Lawrence and Wishart, 1977.

White, Hayden. *Metahistory: The Historical Imagination in Nineteenth-Century Europe*. Baltimore: Johns Hopkins University Press, 1973.

—. 'The Irrational and the Problem of Historical Knowledge in the Enlightenment.' *Tropics of Discourse*. Hayden White. Baltimore: Johns Hopkins University Press, 1978: 135–49.

White, John J. *Mythology in the Modern Novel: A Study in Pre-figurative Techniques*. Princeton: Princeton University Press, 1972.

White, Landeg. 'Poetic Licence: Oral Poetry and History', in Barber and de Moraes Farias, eds (1989): 34–8.

Wilkinson, Jane. *Talking With African Writers*. London: James Currey, 1992.

Williams, Adebayo. 'Ritual and the Political Unconsciousness: The Case of Death and the King's Horseman.' *Research in African Literatures* 24.1 (1993): 67–79.

Williams, Patrick and Laura Chrisman. *Colonial Discourse and Post-Colonial Theory*. New York and London: Harvester Wheatsheaf, 1993.

Williams, Raymond. *Culture*. London: Fontana, 1981.

Winters, Majorie. 'An Objective Approach to Achebe's Style.' *Research in African Literatures* 12.1 (1981): 55–86.

Wright, Derek. 'Stock-taking Soyinkana, 1986-1988.' *Research in African Literatures* 23.4 (1992): 107–16.

—. *Wole Soyinka Revisited*. New York: Twayne Publishers, 1993.

Yai, Olabiyi. 'Issues in Oral Poetry: Criticism, Teaching and Translation', in Barber and de Moraes Farias, eds (1989): 59–69.

—. 'In Praise of Metonymy: The Concepts of "Tradition" and "Creativity" in the Transmission of Yoruba Artistry over Time and Space.' *Research in African*

Literatures 24.4 (1993): 29–37.

Young, Robert. *White Mythologies: Writing History and the West*. London: Routledge, 1990.

Zipes, Frank. *Fairy Tales and the Art of Subversion: The Classical Genre for Children and the Process of Civilization*. London: Heinemann, 1983.

Index

Studies in African Literature
NEW SERIES

*forthcoming

JAMES CURREY
OXFORD